The Modern Chin

The Modern Chinese State is the first book to examine systematically the evolution of the Chinese state from the late Ming dynasty, through the Nationalist and Communist party-states of the twentieth century, and into the twenty-first century. The contributing authors, all leading scholars in the field of Chinese studies, carefully assess the internal organization of the Chinese state over time, the ruling parties that have governed it, the foreign and indigenous systems that have served as models for state-building and political development, and the array of concepts that have guided Chinese thinking about the state.

The Chinese state is the oldest in the world, far predating European and other Oriental state systems, but the party-states in mainland China and Taiwan today both face serious challenges. What are these challenges and can they be surmounted? How are the Chinese adapting? What will the Chinese state of the twenty-first century look like? These contemporary and many more historical questions are explored in this book.

David Shambaugh is Professor of Political Science and International Affairs and Director of the China Policy Program at The George Washington University, and nonresident Senior Fellow in the Foreign Policy Studies Program at The Brookings Institution in Washington, D.C.

Cambridge Modern China Series

Edited by William Kirby, Harvard University

Other books in the series

Warren I. Cohen and Li Zhao, eds., *Hong Kong Under Chinese Rule: The Economic and Political Implications of Reversion*

Tamara Jacka, *Women's Work in Rural China: Change and Continuity in an Era of Reform*

Shiping Zheng, *Party vs. State in Post-1949 China: The Institutional Dilemma*

Edward S. Steinfeld, *Forging Reform in China: The Fate of State-Owned Industry*

Michael Dutton, *Streetlife China*

Jing Huang, *Factionalism in Chinese Communist Politics*

Edmund Fung, *In Search of Chinese Democracy*

Other books by David Shambaugh

Reforming China's Military
The China Reader: The Reform Era (coedited with Orville Schell)
China's Military Faces the Future (coedited with James Lilley)
Is China Unstable? (edited)
Contemporary Taiwan (edited)
China's Military in Transition (edited)
China and Europe, 1949–1995
Deng Xiaoping: Portrait of a Chinese Statesman (edited)
Greater China: The Next Superpower? (edited)
Chinese Foreign Policy: Theory and Practice (coedited with
      Thomas W. Robinson)
American Studies of Contemporary China (edited)
Beautiful Imperialist: China Perceives America, 1972–1990
The Making of a Premier: Zhao Ziyang's Provincial Career

The Modern Chinese State

Edited by

DAVID SHAMBAUGH

The George Washington University

PUBLISHED BY THE PRESS SYNDICATE OF THE UNIVERSITY OF CAMBRIDGE
The Pitt Building, Trumpington Street, Cambridge, United Kingdom

CAMBRIDGE UNIVERSITY PRESS
The Edinburgh Building, Cambridge CB2 2RU, UK
40 West 20th Street, New York, NY 10011-4211, USA
10 Stamford Road, Oakleigh, Melbourne 3166, Australia
Ruiz de Alarcón 13, 28014 Madrid, Spain

www.cambridge.org
Information on this title: www.cambridge.org/9780521772341

First published 2000

Typeface Times Roman 10/13 pt.   *System* Quark [BTS]

A catalog record for this book is available from the British Library.

Library of Congress Cataloging in Publication Data

The modern Chinese State / edited by David Shambaugh
        p. cm. – (Cambridge modern China series)
    Includes bibliographical references.
    ISBN 0-521-77234-6 (hardback) – ISBN 0-521-77603-1 (pbk.)
        1. China – Politics and government – 1644–1912. 2. China – Politics and
    government – 20th century. I. Shambaugh, David L. II. Series.
JQ1510.M66 2000
320.451′09′04 – dc21   99-053435

ISBN-13 978-0-521-77234-1 hardback
ISBN-10 0-521-77234-6 hardback

ISBN-13 978-0-521-77603-5 paperback
ISBN-10 0-521-77603-1 paperback

Transferred to digital printing 2005

In memory of
Professor Franz Michael:
Scholar, Advocate, and Gentleman

Contents

List of Contributors   *page* xiii
List of Illustrations   xvii
List of Abbreviations   xix
Preface   xxi

Introduction: The Evolving and Eclectic
Modern Chinese State
David Shambaugh   1

1   The Late Imperial Chinese State
    H. Lyman Miller   15

2   The Chinese State during the Republican Era
    Ramon H. Myers   42

3   The Evolution of the State in the Republic of China
    on Taiwan
    Bruce J. Dickson   73

4   The Chinese State during the Maoist Era
    Frederick C. Teiwes   105

5   The Chinese State in the Post-Mao Era
    David Shambaugh   161

6   The Chinese Communist Economic State in
    Comparative Perspective
    Jan Prybyla   188

7   The Future of the Chinese State
    Harvey Nelsen   216

Index   237

List of Contributors

Bruce J. Dickson is Director of the Sigur Center for Asian Studies and the East Asian Studies Program in the Elliott School of International Affairs at The George Washington University and Associate Professor of Political Science and International Affairs. His research and teaching focus on the domestic politics of China and Taiwan. His recent publications include *Democratization in China and Taiwan: The Adaptability of Leninist Parties* (1997), "China's Democratization and the Taiwan Experience," *Asian Survey* (April 1998), and "Unsettled Succession: China's Critical Moment," *National Interest* (Fall 1997). He is also associate editor of the journal *Problems of Post-Communism*. He received his Ph.D. in political science from the University of Michigan.

H. Lyman Miller is Senior Fellow at the Hoover Institution at Stanford University, and teaches at the Naval Postgraduate School in Monterey, California. He taught for many years at the Nitze School of Advanced International Studies and in the political science department at Johns Hopkins University. Prior to that he served as an analyst in the U.S. government. He is author of numerous articles on modern China, as well as *Science and Dissent in Post-Mao China* (1996).

Ramon H. Myers has authored, coauthored, and edited twenty books, as well as written essays which have appeared in thirty-two edited works. He is currently the Curator-Scholar of the East Asian Collection and Senior Fellow of the Hoover Institution on War, Revolution and Peace at Stanford University. His most recently published work, coauthored with Linda Chao, is *The First Chinese Democracy: Political Life in the Republic of China* (1998).

Harvey Nelsen is Professor in the Department of Government and International Affairs at the University of South Florida. His book-length studies have dealt with civil-military relations in China and Chinese foreign policy. He has just begun a comparative study of religions in light of the absence of religious wars in Chinese history. His publications include *The Chinese Military System* (1981) and *Power and Insecurity: Beijing, Moscow and Washington 1949–89* (1989).

Jan Prybyla is Professor Emeritus of Economics at Pennsylvania State University. He is the author of *The Political Economy of Communist China* (1970), *The Chinese Economy: Problems and Policies* (1978, 1981), *Issues in Socialist Economic Modernization* (1981), *Market and Plan under Socialism: The Bird in the Cage* (1987), and *Reform in China and Other Socialist Economies* (1990); coauthor of *China and the Crisis of Marxism-Leninism* (1990), and coauthor and coeditor of *Russia and China on the Eve of a New Millennium* (1997). He has taught comparative economic systems at Nankai University, Tianjin, China, in 1987–88, and was a Visiting Scholar at the Institute of International Relations, National Chengchi University, Taipei, Taiwan, in 1989. He is currently working on a book, *China's Two Decades of Economic Reform: Methods, Achievements, Problems*. He lives in Tucson, Arizona.

David Shambaugh is Professor of Political Science and International Affairs and Director of the China Policy Program at the Elliott School of International Affairs, The George Washington University. He is also a nonresident Senior Fellow in the Foreign Policy Studies Program at The Brookings Institution. He has published widely on Chinese politics, foreign relations, security and defense issues, and international relations of the Asia-Pacific region. He has published four books, edited seven others, and served as editor of the *China Quarterly* from 1991 to 1996. He is active in a number of professional organizations and learned societies and associations.

Frederick C. Teiwes received a B.A. from Amherst College and a Ph.D. in political science from Columbia University. He subsequently taught and conducted research at Cornell University, the Australian National University, and, since 1976, at the University of Sydney where he currently holds a Personal Chair in Chinese Politics. He is the author of a number of books on Chinese elite politics including *Politics and Purges in China* (1979, 1993), *Leadership, Legitimacy, and Conflict in China* (1984), and *Politics at Mao's Court* (1990). In recent years he has collaborated with Warren Sun on further studies of Chinese leadership politics, notably, *The Politics of Agricultural Cooperativization in China* (1993), *The Formation of the Maoist Leadership* (1994), *The Tragedy of Lin Biao* (1996), and, most recently, *China's Road to Disaster* (1999).

List of Illustrations

Figure 2.1   The Northern State, 1912–1928   *page* 48
Figure 2.2   Structure of the Nationalist Government,
             1928–1937   56
Figure 2.3   The State Administrative Structure, 1937–1945   67
Figure 5.1   The Chinese State in 2000   169

List of Abbreviations

CCP	Chinese Communist Party
CMC	Central Military Commission
CPPCC	Chinese People's Political Consultative Conference
DPP	Democratic Progressive Party
FFYP	First Five-Year Plan
GED	General Equipment Department
GMD	Guomindang
MAC	Military Affairs Committee
NGO	nongovernmental organization
NPC	National People's Congress
NSC	National Security Council
PAP	People's Armed Police
PLA	People's Liberation Army
PRC	People's Republic of China
ROC	Republic of China
SPC	State Planning Commission
TFYP	Third Five-Year Plan
TVE	township and village enterprise

Preface

This volume owes a debt of gratitude to many. Most of all it owes a special intellectual debt to the memory of Franz Michael (1907–1992), to whom the volume is admiringly dedicated.

Most of the contributors to this volume were either colleagues or students of Professor Michael. Personally, as an undergraduate, he was one of my first teachers of Asian history. He did much to shape my initial understanding of China and Asian civilizations, and he particularly challenged me, as a young liberal, to see how easy it was for unbridled state power to be used in despotic ways. Professor Michael was one of the first Asian scholars to apply the totalitarian paradigm (developed to understand modern fascism and Stalinist communism) to the study of Chinese communism, as he recognized that dictatorships knew no cultural boundaries. This recognition also grew out of his understanding (and debates with Karl Wittfogel) of "Oriental Despotism." His own European heritage and study of Asia blended intellectually in Professor Michael's critical mind.[1]

Franz Michael's impact on the field of Sinological studies was significant. His influence endures in the number of students that he trained in thirty-five years as a professor of history at the University of Washington, George Washington University, and University of Pittsburgh – many of whom pursued careers as China scholars. He also taught large numbers of students who would enter government service and other pursuits in international affairs. However, through his daunting number of articles and books, Franz's scholarly impact reached beyond those in his classroom. His three-volume *The Taiping Rebellion* is still considered the classic work on the subject. Franz also believed in public education and

---

[1] See Marie-Luise Näth, "In Memoriam: Franz Michael (1907–1992)," *The China Quarterly*, No. 138 (June 1994), pp. 513–16.

policy – teaching continuing education courses at the Smithsonian Institution and leading tours to China, testifying before Congress and writing policy papers, and lobbying many in the media. Franz's passion for China was, perhaps, exceeded only by his enjoyment of bird watching and sports car driving.

Franz Michael's own academic training was completed in Germany between the wars. He completed his doctorate with the highest honors at the University of Freiburg in 1933. That year, as the Nazis began their rise to power and anti-Semitism began to spread, Franz abandoned a promising Foreign Office career and went into self-imposed exile in China. After five years teaching German in Hangzhou and traveling throughout the countryside not occupied by the advancing Japanese forces, he accepted a fellowship at Johns Hopkins University and moved to the United States – which would become his adopted home for the remainder of his life.

Throughout his distinguished academic career, Professor Michael was a passionate proponent of the view that one could not understand China unless one understood its bureaucracy and ways in which the state apparat evolved over time and in response to economic and social stimuli. For him, there were two key aspects to China: the gentry and the bureaucracy; together they comprised the Chinese state. Thus the contributors to this volume, and Franz's former colleagues at The George Washington University involved in this project, thought it appropriate that his contributions to the China field be commemorated by commissioning a volume on the modern Chinese state.

The conference that gave rise to this volume was a joint venture between the Institute of Russian, European, and Eurasian Studies (IREES) and the Sigur Center for Asian Studies at The George Washington University. Franz's close colleague Carl Linden must be credited with initiating the idea of a posthumous commemorative volume, and Carl, IREES director James Millar, and I worked closely together in planning the conference. Suzanne Stephenson and Deborah Toy did yeoman's service with all of the complicated logistics. The meeting in October 1998 brought together many of Franz's former students and colleagues, as well as his widow Dolores and daughters, all of whom enjoyed reminiscing about Franz and the former Institute of Sino-Soviet Studies at The George Washington University.

A deep debt of thanks is also due to the contributors, who demonstrated great patience as this volume morphed from a set of conference papers into a scholarly volume. Unfortunately, not all of the papers originally presented at the conference could be included in the volume, but I am still most grateful to all of the original authors for the time and effort expended. Like all edited volumes, the chapters were rewritten several times to take account of suggestions and criticisms from those at the conference and outside peer reviewers for Cambridge University Press. Working with Cambridge University Press has been a real pleasure, particularly with social science commissioning editor Mary J. Child, series editor Professor William Kirby, and copy editor Stephanie Sakson.

The book tries to tackle a big subject and a long expanse of time. Hopefully, it includes some big ideas too, and tries to offer both new students and informed readers an adequate and accurate introduction to the complexities of the Chinese state over the last couple of centuries. As the Chinese state enters its twenty-sixth millennium of organized rule, faced with substantial challenges and abiding questions about its efficacy, pundits may do well to consider its evolution along a longer continuum. This volume should help to fill that need.

David Shambaugh
Washington, D.C.
May 1999

Introduction:
The Evolving and Eclectic
Modern Chinese State

DAVID SHAMBAUGH

THERE are few issues that have interested China scholars over the years as the evolution of the Chinese state.[1] As the following chapters illustrate, the Chinese state in the modern era has been a particularly dynamic entity. While it has evolved, the Chinese state has shed and absorbed a variety of organizational and normative features – becoming, over time, an eclectic amalgam.

CHINA'S ECLECTIC STATE

Unlike many Western polities that have evolved over the same period of time generally within a singular liberal paradigm, the modern Chinese state has undergone several macro transitions: from imperial to republican to revolutionary communist to modernizing socialist and, in Taiwan, to democratic phases. While radically different in its basic ethos and organizational structure in each phase (monarchical-republican-Leninist-liberal), the Chinese state on the mainland has had three enduring missions: modernization of the economy, transformation of society, and defense of the nation against foreign aggression. The intended goals of social transformation varied (from neo-Confucianist to neofascist to radical Maoism to pragmatic Dengism), but for more than a century these have been the central and consistent missions of the Chinese state regardless of their fundamentally different cast. As one evolved to the next, some elements of the past survived each transition and were woven

---

[1] Recently, for example, see the masterful study by R. Bin Wong, *China Transformed: Historical Change and the Limits of European Experience* (Ithaca: Cornell University Press, 1997).

into new institutional frameworks. Each new departure was never total, although all were sharp and each sought to "overthrow" and replace the former. In reality, though, each new Chinese state maintained certain features of the old. Moreover, in each phase, different foreign elements were imported and grafted on to the evolving indigenous root, creating an ever-more complex hybrid. This eclectic state is apparent from examining the evolving tables of organization of successive Chinese states, but is particularly evident when one speaks with bureaucrats and officials of different government ministries, different components of the military and security apparat, and educational institutions. In interviewing Chinese officials, bureaucrats, and cadres on the Chinese mainland and Taiwan today, one encounters distinct institutional identities, which seem to derive, at least in part, from the different foreign nations that served as "models" of administrative development and trained officials accordingly. These organizational identities exist apart from bureaucratic missions and "turf," as they help to form a kind of "inner ethos" within different state organs – thus giving rise to multiple, coexistent, and competitive subidentities within the eclectic modern "Chinese state."

As the Chinese state evolved over time and took on different missions, it varied in size, scope, and organizational complexity. The ensuing chapters in this volume elaborate this in great detail. The late imperial state, from the late Ming dynasty through the "High Qing" period, expanded constantly to manage the ever-growing state monopolies over key commodities, irrigation and agriculture, local taxation, and management of commercial and diplomatic interactions with foreign "barbarians" as well as those in the "Sinic zone" of the "tributary system." Late Qing efforts at military modernization, the policy of building "shipyards and arsenals," also spawned new industrial structures and bureaucracies. By the time of its collapse, the imperial Chinese state was a sprawling and unwieldy set of bureaucracies (one might say that it collapsed under its own weight). The early republican government, after the revolution of 1911 (*Xinhai Geming*), produced a more circumscribed state apparatus, although it never fully took shape and soon was limited to a finite sphere of activity as warlords dominated and administered different sections of China. When the Nationalist state finally eliminated warlordism and constituted a new government in Nanjing in 1928, the Chinese state had shrunk and been functionally redefined from its imperial predecessors. The Nanjing Government was an eclectic mix of some late imperial organs, but it also drew on a range of foreign institutional models: Japanese, German, British, Soviet, and American.[2] Despite these reforms, the "reach of the state" remained geographically and functionally limited; the rule of law did not underpin government activity; while a variety of neofascist paramilitary thugs, secret police, and gangs coerced the populace to comply with supposed government edicts. After the Japanese invasion, the Nationalist state, as a functioning national entity, collapsed for all ostensible purposes. With the victory of the Chinese Communists in 1949, the state began to grow again. While retaining some elements of the imperial and Nationalist organizational structure, it essentially morphed into a cloned version of the "High Stalinist" Soviet communist state. This produced a variety of new structural and functional hierarchies. Mao's various attempts at social engineering and transformation also contributed to the growth of the party-state, particularly at the local level.[3] With the post-Great Leap economic reforms of the early 1960s, the state and its purview grew further – which had much to do with Mao's attempts to attack and reduce it during the Cultural Revolution (1966–76). With post-Mao economic, scientific, and military reforms under Deng Xiaoping, the Chinese state was reconfigured and grew in size yet again, although its scope of activity was reduced. By the 1980s, however, the size of government had become an impediment to economic, scientific, and military modernization. As a result, the government undertook four successive waves of retrenchment, downsizing, and streamlining (1982, 1988, 1993, 1998) in attempts to improve efficiency and economies of scale. Still, the Chinese state today remains a sprawling set of functional and territorial bureaucracies, and possesses the largest number of bureaucrats of any government in the world.

THEMES

The contributors to this volume trace this historical evolution of successive Chinese states, and ably capture the complexities of each distinct phase. In the process, vast amounts of information are distilled for the reader.

H. Lyman Miller begins (Chapter 1) with an overview assessment of the late imperial state, from the mid-sixteenth century to the 1911 Revo-

---

[2] This is recognized, for example, by Julia Strauss in her *Strong Institutions in Weak Polities: State Building in Republican China, 1927–1940* (Oxford: Clarendon Press, 1998).
[3] See Timothy Cheek and Tony Saich, eds., *New Perspectives on State Socialism in China, 1949–1965* (Armonk, N.Y.: M.E. Sharpe, 1997).

lution. He sets forth a number of themes and identifies several components of the modern Chinese state that are seen in subsequent chapters. Students and scholars of twentieth-century Chinese states will be struck by the numerous continuities with China's *ancien régime*. Despite the twin revolutions of the twentieth century (1911 and 1949) and the reinvention of the Nationalist state on Taiwan after 1949, Miller's chapter is a refreshing reminder that, organizationally and behaviorally, the Ming and Qing state practices presaged their twentieth-century counterparts. Consider the following examples noted in Chapter 1.

The legitimization of the late-imperial state was the product of, among other things, a moralistic ideology (neo-Confucianism), which was propagated through a variety of state organs. Concomitantly, the educational system was highly elitist and a tool for propagating and inculcating the official cant in the educated literati who staffed the state – who, in turn, were co-opted and patronized by central and local elites. With neo-Confucian orthodoxy the ethical-moral basis of rule, there was a natural ritualistic basis of state authority. Regime change in such a system was thus precipitated more by the perceived loss of moral authority (the "Mandate of Heaven") than as the result of the incompetence of rulers or their unpopular policies. Needless to say, there was no routinized process of elite turnover or regime change. Miller notes the longstanding, and chronic, Chinese inability to manage what nowadays is called leadership succession. In traditional China, as today, leaders stay in office until they become incapacitated, die, or are overthrown by rivals. He further calls attention to the endemic maneuvering for power among the elite in the imperial court, eunuchs, and members of the emperor's clan.

It is important that Miller's chapter also delineates how the Chinese state was structured and ruled over the millennia, and how imperial China established a "modern" state structure long before the West. The precursor of the centralized administrative system established in France under Louis XIV had existed in a highly complex and functional form in China at least since the Song dynasty – indeed, as noted by French historian Jacques Gernet, the totality of imperial Chinese state control over the population, economy, and military far exceeded that of the embryonic modern European state.[4] While reaching its zenith in the Song and

---

[4] Jacques Gernet, "Introduction," in Stuart R. Schram, ed., *Foundations and Limits of State Power in China* (Hong Kong: Chinese University Press and London: School of Oriental & African Studies, 1987), pp. xxii.

Ming dynasties, the Chinese state dates to the third century B.C. – easily the earliest known government in human history. By the "High Qing" period, as Miller notes in his chapter, many of the attributes now associated with the "modern" state functioned smoothly in China. China developed functionally defined and highly specialized civil and military bureaucracies, stretching vertically from capital to localities. Central edicts and laws (and indeed this was a system based on law and an extensive codified judicial system) were implemented by an extensive corps of civil servants, the "mandarinate," who underwent lengthy exam-based training and were subject to meritocratic criteria of performance and promotion. The military was a similarly elite system, with strategically garrisoned troops. Miller also describes the system of internal government communications, and the internal organization of the imperial court, which were also highly advanced and specialized.[5] The central state established procedures and humiliating rituals for dealing with foreigners, particularly non-Sinic "barbarians." It also established state monopolies over the production and distribution of key commodities, such as salt, water, and bronze.

Despite the reality of the highly advanced imperial Chinese state, Miller also draws attention to its limits. Fiscally, the late imperial state had a weak capacity to extract resources and revenue from the populace. One result of this inability was that the central state did not possess the means to redistribute resources to needy sectors or invest in strategic priority projects. A value-added tax on commerce would have gone far to fill state coffers and stimulate growth in key industries. Many historians, notably the late Joseph Needham, point to this fact as one of the key reasons that China remained, in essence, a handicraft economy and never industrialized when the West did in the eighteenth and nineteenth centuries. He further argued that, while science was highly developed in imperial and late imperial China, there were few commercial incentives to create the investment necessary to convert "basic" science into "applied" technology. The social stratification of society, which placed merchants at the bottom of the social ladder, was a further impediment.

Finally, Miller's chapter discusses the limits on state power at the local level and the persistent centrifugal forces in Chinese history that have always made it difficult for the sovereign to extend total rule over its sub-

---

[5] Also see Beatrice S. Bartlett, *Monarchs and Ministers: The Grand Council in Mid-Ch'ing China* (Berkeley: University of California Press, 1991).

jects in such a far-flung empire. The lowest representatives of the imperial state were the district and county magistrates, but their writ of rule
was extremely circumscribed as their jurisdictional responsibilities numbered hundreds of thousands of subjects. In an effort to maintain some
semblance of control over local security and trade, Miller notes, the
baojia and *lijia* systems, respectively, were established. But this was not
sufficient – the local magistrates had to enter into an extensive web of
patron-client ties with local elites, the rural gentry, and militias.[6]

Thus Miller paints a picture of the late imperial state as having developed a highly centralized and specialized bureaucracy, but one that
encountered real difficulties extending its writ over society. The "minimalist state" reigned, he argues, but did not really rule. It was only with
the establishment of the republic, after 1911 and particularly after 1937,
that the penetrative, mobilizational, and extractive elements associated
with strong state capacity were truly established – and these were, of
course, taken to an extreme under Mao Zedong and the Chinese Communist state.

The steady erosion of late imperial state capacity, described by Miller,
set the stage first for the "Self-Strengthening Movement" (*Zi Qiang
Yundong*) of the 1870s and then the attempted reforms of 1898 – which,
while ultimately failing, served as the bridge to the twentieth century,
republicanism, and a more modern state for China. Together they set the
Chinese state on the paths of modern industrialization, military modernization, scientific inquiry, and Western educational reform. These twin
movements were inspired by studying a combination of Japanese Meiji
reforms, European industrial and military strategies, and American
science and education. To be sure, the dismemberment of China at the
hands of Western powers and Japan spurred the urgency of the mission.
From that point on, state-building in modern China was equated with
nation-building, and the majority of Chinese elites agreed that a strong
state was necessary to guide economic and military development. Only
with a strong nation could China overcome its weaknesses, repel aggres-
sors, and regain China's rightful place in the world as a modern power
with dignity and self-respect. This has been the singular mission of
Chinese statesmen ever since.

The Chinese state during the republican era is the subject of Chapter
2, by Ramon Myers. The republican era (1911–1949) was one of a series

---

[6] See, for example, Frederic C. Wakeman, Jr., and Carolyn Grant, eds., *Conflict and Control
in Late-Imperial China* (Berkeley: University of California Press, 1975).

of abortive initiatives, failed constitutionalism, and persistent militarism and war. In such an environment, the new republican state was constantly on the defensive – against bandits and warlords, opposition communist armies, invading Japanese forces, rebellious commanders, incompetent and corrupt officials, a factionalized and bloodthirsty political elite, personalistic rule, and the dictatorial persona of Chiang Kai-shek. This was not the way the father of modern China, Sun Yat-sen, had envisioned it. Sun's Three People's Principles (nationalism, people's rights, and people's welfare) offered a blueprint for a modern democratic state, a modern society, and a modern economy. But, as Myers shows, not all agreed with Sun's vision. Influential intellectuals such as Liang Qichao disagreed that the Chinese people were ready for such modernity, arguing instead that an extended "enlightened autocracy" was required for an indeterminate period of tutelage (just prior to his death, Sun agreed). Myers cites Thomas Metzger's belief that these two differing visions were not only different in terms of their estimate of China's social structure, but they also represented, respectively, "transformative" (Sun) versus "accommodative" (Liang) modes of statecraft. These differing approaches illustrate the two distinct strands of Chinese statecraft – sweeping "totalism" versus incremental pragmatism – which later became manifest during the People's Republic in the contrasting approaches of Mao Zedong and Deng Xiaoping.

The republic's first president, Yuan Shikai, advocated state-strengthening and had little time for the constitutional constraints on executive power or his rule. Myers shows how Yuan Shikai ruled as an autocrat and schemed to install his militarist cronies in power. Yuan even attempted to restore the monarchy and crown himself emperor in 1916, but this effort failed and he died a year later. Various military strongmen vied for the control of the national government and north China for the ensuing twelve years, a period during which centralized rule and national unity collapsed in the face of warlords, personalistic rule, and constantly shifting factions and coalitions.[7] During this period the central state, in effect, collapsed. The anarchic period came to an end when a coalition of military forces, led by Chiang Kai-shek, launched the "Northern Expedition" from Guangdong in 1927, and swept up to the Yangzi Valley. This effort was ultimately successful in unifying much of the country under a single government, established in Nanjing in 1928.

---

[7] See Edward McCord, *The Power of the Gun: The Emergence of Modern Chinese Warlordism* (Berkeley: University of California Press, 1993).

Thereafter, for the next decade prior to the full Japanese invasion, the Nationalist state in Nanjing reestablished and reconstituted itself (the "Nanjing Decade"). Unfortunately, as Myers traces in illuminating detail, the Guomindang (Nationalist) party-state fell prey to many of the same machinations and bad luck that beset its predecessor. Nonetheless, the Nanjing government was able to constitute itself organizationally and programmatically to a considerable extent.[8] Myers interestingly shows how Sun Yat-sen's ideology combined with neo-Confucian values and Leninist organizational techniques during this period to constitute a unique hybrid form of Chinese state. The underside of this state was the neofascism expressed in Chiang Kai-shek's New Life Movement and gangster-like terror against political enemies. Myers also shows how this was a period of bureaucratic growth and economic development. Unfortunately, domestic and international security concerns preoccupied Chiang and his government, requiring the diversion of substantial resources not only into the military and paramilitary security services, but also into defense industries. The Nanjing Government also fell prey to the same cancer that plagued the late imperial state (and present-day regime): fiscal insolvency due to a weak tax base and deficit spending. Following the anti-Japanese war the hyperinflationary spiral caused by deficit spending, poor macroeconomic management, and an uncontrolled money supply left the nation bankrupt and the populace destitute. This was a major contributing factor to the collapse of the Nationalist state, causing the government to flee to Taiwan.

Once on Taiwan, the Guomindang-led Nationalist state reconstituted itself, under the protection of the United States. This is the subject of Chapter 3, by Bruce Dickson. As Dickson notes at the outset, from the vantage point of the end of the twentieth century and after five decades of growth, the Nationalist state on Taiwan appears to be a textbook case of a modern and democratic Chinese state. Dickson reminds us, however, that this has not always been the case, and that the Nationalist state on Taiwan also had a long, dark history of oppression and authoritarianism under martial law. But, throughout, Taiwan reaped the benefits of state-led development – doing much to coin the term "the developmental state."

Dickson shows how the state on Taiwan evolved over time and drew upon an "uneasy amalgam of traditions" from imperial China, the Nationalist era on the mainland, as well as distinctive features of Taiwan.

---

[8] See Strauss, *Strong Institutions in Weak Polities*.

It also drew heavily upon American advice and advisors. Taiwan's political elite since has been almost entirely U.S.-educated.

The Guomindang transferred the five-branch organization of government from the mainland to Taiwan, and for awhile this centralized "national" system was superimposed on the "provincial" government on the island, but this bifurcated fiction eventually gave way to a unified system in 1997 when the provincial level of government was abolished. Once this was formally done, any pretense to the Nationalists' claim to sovereignty over the mainland disappeared. Subsequently, the Nationalist state on Taiwan has maintained that there exists a situation of "one nation, divided country" with two ruling "political entities" which should deal with each other on the basis of "special state-to-state relations." For many years the new Nationalist state on Taiwan was merely a tool in the Guomindang's hands, during the long period of martial law under Chiang Kai-shek. But following the Generalissimo's death in 1975 and the ascent of his son Chiang Ching-kuo, martial law was gradually relaxed until its formal elimination in 1987. This decree opened the door, under Chiang Ching-kuo's successor, native Taiwanese Lee Teng-hui, to amend the Constitution, disband the security state and release political prisoners, give increasing power to the legislative branch, permit opposition parties, institute island-wide elections, and establish – for the first time in Chinese history – a true democratic and popularly elected state/government. To be sure, this has been (and still is) a bumpy political process, as the system is still fraught with corruption and vote-buying. Although immature, the democratic Nationalist state on Taiwan has provoked extreme displeasure from Beijing, which tried to influence the first-ever presidential elections in 1996 with a barrage of ballistic missile "tests" near the island, aimed at intimidating voters. President Lee has also successfully overhauled the Guomindang by bringing large numbers of native Taiwanese, like himself, into the party at all levels. As a result, Dickson notes that the Nationalist state on Taiwan can no longer be regarded as an unwelcome occupying force. Yet the twin processes of Taiwanization and democratization have precipitated a profound identity crisis for the inhabitants of the island: Are they Chinese, Taiwanese, or both? Is Taiwan part of or separate from China? These are core issues that will continue to plague the collective identity of Taiwan's citizens and politicians, as well as the governments in Beijing, Washington, and throughout East Asia. Despite this uncertain identity, the Nationalist state on Taiwan is unique in Chinese history.

The "democratic breakthrough" on Taiwan contrasts sharply with

Communist Party rule on the Chinese mainland. Chapter 4, on the Maoist state, by Frederick Teiwes, elucidates the "totalistic state" that Mao and his comrades built after 1949, which was torn asunder in 1966–67 during the "Great Proletarian Cultural Revolution." Teiwes distinguishes Maoist totalism from classic totalitarianism on the basis of several indicators: the mode of policy implementation, the broad relationship of state to society, the nature of the party-army relationship, the degree of factionalism among the political elite, and the degree to which state control was founded on perceived legitimate authority or simply brute force. Teiwes further finds that the unique revolutionary experience of the Chinese Communists had much to do with how they adapted Soviet Leninist practices to create the totalist Maoist state. From its outset, Teiwes finds, the Chinese Communist Party (CCP) embraced a far more devolved and decentralized model of rule than its Soviet counterparts, and the "mass line" and "united front" strategies contrasted sharply with the insular and conspiratorial style of the Bolsheviks. He also notes that Chinese Communist leaders adopted a greater degree of collective decision-making, at least until Mao gained unquestioned preeminence. Yet, normatively, Teiwes argues that the CCP implemented strict Leninist discipline within the party and adopted the "organizational weapon" of the "dictatorship of the proletariat" to extinguish domestic political enemies as well as significant segments of the populace. The harsh reality of China under Mao was that tens of millions perished in political "campaigns" (*yundong*), targeted purges, or as the result of state and nature-induced famine.

Organizationally, Professor Teiwes sketches the structure of the Maoist state and finds that there was "considerable structural continuity" throughout the period 1949–76. Of course, during the Cultural Revolution (particularly 1966–72) the central and provincial party and state apparat was decimated, and much of it ceased functioning. In its place, new structures – such as Revolutionary Committees – were formed, and the "affirmative action" policies of putting workers, peasants, and soldiers (*gong-nong-bing*) in positions of governmental and enterprise authority were implemented. Teiwes provides a detailed description of the structure and functioning of the CCP and its constituent Central Committee departments. This vertical hierarchical party-state system borrowed from the Soviet Union formed the backbone of Chinese Leninism and penetrated society to an extent far greater than imperial, late imperial, or the series of Nationalist governments were ever capable of. Central to this apparat was the Leninist *nomenklatura*, the role of internal security forces, and the military. Teiwes shows how the party penetrated the government, society, and economic units through the *nomenklatura* system, and how the military, too, became a creature of the party instead of the government. Indeed, the Chinese state under Mao was the party! Coercion, and the threat of it, was fundamental to the system. If the party-state chose not to suppress, it co-opted. Various professional groups and local elites were given an essential choice: join the party-state or be suppressed by it. Over time the various organizations and instruments of totalistic rule developed by Mao and his communist comrades were deployed in support of different attempts at class-leveling and social engineering. In the process, they ceased to perform some of their original intended bureaucratic purposes and became tools in the hands of Mao and his utopian kindred spirits. Following the zenith of Cultural Revolution anarchy and the suspicious death of Mao's would-be successor Lin Biao in 1971, the bureaucratic party state began to be rebuilt by Premier Zhou Enlai and Vice-Premier Deng Xiaoping. Zhou and Deng met with limited success in the nadir of the Cultural Revolution and toward the end of Mao's life, but their initiatives sowed the seeds of fuller reforms following Mao's death.

This is the subject of my Chapter 5. Once rehabilitated, Deng Xiaoping inherited a difficult situation, described by Teiwes as: "a fractured and grievance-riddled society, a party-state with reduced legitimacy and weakened dominance over society, faction-infested institutions, ambiguous social norms, and a divided top leadership." Deng quickly set out to rectify these anomalies, realizing fully that the CCP's legitimacy and longevity were at stake and that China's economy and standard of living had fallen far behind much of the world. Deng was a man in a hurry. He faced the contradictory task of rebuilding the atrophied party-state, while at the same time relinquishing much of its former totalistic purview. Devolution and decentralization of power were the order of the day under Deng. While the Communist Party maintained its hegemonic monopoly on political power, in many ways the party-state "withdrew" from society and its former all-intrusive controls. As a result, China's farmers, workers, and entrepreneurs were liberated to an unprecedented extent. The economy boomed and society pluralized.

My chapter on the post-Mao state also elucidates three principal arenas of change: structural, normative, and spatial. I argue that, organizationally, the post-Mao state has not changed all that much from its predecessor, but organically it has evolved substantially. By this I mean that the party's control over the two other principal pillars of institutional power, the government and the military, has loosened considerably. Even in terms of the *nomenklatura*, composition and scope of party committees, control over propaganda and the media, the "interlocking directorate" of party/government/military elites, and other core elements of the Leninist apparat, the post-Mao era has witnessed qualitative and fundamental change. Normatively, the functions and policy-making procedures of the state have also changed dramatically. Factionalism has declined markedly, while decision-making has become more consensual, consultative, and collective. Spatially, the "withdrawal of the state" meant devolving decision-making authority to the locality and enterprise, loosening the work unit (*danwei*) cradle-to-grave employment and welfare systems to permit the growth of a private sector and nongovernmental organizations, relaxing the controls of security organs and party cells, permitting much-expanded individual freedoms and a "public sphere," and so on.

These reforms have had a profound effect on the Chinese state and society: The state's control over society and grip on power is looser than ever in the half-century of Communist Party rule. The more the party-state loosened its previously hegemonic grip, the more pressure there has been for further reform. The political pressures for interest articulation grow and, along with them, the pressures for enfranchised civil society. Without creating the channels of expression, frustrations build and pressures from below grow. Sooner or later it erupts, as it did in the popular demonstrations across China in 1989. These reformist changes and rising pressures raise serious questions about the survivability of CCP rule, a subject taken up in the concluding chapter.

Economist Jan Prybyla's insightful Chapter 6 examines the full sweep of the fifty years of the Chinese Communist "economic state" in comparative perspective. This subject is treated separately from the preceding two chapters, as the economy and economic organizations during the People's Republic are so important and complex as to warrant individual consideration. Prybyla's chapter traces the evolution from the centralized, commandist, hierarchical, all-pervasive, and overly bureaucratized Maoist economic state to the decentralized condition of the Deng and post-Deng era. Prybyla sees economic commandism and centralization as the twin of political totalitarianism and he shows how the Chinese Communists nationalized, centralized, socialized, collectivized, and homogenized economic production through a series of Maoist campaigns and Soviet-style takeovers during the 1950s. But Prybyla also demonstrates how the Chinese began to chafe under Soviet tutelage and how differing approaches to development played a key role in Mao's 1958 launch of the Great Leap Forward and commune movement, and two years later in the Sino-Soviet rupture.[9] The post-Soviet phase of economic development in 1962–65 hesitantly embraced markets, material incentives, and limited property rights – before succumbing to "Maoism II": the Cultural Revolution. This flirtation with autarky and mass mobilization proved devastating to China's development. Only with Deng Xiaoping's return to power and the post-1978 economic reforms did China begin to enjoy unprecedented productive growth and prosperity.[10] These reforms required substantial institutional change in state structure and the purview of the state. While a large portion of the Chinese economy (55%) now lies outside the state structure, the remnants of the socialist economy are far from eliminated and, in fact, serve as a huge drag on the economy as a whole. They also have resulted in perhaps the greatest threat to the sustainability of the party state: fiscal insolvency. As has been noted above and is seen in Chapters 1 and 2, the incapacity to collect taxes was a major factor imperiling the late imperial and republican states.

Certainly the Chinese state at the outset of the twenty-first century faces many complex challenges on multiple fronts. China is not necessarily a stable country and some China specialists deem the communist party-state to be weak and vulnerable.[11]

In the concluding chapter, Harvey Nelsen attempts to examine the unpredictable: the future of the Chinese state. He begins by noting that Communist China has passed through fairly predictable stages of development, particularly as noted by the late German political scientist Richard Lowenthal: mass mobilization and social transformation followed by state building, professional specialization, rationalization, and economic modernization. In the process, revolutionary aspirations give way to bureaucratic inefficiencies, corruption, and the need for coercion. In the late twentieth century, Nelsen notes, these phenomena were exacerbated by the processes of globalization – which not only undermined protectionist economies, but also subverted political hegemony. Nelsen,

---

[9] Also see Odd Arne Westad, ed., *Brothers in Arms: The Rise and Fall of the Sino-Soviet Alliance, 1945–1963* (Washington, D.C., and Stanford, Calif.: Woodrow Wilson Center Press and Stanford University Press, 1998).

[10] Also see Orville Schell and David Shambaugh, eds., *The China Reader: The Reform Era* (New York: Random House, 1999).

[11] See the contributions in David Shambaugh, ed., *Is China Unstable?* (Washington, D.C.: Sigur Center for Asian Studies, 1998).

borrowing on the work of Samuel Huntington and Bruce Dickson, asks whether the CCP party-state is capable of "adaptation" to meet the demands of economic efficiency and political pluralism, but arrives at a essentially pessimistic conclusion. Will "democracy" replace the CCP and blossom in China? Here too he is also dubious. Nelsen is more optimistic about the possibilities of federalism for China – and, in fact, he sees it as having been under way for a number of years. Yet he is uncertain that China's unitary political traditions and culture can be reconciled with the demands of federalism.

Will the CCP endure? Nelsen concludes by offering seven reasons why it will:

- The regime will invoke threats to justify its rule;
- There is an absence of likely alternatives to the regime;
- The regime, post-1989, is resolved to use force to maintain itself in power;
- The regime will manipulate nationalism for its own ends;
- Economic growth will slow but not stop;
- The political system remains, in essence, a Leninist one;
- The legal system is gradually developing.

Nelsen concludes that the world should be prepared to live with a "Market-Leninist" China for years to come, but that enough complex variables exist that – if certain ones coalesce – the entire ruling party-state could come crashing down.

In sum, this volume looks at a long span of Chinese history and a long line of successive Chinese states. In organization, missions, constitution, and composition, they are all quite different: dynastic, republican, socialist, democratic. While the Chinese state has been evolving for more than four millennia, its makeup and nature in the twenty-first century remains an open question – but the pages that follow should sober readers to expect both further evolutionary (even dramatic) change as well as some essential continuities in the Chinese state.

1

The Late Imperial Chinese State

H. LYMAN MILLER

WESTERN historical scholarship on late imperial China seems less settled than ever. In recent years it has evolved in directions that significantly alter longstanding interpretations of the late imperial state. Once-definitive perspectives regarding the scope of the late imperial state, its processes and institutional trends, and its reach into Chinese society have been reopened. New frameworks built on different lines of inquiry and evidence have challenged enduring views on the reasons both for the unprecedented longevity of the Qing dynasty as an alien conquest regime and for its decline in the nineteenth century and demise in the early twentieth century. Presumed continuities between the late imperial past and the authoritarian present no longer seem as compelling as they once did. In their place a renewed appreciation of patterns of dynamism and change has suggested more fertile approaches to making the past serve the present. With all of these changes, alternative chronologies built around newly recognized historical turning points reorganize what seems useful in understanding how we got to the Chinese present from its late imperial past. More than ever, historians seem to speak with contending voices, not consensus regarding state and society in late imperial times.

For historians of China's late imperial era – here defined as China from the mid-sixteenth century until the 1911 Revolution – the emergence of these changes in the historiography of the late imperial era has seemed evolutionary and gradual. For them, they are the familiar consequences of the normal functioning of a now well-established disciplinary com-

The author is grateful to Frederick W. Mote, professor emeritus at Princeton University, and Professor William T. Rowe of Johns Hopkins University for extensive helpful comments on an earlier draft of this chapter.

munity. Older answers to fundamental questions raise new questions whose answers in turn refine, modify, and sometimes transform previous work. New forays into the vast corpus of late imperial records and writings and new approaches to using previously worked bodies of evidence set older generalizations in new contexts. Sometimes, in so doing, some new conclusions have turned earlier generalizations about the late imperial state upside-down. But the changes have emerged gradually.

For students of contemporary China – long the preserve of political science – the historians' discussion of the late imperial state and society will seem foreign. Pursuing a different analytical agenda with respect to a very different China, many contemporary China specialists do not read the work of their colleagues in late imperial history.[1] Their understanding of China's late imperial past often reflects conclusions and generalizations that are no longer universally embraced. And so the changes in late imperial historiography will seem to them revolutionary, not evolutionary.

This is unfortunate. Many of the questions that specialists of contemporary China ask today about the evolution of the contemporary communist regime and its relationship to a rapidly changing Chinese society are the kinds of questions that historians ask about the late imperial era. In a particularly uncertain present, history may be the best guide. And so now it seems more appropriate than ever to reconsider explanations of the past. Certainly Franz Michael, whose work spanned both China's late imperial past and its contemporary present, would have agreed.

This chapter sketches some aspects of recent historiographic trends in understanding the late imperial state. In doing so, it uses the work of Franz Michael as a point of departure. Michael made several important contributions to the history of that era. These include his argument regarding the preconquest adoption by the Manchus of Chinese techniques of governance as an explanation for their dynasty's effectiveness

---

[1] Nor do historians venture much into the work of their political science colleagues on the contemporary Chinese state. In a very useful review of some of the major trends in late imperial and modern Chinese social and economic history, Hans van de Ven, for example, recognizes the import of many of the large questions recent work in these areas pose for understanding contemporary China, but stops short at 1949 "as the history of the People's Republic has been colonized by political scientists." Hans van de Ven, "Recent Studies of Modern Chinese History," *Modern Asian Studies*, vol. 30, no. 2 (1996), 225.

and staying power; his collaborative effort with Zhang Zhongli to dissect the roles of late imperial China's strategic elite, the Chinese "gentry"; and his long-standing interest in tracing the emergence of political and military regionalism in the twentieth century in the decline of centralized imperial power in the nineteenth. In some areas, recent work has significantly altered or modified perspectives that he pioneered; in others, the thrust of his work has been affirmed. After this survey, the chapter concludes by examining some of the implications of this evolving historiography of the late imperial period for the study of contemporary China.

THE LATE IMPERIAL POLITICAL ORDER

Since several detailed analyses of the late imperial state are readily available, only the primary features of its institutions and processes are sketched here.[2]

China in the late imperial period was governed by a bureaucratic monarchy. The seat of political authority resided in the person of the emperor. The emperor's purview was in principle comprehensive, and so his pronouncements were authoritative in every arena of human thought and action. He was at once the final author of the state's political decisions – all officials ultimately acted in his name. He was its supreme lawgiver and commander of its military forces. He was the highest patron of the realm's religious orders and foremost sponsor of its arts and letters.

His authority was legitimated by a Confucian cosmology that placed him at the pivot between the cosmic natural order and the human social order – the "Son of Heaven" (*tianzi*). Paralleling the role of the family

---

[2] The best analytical portrait of the late imperial state is Frederick W. Mote, "Political Structure," in Gilbert Rozman, ed., *The Modernization of China* (New York: Free Press, 1981), 47–106, upon which the discussion in this section relies heavily. A full description of the Qing political system is in Xiao Yishan, *Qingdai tongshi* (Taipei: Taiwan Shangwu Yinshuguan, 1966), vol. 1, pp. 501–610. Also useful are two works by the dean of Chinese institutional history, Charles O. Hucker, *The Ming Dynasty: Its Origins and Evolving Institutions*, Michigan Papers in Chinese Studies No. 34 (Ann Arbor, 1978), and the chapters of his text *China's Imperial Past* (Stanford: Stanford University Press, 1975), 303–328. See also the survey of Albert Feuerwerker, *State and Society in Eighteenth Century China: The Ch'ing Empire in Its Glory* (Ann Arbor, Michigan Papers in Chinese Studies No. 27, 1976), and Richard J. Smith, *China's Cultural Heritage: The Qing Dynasty, 1644–1912*, 2nd edition (Boulder: Westview Press, 1994), 41–67. Franz Michael offered a brief sketch of the late imperial state in his textbook, with George Taylor, *The Far East in the Modern World*, 3rd edition (New York: Holt, Reinhart and Winston, 1975), 34–40.

in observing proper ancestral rites in folk religion, the emperor's character and behavior – particularly his observance of proper rituals and ceremonies – and by extension the ethical conduct of the officials of his regime ensured harmony between and within the natural and social orders. If the emperor's character was upright, if he performed the proper rites, and if his administration was just, then peace and order would prevail. The seasons and celestial cycles of the natural order would progress predictably and would benefit the realm with the right climate and rainfall for abundant harvests. By the same token, deficiencies of the emperor and his government in any of these respects could be expected to bring disorder in the natural and social worlds: floods, droughts, earthquakes, and unanticipated celestial events such as eclipses, comets, and meteor showers in the former, and social disorder and rebellion in the latter. In hindsight, the collapse of a dynastic house and its replacement by another could be understood and so legitimated in terms of this moralistic cosmology, positing the cyclical lapse of the former dynasty's degenerate last emperors' neglect of the proper rites and ceremonies and their restoration by the upright founders of a new dynastic regime.

Under the Qing, this ideology was reflected in institutions at the court. An Imperial Board of Astronomy (*Qintianjian*) managed the politically sensitive tasks of compiling the annual calendar and recording significant celestial and meteorological observations, while a Court of Sacrificial Worship (*Taichangsi*), together with a Board of Rites (*Libu*) and several other palace offices, attended to the emperor's ritual duties.

Imperial succession in the Qing differed from the Ming practice whereby the eldest son of the emperor's empress became heir apparent. Before the Qing conquest of China proper, Hongtaiji, the eighth son of Nurhaci, succeeded his father as Khan of the later Jin in 1626 following Manchu custom. After the Qing was established in Beijing, Hongtaiji's successor Fulin, the Shunzhi Emperor, broke Chinese tradition by designating his seven-year-old third son Xuanye, who became the Kangxi Emperor Shengzu, as heir as he lay dying of smallpox in 1661 because Xuanye was immune to the disease.[3] Xuanye designated his second son

---

[3] Arthur W. Hummel, ed., *Eminent Chinese of the Ch'ing Period* (Washington: United States Government Printing Office, 1943), vol. 1, 328, and Frederick W. Mote, *Later Imperial China, 900–1800*, forthcoming. I am grateful to Professor Mote for allowing me to read portions of his magisterial history relevant to this chapter.

Yinreng heir apparent in 1676, only to depose him in 1704. In the end, Xuanye's fourth son Yinzhen emerged in 1721 through an uncertain succession to become the Yongzheng Emperor Shizong. Thereafter Yinzhen established the practice of predetermined secret succession in 1723.[4] The imperial lineage through the Aisin Gioro clan itself occupied a special position within the broader Qing conquest elite that entitled them to stipends, titles, and ranks and whose affairs were managed by an Imperial Clan Court (*Zongrenfu*) instituted in 1652. In addition, several other palace offices and courts served the personal needs and functions of the emperor and his house.

The imperial clan was part of the broader military aristocracy that Qing founders Nurhaci and Hongtaiji welded together under the banner system of organization in Manchuria before the conquest of China. Under this arrangement Manchu warriors were grouped into *niru* ("arrows," or companies), the basic Manchu fighting unit, which in turn were grouped together into larger forces called *gusan*, or "banners," distinguished in formation by flags of different color. Gradually by accretion eight Mongol and eight Manchurian Chinese banners were established alongside the eight Manchu banners organized by Nurhaci in 1616, creating the Qing conquest elite of twenty-four banners. More than simply military units, the banners became institutions of social standing, economic entitlement, and political competition. The banner elite was graded into ranks of varying nobility, and after the conquest the banners received tracts of land surrounding the capital for their support. In addition, a separate system of military examinations was maintained for bannermen, and members of the conquest elite routinely filled out both military and civil posts slotted for them in the Qing institutional hierarchy.

The Qing civil administration was founded generally on Ming precedent but deviated where considerations of dynastic security, power, and efficiency demanded. The Grand Secretariat (*Neige*) was retained from the Ming as the critical coordinating center of imperial decision-making in the early reigns of the Qing, although its position in this role was never secure. Ultimately it was superseded in the Yongzheng reign by a new Grand Council (*Junjichu*) within the emperor's

---

[4] Mote, *Later Imperial China*; Harold L. Kahn, *Monarchy in the Emperor's Eyes* (Cambridge: Harvard University Press, 1971), 239–241; and Silas H. L. Wu, *Passage to Power: K'ang-hsi and His Heir Apparent, 1661–1722* (Cambridge: Harvard University Press, 1979), 31–38 and 112–183.

inner court, which thereafter remained the central arena of imperial decision-making.

The Qing also retained the six ministries (*liubu*) of the Ming,[5] each responsible for specific functional areas. The Board of Civil Appointment (*Cibu*) supervised appointment in the larger civil bureaucracy; a Board of Finance (*Hubu*) managed the realm's land and labor corvée tax registers and tax collection and supervised state financial affairs. The Board of Rites *(Libu)* supervised the state's broader ceremonial affairs, including the system for tributary relations with some foreign peoples, and the three-level civil service examination system; the Board of War (*Bingbu*) managed the system of military appointment and the separate system of military examinations. The Board of Public Works supervised maintenance of the realm's larger irrigation and waterway systems, including the Grand Canal and other infrastructures, and the Board of Punishments (*Xingbu*) supervised application of the regime's criminal codes. In addition, the Censorate (*Duchayuan*) provided disciplinary surveillance to the broader civil bureaucracy as the emperor's "eyes and ears," but also had the right and duty to remonstrate against instances of impropriety on the part of the emperor himself.

The Qing solidified the Ming system of regional administration, dividing China proper into provinces (*sheng*) and a separate metropolitan capital region (Zhili). The Ming had thirteen provinces and two capital areas (Nanzhili and Beizhili); by the nienteenth century China under the Qing had eighteen provinces. Each province was presided over by a governor (*xunfu*), also substantively regularized from the preceding Ming "grand coordinators" (signified by the same Chinese term). The Qing also regularized the Ming office of governor-general (*zongdu*), a post holding supervisory powers over both military and civilian affairs, normally over two or three contiguous provinces. In the Qing there were eight governors-general (nine in the nineteenth century). In addition, regional administration of fiscal and judicial affairs was conducted by provincial financial commissioners (*buzhengshi*) and judges (*anchashi*), and most provincial administrations also included a controller over the state's salt monopoly, educational directors, and tribute grain intendants. Beneath the provincial level, with some regional variation throughout China proper, a system of circuit intendants (*daotai*) and several subprovincial

---

[5] The *liubu* are conventionally referred to as the Six Boards, not ministries, with respect to the Qing, following I. S. Brunnert and V. V. Hagelstrom, *Present Day Political Organization of China* (Taipei: Book World Co., 1911).

prefects (*zhifu*) reported to the governors and governors-general and their subordinates in functional areas of administration.[6]

The basic level of the late imperial state in China proper was the district (*xian*), presided over by a district magistrate (*zhixian*). In the late seventeenth century, during the Kangxi reign, there were 1,261 districts; in the late nineteenth century, 1,303.[7] The district magistrate's administration included a small number of civil service assistants, together with a staff of clerks and runners paid by the state to conduct the district's affairs. In addition, as district magistrates faced increasing problems of governing a mounting population and a changing society, they recruited and maintained personal staffs of private secretaries and assistants having expertise in various specialized facets of administration and practical affairs.[8]

Within local society, state purposes were served with differing degrees of consistency and success by a variety of systems under the district magistrate's supervision and management. Police and militia functions were carried out through the *baojia* system of registration and surveillance, which organized groups of ten households into *pai*, ten *pai* of 100 households into *jia*, and ten *jia* of a thousand households into *bao*. The *lijia* system similarly organized households into comparable pyramids for tax collection purposes. The districts also managed a system of granaries (*changpingcang*, the "ever-normal granaries") for purposes of famine relief, while a system of semimonthly readings – the *xiangyue* – based on the Kangxi Emperor's "Sacred Edict" of 1670 and formalized by the Yongzheng Emperor in 1724 was intended to promote ideological edification among the district's population.[9]

The civil service officialdom was drawn both from the conquest banner elite and Chinese. A pattern of dual appointments was used in the top levels of the Grand Council, Grand Secretariat, the six boards, and other metropolitan offices. A board, for example, normally had both a Manchu and a Chinese president and two Manchu and two Chinese vice-

---

[6] Ch'u T'ung-tsu, *Local Government Under the Ch'ing* (Cambridge: Harvard University Press, 1970), 4–7; Mote, "Political Structure," 83.

[7] Ch'u T'ung-tsu, *Local Government*, 2.

[8] Mote, "Political Structure," 83–84; Ch'u T'ung-tsu, *Local Government*, 14–115; and John R. Watt, *The District Magistrate in Late Imperial China* (New York: Columbia University Press, 1972), 11–22.

[9] Each of these systems is described and assessed in Hsiao Kung-ch'uan, *Rural China: Imperial Control in the Nineteenth Century* (Seattle: University of Washington Press, 1960), 43–258.

presidents. Appointments to the posts of governor-general and governor followed a similar division, with one post going to a member of the Manchu, Mongol, or Chinese banner elite and the other to a Chinese.

Selection and appointment among the Chinese officialdom operated in principle on standards of meritocratic rationality. Chinese appointees were recruited from among the pool of successful candidates from the three-level system of triennial examinations presided over by the emperor and managed by the Board of Rites. This system ensured an abundant supply of highly literate officials thoroughly educated in a Confucian social and political ethic that emphasized both loyalty to the sovereign and commitment to public service. Although in some periods, special degrees could be bought, appointment in the civil service came mostly from success in the examinations, making this institution the gateway to political standing and social status. The civil service bureaucracy as a whole was graded into a structure of nine ranks and eighteen subranks. The top candidates of the metropolitan and palace examinations could hope for appointment somewhere in the middle ranks of this structure. Promotion to higher posts rested on a system of recommendation by officials in supervising posts.

The late imperial state's civil administration operated on a well-articulated system of internal communications. A system of routine memorials (*tipen*) were forwarded from the central bureaucracies and provincial offices to the Grand Secretariat, whose secretaries drafted rescript responses for consideration by the emperor. Begun under the Kangxi Emperor and formalized under the Yongzheng Emperor, a separate system of confidential memorials (*zouben*) bypassed the Grand Secretariat and went directly to the emperor, providing him with detailed information on events and trends and furthering efforts to reduce the political power of the Manchu nobility and to assert better control over the central bureaucracy.[10] A system of postal stations maintained by the Board of War tied the provinces together and to the capital. An express letter dispatched from Canton on the southeastern coast could reach the capital in sixteen days under this system, although routine dispatches took twice that long.

At the height of Qing power, the dynasty maintained military forces of roughly 200,000 banner troops stationed at strategic points around the

---

[10] These memorial systems are analyzed comprehensively in Silas H. L. Wu, *Communication and Imperial Control in China* (Cambridge: Harvard University Press, 1970), 27–78.

empire. In addition, it maintained garrisons of some 600,000 Green Standard armies built originally out of Chinese forces joining or surrendering to the Manchus in the conquest era. In the late seventeenth century and throughout the eighteenth, these forces were capable of maintaining the peace in China proper while repeatedly defeating successive Mongol challenges in Central Asia, incorporating the far southwest under Qing rule in the 1720s and '30s, and bringing Tibet under Qing hegemony (though *not* its outright incorporation) by the 1740s. Through these campaigns, the Qing empire doubled the size of territory directly under Ming sovereignty, to the present-day boundaries of the People's Republic. Only by the end of the eighteenth century did the military capacities of the Manchu dynasty begin to fray visibly, when suppression of the White Lotus rebellion in the southwest required resort to local gentry-led militia building.[11]

The late imperial state's fiscal base rested heavily on China's agrarian economy. The conjoined land and labor service taxes, monetized into payments of silver, provided the overwhelming bulk of the state's revenue. In addition, state monopolies over the production and distribution of several commodities such as salt, tobacco, and alcohol provided revenue, the most important of which was salt. Taxes on commerce were insignificant until the institution of the *lijin* (likin) in the mid-nineteenth-century effort to suppress the Taiping rebellion.[12]

Overall, the late imperial state provided stable governance of a vast, diverse empire for long periods of time. It featured institutions and processes – its meritocratic civil bureaucracy, for example – that in many respects were, to borrow Gilbert Rozman's characterization, "precocious in their modernity." It had the capacity to extract sufficient resources from the society and economy it governed to permit the Kangxi Emperor in 1712 to freeze the land and labor tax while still maintaining an impressive display of imperial splendor in monument and lifestyle and, for most of the eighteenth century, major military expeditions against foes to the north, west, and south. Even to Western observers of the time, the power, effectiveness, and wealth of the late imperial state commanded admiration.

---

[11] On the use of *tuanlian* militia organization to defeat the White Lotus rebellion, see Philip A. Kuhn, *Rebellion and Its Enemies: Militarization and Social Structure, 1796–1864* (Cambridge: Harvard University Press, 1970).

[12] Mote, "Political Structure," 73; Wang Yeh-chien, *Land Taxation in Imperial China* (Cambridge: Harvard University Press, 1973), 8–12 and 79–83.

MANCHUS AND CHINESE

Franz Michael contributed to Western understanding of the late imperial state in several significant ways. His first and one of his most enduring contributions was his classic work *The Origin of Manchu Rule in China: Frontier and Bureaucracy as Interacting Forces in the Chinese Empire*, published in 1942. The question Michael sought to answer in this path-breaking study was how it was that a tiny frontier tribal society was able not only to conquer but also then to govern a sophisticated Chinese society many times its size for more than 200 years. Building on the work of Owen Lattimore on China's historical interaction with its inner Asian frontiers and using primarily Chinese sources sponsored by the Qing at its imperial height, such as the *Huang Qing Kaiguo Fanglue*, Michael located the unique effectiveness of the Qing among alien conquest dynasties in their adoption of Chinese ruling techniques on the frontier of a declining Ming in governing previously Chinese-controlled portions of the Liaoning plain before the conquest. It was neither superior military power nor assimilation but rather flexibility in political organization that gave the Manchus the capacity to appeal to vacillating armies of the Ming, to pacify large populations of Chinese, and then to govern China itself effectively for more than two centuries.[13]

Although Michael did not argue explicitly so in his book, the thesis of *Origins* comported with a larger view of the Qing as an example of the assimilative power of Chinese political tradition. On this view, the Qing was a synarchic regime in which the ruling Manchu house became so submerged in Chinese traditions of governance as to have lost any distinctive identity apart from the Han Chinese they governed. The longevity of their regime proved once again the adage that "the empire might be conquered on horseback but it could not be governed so."

Recent scholarship has called this larger view into question. Impetus in this work has come in part from a new appreciation of the value of Manchu-language sources in Qing history alongside previous work in Chinese sources alone, abetted by access to the imperial Number One Archive in Beijing and by publication of Manchu-language documents by Taipei's National Palace Museum since the late 1970s.

Studies in this vein by Evelyn Rawski, Pamela Crossley, Beatrice Bartlett, and others have asserted a "Manchu rather than Han-centered

[13] Franz Michael, *The Origin of Manchu Rule in China: Frontier and Bureaucracy as Interacting Forces in the Chinese Empire* (New York: Paragon Books, 1972).

perspective" in Qing conceptions of rulership, empire, and cultural and political interaction with the Chinese and other peoples they governed.[14] Their work has shown that Manchu distinctiveness did not evaporate in the early reigns of the dynasty. Instead, these studies find, Manchu language and traditions remained prominent, though steadily fading from the beginning of the eighteenth century, at least up through the Jiaqing reign. Their studies argue, for instance, that Manchu remained the standard language for memorials among the banner elite and among campaigning generals throughout the eighteenth century. One recent study asserts that deliberations of the Grand Council (*Junjichu*), the coordinating center created by the Yongzheng Emperor in the late 1720s, were routinely conducted in Manchu through the Qianlong reign.[15] Partly in reaction to the accommodating approach toward Chinese traditions of the Kangxi Emperor and to relentless pressures of assimilation, the Yongzheng and Qianlong Emperors took steps to institutionalize Manchu heritage, consolidating traditions of Manchu origins and explicating the dynasty's legitimacy in succeeding the Ming.[16]

One major avenue opened up by this work has been a reconsideration of the Manchu dynasty's relations with non-Chinese peoples in Central Asia. From this perspective, the seventeenth- and eighteenth-century Qing expansion, subsuming vast regions and diverse peoples under the dynasty's suzerainty, reflected not its systematic assimilation of Chinese traditions and techniques, but rather its flexibility in deploying non-Chinese traditions and alternative institutional approaches in dealing with various Mongols, Tibetans, and other peoples.

From this perspective, the Qing dynasty was not simply the last of the great dynasties of China; it was a multiethnic empire utilizing a diversity of governing institutions and routines. Nor was the Qing emperorship coterminous with the position of emperor of China. The Manchu ruler in

---

[14] Particularly useful in summarizing aspects of this new work is Evelyn Rawski's 1996 presidential address to the Association for Asian Studies, "Reenvisioning the Qing: The Significance of the Qing Period in Chinese History," published in *Journal of Asian Studies*, vol. 55, no. 4 (November 1996), 829–850. See also Pamela Crossley's review article, "The Rulerships of China," *American Historical Review*, vol. 97, no. 5 (December 1992), 1468–1483. For a concerted rejoinder to the thrust of much of this work and to Rawski's address in particular, see Ping-ti Ho, "In Defense of Sinicization: A Rebuttal of Evelyn Rawski's 'Reenvisioning the Qing,'" *Journal of Asian Studies*, vol. 57, no. 1 (February 1998), 123–155.

[15] Rawski, "Reenvisioning the Qing," 829.

[16] Pamela Kyle Crossley, "*Manzhou yuanliu kao* and the Formalization of Manchu Heritage," *Journal of Asian Studies*, vol. 46, no. 4 (November 1987), 761–790.

Beijing was indeed the emperor of China, as Chinese historiography abundantly attests. But he was also the "Khan of Khans" to the Mongols the Manchus defeated and allied to their cause, as well as *cakravartin*, the "wheel-turning" universal ruler of Buddhist tradition. The Qing conception of the emperor thereby encompassed authority and corresponding roles beyond the Confucian traditions at the foundation of China's imperial order and reflected a symbiotic synthesis of traditions pursued by earlier Inner Asian conquest dynasties.[17] Qing success in embracing these traditions enabled the dynasty to maintain suzerainty over vast non-Chinese territories and peoples for the most part until the end of the dynasty in 1912, bequeathing both China's present boundaries and its internal ethnic tensions.

This alternative appreciation of the Qing conception of rulership has also had significant application in reevaluating the dynasty's interactions with the West. James Hevia's fascinating study of the ritual interactions between the Qing court and the 1793 Macartney Mission builds on the new Manchu-centered historiography in a skillful dissection of the Qing realm as having "multiple centers and multiple powers" and so "a multitude of lords," whereby the Qing court manipulated ceremonies and symbolisms of several traditions in establishing its authority. In Hevia's analysis, the Macartney encounter with the Qianlong court reflected not cultural blindness and inertia within the constraints of the tributary system on the Qing side, but the interaction of two complex "imperial formations," each sensitive to the implications of ceremony for its own authority.[18]

IMPERIAL AUTHORITY AND POWER

The "Manchu-centered" perspective has had implications for understanding imperial politics within China proper as well. This perspective complements other work using Chinese-language sources that has helped to illuminate the complexities of politics under the Qing. In such studies it is the competition of elites at the court and the practical limits of imperial power that have stood out rather than the subservience of

---

[17] Rawski, "Reenvisioning the Qing," 831–832 and 833–838; Crossley, "The Rulerships of China," 1472–1473; Crossley, *The Manchus* (Cambridge, Mass.: Blackwell, 1997), 112–122; and Thomas J. Barfield, *The Perilous Frontier: Nomadic Empires and China, 221 BC to AD 1757* (Cambridge, Mass.: Blackwell, 1992), 275–294 and 299ff.

[18] James L. Hevia, *Cherishing Men from Afar: Qing Guest Ritual and the Macartney Embassy of 1793* (Durham: Duke University Press, 1995), 1–56.

officials, nobles, and bureaucrats to the despotic authority of the emperor.

The conventional image of the emperor in Chinese politics, not so much among historians of the late imperial past but frequently among those who focus on the communist present, is one of unchallengeable power. The most extreme analysis of imperial power along these lines was Karl August Wittfogel's *Oriental Despotism: A Comparative Study in Total Power*. Wittfogel's analysis traced what he believed to be the foundations of traditional despotism to China's use of massive irrigation systems in agriculture. Mobilization of the great numbers of people necessary to construct and maintain works of this scale required authoritarian social values and ultimately autocratic political institutions that centralized power to a degree far higher than in most other traditional societies – only the pharaohs of ancient Egypt seemed to rival the authority of China's traditional emperors. This extremely authoritarian order prefigured the totalitarianism of the communist era, Wittfogel argued, because the nature of economic production in contemporary China had not changed much into modern times.[19]

Wittfogel's views on the roots of Chinese autocracy were not broadly accepted by Western historians of the late imperial era.[20] But the image

[19] Karl A. Wittfogel, *Oriental Despotism: A Comparative Study of Total Power* (New Haven: Yale University Press, 1957).

[20] There appears to be a complete misreading of the reception of Wittfogel's views among those associated with the Modern Chinese History Project at the University of Seattle, including Franz Michael. In a recent essay Frederic Wakeman suggests that Wittfogel's concept of "Oriental Despotism" was the prevailing framework adopted by Frederick Mote, Zhang Zhongli, Hsiao Kung-ch'uan, Vincent Shih, and Michael in their writings of the 1950s and 1960s. According to Wakeman, who cites work by all of these scholars from this period, the Seattle group followed Wittfogel in describing an "essentially changeless history," with "one imperial dynasty after another participating in the steady growth of autocracy." The Taiping rebellion disrupted this "self-maintaining system of Sino-barbarian imperial despotism," leading to the collapse of the imperial system later. Once the imperial system disappeared, "there was absolutely nothing to prevent a Chinese Stalin from appearing in the form of Mao Zedong," recreating Oriental Despotism anew in contemporary China. In a somewhat different direction, Pamela Crossley has also suggested Wittfogel's thesis dominated historiography at Seattle. "Wittfogel's student Franz Michael," according to Crossley, "in his work on the Taiping rebellion, suggested that the Taiping movement had in fact been a precursor of communist revolution," breaking the cycle of dynastic power and arousing a "mass politics" that "culminated at length in the establishment of a communist state." Both views seriously misconstrue the thrust of these scholars' writings, which was in a direction diametrically opposed to Wittfogel's thesis. Michael, moreover, was not Wittfogel's student, as Professor Crossley believes. Her depiction of the Taipings as the forerunners of mass egalitarian revolution, moreover, better suits the views of John King Fairbank than Michael, who

27

of comprehensive imperial power it sought to explain fit well with commonplace presumptions about imperial authority transported from official Chinese historiography and among those who sought parallels for the penetrative and mobilizing power of the communist regime. In this view, the Kangxi Emperor epitomized the height of imperial power, ruling with sagacity and decisiveness, patronizing Confucian literati while also campaigning vigorously against Mongol enemies, and presiding over his court without limit on his prerogatives and authority. His reign presented a paradigm of imperial power akin to the absolutist reigns of Louis XIV in France and Peter the Great in Russia, marred only by the factionalism around his potential successors as his vigor declined in his last years.

Recent writings on Qing politics build on earlier studies of the late imperial era in presenting a grittier, more realistic view of court politics and imperial power, both in the early reigns and later. Such writings show a conflict of ruling traditions in the early reigns, in which a "separate and unequal" but far from monolithic conquest elite struggled to inhibit the consolidation of imperial power along traditional Chinese lines, while a fragmented Chinese officialdom competed for position and influence at court. Banner chiefs sought to preserve the more federative institutions of the pre-conquest period – such as the Deliberative Council of Princes and Ministers (*Yizheng Wang Dachen Huiyi*) – against imperial efforts to adopt more hierarchical Chinese imperial concepts and routines, and they struggled among themselves for power and standing using the banner institutions as bases of power. Chinese factions in the civil bureaucracy sought out Manchu patrons or coalesced around the emperor himself in seeking to establish themselves and their associates at the court. Emperors meanwhile renewed the longstanding efforts of their Chinese predecessors to enhance their own power by tinkering with inner court institutions to displace and circumvent the limitations on their power of the outer court civil bureaucracy.[21]

explicitly rejected that line of argument. Cf. Franz Michael, *The Taiping Rebellion* (Seattle: University of Washington Press, 1966), and Fairbank, *The United States and China*, 4th edition enlarged (Cambridge: Harvard University Press, 1983), 181. See Frederic Wakeman, "Models of Historical Change: The Chinese State and Society, 1839–1989," in Kenneth Lieberthal et al., eds., *Perspectives on Modern China: Four Anniversaries* (Armonk, N.Y.: M. E. Sharpe, 1991), 68–102; and Pamela Kyle Crossley, "The Historiography of Modern China," in Michael Bentley, ed., *Companion to Historiography* (New York: Routledge, 1997), 644–645.

[21] Rawski, "Reenvisioning the Qing," 832–833, includes a general discussion of the "Manchu-centered" perspective for understanding Qing court politics.

Robert Oxnam's study and my own doctoral dissertation analysis of court politics during the first half of the Kangxi reign, written under Franz Michael's direction, showed, for example, the Oboi regency (1661–69) to have been a period of intense Manchu conservatism, during which banner elders overturned the earlier efforts of an ineffectual Shunzhi Emperor to enhance his own power using Chinese institutions. My own study attempted to show further that the Kangxi Emperor's landmark decision to retire the three southern feudatories played out against a contest among different generations of the banner elite in coalition with regionally derived Chinese factions at the court. Only through cautious manipulation of contending factions, after broadening his political base by using inner court institutions like the Southern Library (*Nanshufang*), could the emperor attain in the 1680s a predominant position at the court through balance-of-power tactics.[22]

Similarly, Beatrice Bartlett's painstaking analysis of the founding and operation of the Grand Council by the Yongzheng Emperor depicts the new decision-making center as yet another attempt by an emperor "to reach out for power over matters previously not directly susceptible to his will." The Grand Council thus began as the Yongzheng Emperor's attempt to establish "a secure separate inner-court sanctuary where the monarch and his highest ministers would preside over as much of the government as possible . . . set apart from the distant activity of outer-court bureaucrats." Over the long term, nevertheless, paralleling the evolution of the Grand Secretariat in the Ming, the Grand Council and its processes were gradually formalized in a manner that compromised its effectiveness as an imperial inner court decision-making preserve against the routinizing propensities of outer court officialdom. "In fact," Bartlett concluded, "instead of supporting what has been viewed as the increasing imperial despotism of the eighteenth century, the rise of the Grand Council created a government that could run effectively whether or not a strong monarch prevailed in Peking."[23]

What emerges from such studies is a picture of imperial power severely limited by the practical realities and complexities of elite politics. Emperors in the late imperial era reigned far more frequently than they ruled.

---

[22] Robert B. Oxnam, *Ruling from Horseback: Manchu Politics in the Oboi Regency, 1661–1669* (Chicago: University of Chicago Press, 1975); H. Lyman Miller, "Factional Conflict and the Integration of Ch'ing Politics, 1661–1690," Ph.D. dissertation, the George Washington University, 1974.

[23] Beatrice Bartlett, *Monarchs and Ministers: The Grand Council in Mid-Ch'ing China, 1723–1820* (Berkeley: University of California Press, 1991), 17 and 278.

As Bartlett observed, "if a monarch wished to rule as well as reign, he had to develop his own administration, both through links to civil servants in the outer court and in the provinces and through a strengthened inner court."[24] Both the classically paradigmatic Kangxi and Qianlong Emperors managed this for portions of their long reigns but could not sustain it throughout. Only the Yongzheng Emperor seemed truly effective in maximizing the power inherent in imperial authority throughout his relatively short thirteen-year reign. He emerges in hindsight as probably the most powerful autocrat since Ming Taizu. But because of the ruthlessness of his tactics in establishing his power, he has never seemed the exemplar of traditionally defined imperial rule.

In this perennial balance of power in imperial politics, of course, emperors could on occasion assert overwhelming autocratic power unpredictably, as Philip Kuhn's study of the politics of the "soul-stealing" sorcery scare of 1768 illustrates. Hungli, the Qianlong Emperor, moved ruthlessly with a nationwide campaign to exterminate a spreading panic among a superstitious populace, partly out of security concerns about the potential for sedition in social unrest, but also to render court and provincial officials preoccupied with their own interests and routines more susceptible to his direction and control. Hungli, however, could press the campaign only so far without raising doubts about himself, and in the end the imperial bureaucracy – buffeted between aroused and unpredictable monarchical power and a volatile and panicked public – gets "two cheers" from Kuhn. The larger corps of imperial officials deploying the "ingrained practices" of "prudential concealment of information, self-protective dithering, cover-ups to protect personal relationships, and an unshakable preference for routine procedures," together with a few courageous high officials who invoked "the superior code under which all human governments might be judged" afforded by the Confucian ideology, enjoined prudence from Hungli and once again curbed the arbitrary exercise of imperial power in the absence of formal constitutional constraints.[25]

THE REACH OF THE STATE

Perhaps the most dramatic changes in perspective on the late imperial state have emerged from the work of historians on local society. From

---

[24] Ibid., 24.
[25] Philip A. Kuhn, *Soulstealers: The Chinese Sorcery Scare of 1768* (Cambridge: Harvard University Press, 1990).

such work has emerged a new understanding of the diversity of local social elites, the evolving range of their activities in local society, and their complex interrelationships.[26] From these studies an altogether different picture of the reach of the late imperial state into society has emerged which has stood on their heads the presumptions of previous approaches to state-society relations in the late imperial period.

Earlier understandings of the composition and power of local elites with respect to the imperial system drew on impressions of local society of nineteenth-century Western observers combined with the penetrating sociological insight of Max Weber. Pioneering studies of the Chinese "gentry" focused on the role of the imperially sponsored examination system in defining a literati elite who collaborated in constituting the imperial order by aiding the governance of local society on one hand and staffing the emperor's officialdom on the other. Such foundational studies of the gentry differed somewhat in the degree of subservience versus autonomy with respect to imperial power, and they varied in definition. Ch'u T'ung-tsu's study of local government saw the gentry as a class essentially created by the imperial system through the examination system and by the privileges the state granted them.[27] Ho Ping-ti's study of social mobility in the Ming and Qing periods applied a more restrictive definition of the elite, confined to those who had passed the second level (*juren*) of the examination system.[28] Zhang Zhongli offered the broadest definition of the gentry, delineating an elite stratified into an upper level of *jinshi* and *juren* examination degree-holders and a lower level that included those who had passed the first level of the examinations (*shengyuan*) and those who had acquired degrees through purchase (*jiansheng*). Zhang's work also underscored the diversity of roles played by the gentry in local society, as well as elucidating the diversity of its sources of income – derived from not simply landowning but other occupational and professional roles, including commerce – in some ways prefiguring the direction of later studies.[29]

---

[26] A very useful review of this literature is Joseph Esherick's and Mary Backus Rankin's "Introduction" to the conference volume they edited, *Chinese Local Elites and Patterns of Dominance* (Berkeley: University of California Press, 1990), 1–24.

[27] Ch'u T'ung-tsu, *Local Government*, 169–173.

[28] Ho Ping-ti, *The Ladder of Success in Imperial China: Aspects of Social Mobility, 1368–1911* (New York: Columbia University Press, 1962), 17–41.

[29] Chang Chung-li (Zhang Zhongli), *The Chinese Gentry: Studies on Their Role in Nineteenth-Century Chinese Society* (Seattle: University of Washington Press, 1955), and *The Income of the Chinese Gentry* (Seattle: University of Washington Press, 1962).

These studies also differed in the degree of autonomy the gentry enjoyed with respect to the imperial state. Ch'u and Ho tended to emphasize the preponderant power of the state. Zhang saw the interests of the gentry as rooted both in the imperial order and in local society, giving them a degree of autonomy not apparent in the studies by Ch'u and Ho. Franz Michael, who worked closely with Zhang, emphasized the latter view in his own writings. In his introductory chapter to *The Taiping Rebellion*, Michael emphasized "the strength and autonomy of the social order, which the dynastic state affected only to a limited degree." Following Zhang, Michael stressed the critical "dual role" the gentry played in local society in handling "a large number of public affairs" distinct from the relatively small range of functions managed directly by the imperial state itself.[30]

Recent studies have moved considerably beyond these pioneering works, redefining and delineating local elites according to criteria of local role and wealth, not simply examination degree. These studies of local elites complement and draw impetus in part from the burgeoning studies of economic and social history of the late imperial era. Taken together, these studies show a China in the midst of dynamic demographic, economic, and social transformation since the sixteenth century, with corresponding import for the changing composition of local elites and for governance by the imperial order.

Many of these studies, while focusing on very different aspects of local and regional change in late imperial China, all seem to point in a similar direction. Several have shown the failure of the imperial state to expand in step with the unprecedented growth in population through the Ming and Qing eras. Effectively the number of districts and thus magistrates remained frozen as population surged into the eighteenth century, increasing the need for magistrates to rely more and more on local elites for assistance in performing fundamental tasks of governance. Philip Kuhn's analysis of gentry-led militia-building in the period from the White Lotus rebellion of the late eighteenth century through the Taiping rebellion in the mid-nineteenth century, as well as his later studies on the usurpation of local governance functions by local elites into the twentieth century, show a similarly declin-

---

[30] Michael, *The Taiping Rebellion*, vol. 1, pp. 4–5.

ing capacity of the central imperial state to assert control in local society.[31]

Studies of the impact of economic change – and particularly of the commercial expansion accelerating since the mid-sixteenth century through the nineteenth – detail the proliferating social complexity that accompanied economic diversification and specialization, the blurring of social class lines, and the retreating capacities of the imperial state to maintain direct control over a rapidly changing society. William Rowe's study of the mammoth entrepôt Hankow depicts the elaboration of an urban commercial elite, its performance of public functions in aiding local governance, and its promotion of a separate urban culture alongside the roles and concerns of the official elite traditionally associated with China's administrative cities.[32] A provocative chapter in *The Cambridge History of China* by Philip Kuhn and Susan Mann – uncharacteristically so given the purposes of that series – recast changes afoot in the late eighteenth and early nineteenth century long taken as symptoms of the age-old dynastic cycle as instead the consequences of commercialization and social change in that era. "[C]ommercialization as well as corruption, increasing social complexity as well as decadence, were among the forces altering Chinese society and the distribution of power within it, on the brink of modern times," they concluded. "As the monarchy lost its capacity to defend its realm against the assertion of private interests, the role of the central government itself in dominating and defining the sphere of public interest was being irreparably damaged."[33]

Other studies have depicted accelerating elite activism in the last decades of the nineteenth century in public affairs and government at the local level that drew strength from several sources, including the

---

[31] Philip Kuhn, *Rebellion and Its Enemies*; "Local Taxation and Finance in Republican China," in Susan Mann Jones, ed., *Select Papers from the Center for Far Eastern Studies*, no. 3, University of Chicago Press, 1979; "Local Self-Government Under the Republic," in Frederic Wakeman and Carolyn Grant, eds., *Conflict and Control in Late Imperial China* (Berkeley: University of California Press, 1975), 257–298; and "The Development of Local Government," in Denis Twitchett and John King Fairbank, eds., *The Cambridge History of China*, vol. 13 (New York: Cambridge University Press, 1986), 329–360.

[32] William T. Rowe, *Hankow: Commerce and Society in a Chinese City, 1796–1889* (Stanford: Stanford University Press, 1984), and *Hankow: Conflict and Community in a The Chinese City, 1796–1895* (Stanford: Stanford University Press, 1989).

[33] Philip Kuhn and Susan Mann Jones, "Dynastic Decline and the Roots of Rebellion," in John King Fairbank, ed., *The Cambridge History of China*, vol. 10 (New York: Cambridge University Press, 1978), 161–162.

impact of the Taiping rebellion on central constraints on local initiative, patterns of gentry-merchant collaboration as the commercialization of the economy proceeded, and the impact of the treaty ports. This activism was expressed in enthusiasm for and interest in alternative institutional forms of public and political association – chambers of commerce, professional organizations (*fatuan*), and ultimately the self-government and constitutional movements – once the ban of such activity was lifted at the beginning of the late Qing "New Reforms" after the turn of the century.[34]

The thrust of all of these studies alters in at least two fundamental ways our understanding of the reach of the late imperial state into society and of the dynamic of change under way in late imperial China. First, the long standard picture of a powerful imperial state possessing the capacity to intrude deeply into society for purposes of authoritarian – even totalitarian – control has been inverted. In its place emerges a picture of a limited imperial state that governed flexibly and lightly according to an official ideology of "benevolent government" (*renzheng*) and that possessed only modest ambitions with respect to the society it governed.

In its administration of local society, the late imperial state relied on its ability to co-opt local elites and harmonize their interests with its own, not on displacing them and penetrating beyond them to the lowest levels. In the core Han areas, district magistrates and other officials collaborated with heterogeneous, segmented local elites who "brokered" state interests through overlapping hierarchies of local market, kinship, religion, and water control networks and patron-client relationships. By drawing on what Prasenjit Duara has called the "cultural nexus of power," the imperial state "used various channels, such as corporate merchant groups, temple communities, myths, and other symbolic resources embedded in popular culture to reach into local communities" and maintain order indirectly.[35]

In non-Han frontier areas, the late imperial state deployed similarly flexible techniques of cooptation. In keeping with the multiplicity of its ruling identities, the Qing thus did not mechanically impose in such areas the traditional Chinese institutions it inherited and maintained in the Han core areas. Instead it pragmatically incorporated local headmen,

---

[34] Mary Backus Rankin, *Elite Activism and Political Transformation in China: Zhejiang Province, 1865–1911* (Stanford: Stanford University Press, 1986).

[35] Prasenjit Duara, *Culture, Power and the State: Rural North China, 1900–1942* (Stanford: Stanford University Press, 1988), 15–41.

tribal chieftains, and religious hierarchies and adapted possible existing structures and techniques in Taiwan, the southwest, Tibet, Xinjiang, and other frontier areas.

This co-optive approach manifested a minimalist ambition in governance. The Qing approach to governing areas outside the Han core, as John Robert Shepherd's study of the evolution of Qing administration of Taiwan has shown, followed a calculus that balanced considerations of security and cost to the state. Security concerns permitting, the Qing opted for direct Chinese-style administration only when local revenue sources could support the costs of such rule; otherwise it adopted indirect techniques. In the early decades after its conquest of Taiwan in 1683, according to Shepherd, the Qing left local administration in the hands of aboriginal chiefs, quarantined the island against further Han Chinese immigration, froze reclamation of land that would have served Chinese-style agriculture by immigrating Han farmers and might have provided the basis for tax revenue under traditional Chinese administration, and relied on aboriginal militias to maintain local order. By the Yongzheng period, illicit Han immigration had tilted the Han-aborigine balance and was creating chronic social tensions and unrest between the two ethnic groups. The Qing then resorted to a more aggressive colonization policy that promoted Han immigration, authorized land reclamation for Chinese-style agriculture, and expanded land registration to raise the level of tax revenue needed to maintain a Han-based agrarian order.

By the Qianlong period, however, the costs of this colonization policy outpaced the expansion of tax revenue, and so the Qing court imposed new constraints on Han immigration and land reclamation and used hybrid techniques to administer a divided aboriginal-Han populace. By the late nineteenth century, as Western and Japanese threats to Qing sovereignty of the island emerged, the court moved to upgrade its military and administrative presence despite the expense to itself. As Shepherd shows, a parallel calculus of security, cost, and revenue potential guided Qing approaches to other frontier zones.[36]

The minimalism of the late imperial state was also evident with respect to the economy. Peter Perdue's study of the role of the late imperial state in the Hunan rice economy during the late Ming and Qing periods shows officials adopting changing strategies to encourage agricultural produc-

---

[36] John Robert Shepherd, *Statecraft and Political Economy on the Taiwan Frontier, 1600–1800* (Stanford: Stanford University Press, 1993). In particular, see Shepherd's comparative analysis in his concluding chapter, 395–410.

tion both to ensure a stable flow of revenue from the land tax and to foster social stability. In the early Qing official policies sought to expand production extensively through tax relief, incentives for land reclamation and irrigation infrastructure, and other measures. In the early eighteenth century, as these policies approached their natural limits, they sought to expand agriculture intensively by raising productivity through technological and other means. As commercialization of the agricultural economy accelerated, the state began to privatize functions it had taken on in the previous century. The state also worked to stabilize grain prices by means of a network of state granaries that bought up stores of grain during surplus harvests and sold them off during seasons of grain shortfall. By the nineteenth century, the *repertoire* of strategies was exhausted by the effects produced by the very success of official policies: demographic growth, expanding commercialization and surging consumption, and ecological depletion.[37]

Where conventional views of the late imperial state long emphasized its stifling role on the traditional economy – antimerchant policies and the lack of a commercial code, heavy taxation of both agriculture and commerce, and predatory official corruption – studies like Perdue's and others suggest a more positive role. In addition to efforts to stabilize grain prices through the "ever normal granaries," the state promoted commercialization of the economy by monetizing taxation (beginning with the sixteenth-century "single whip" tax reform), maintaining relatively low levels of taxation, adopting laissez-faire policies toward commerce and tolerating internal labor migrations, providing the legal foundation for upholding contracts, and actively working to level incomes.[38]

Second, the recent scholarship presents a picture of decline of the late imperial order that derives from causes that cannot be encompassed by explanations based on the latest turn of the hoary dynastic cycle, the mechanism long transported from imperial historiography into Western writing to explain dynastic decline. The imperial order itself was being transformed by larger, historically unprecedented indigenous processes under way in China – demographic growth, commercialization and economic transformation, and accelerating social change – preceding the

---

[37] Peter Perdue, *Exhausting the Earth: State and Peasant in Hunan, 1500–1800* (Cambridge: Harvard University Press, 1987).

[38] Madeleine Zelin, "The Structure of the Chinese Economy During the Qing Period," in Kenneth Lieberthal et al., eds., *Perspectives on Modern China: Four Anniversaries*, 31–67. See especially 53–55.

encroachments of the West in the nineteenth century. The state did not expand as society itself grew in directions that ultimately hollowed out the foundations of the late imperial state and sought new forms of government.

CENTER AND REGION

The last major perspective on the late imperial era with which Franz Michael was associated is his thesis regarding the emergence of military regionalism in the nineteenth century. In a landmark 1949 essay in *Pacific Historical Review* and in an introduction to Stanley Spector's 1964 study of Li Hongzhang, Michael built on earlier work by Lo Erh-kang in tracing the militarization of politics and the emergence of the warlords in the twentieth century to the devolution of central power into the hands of regional leaders in the mid-nineteenth century. Unable to defeat the Taiping rebels using standing forces, the Qing permitted regional leaders like Zeng Guofan, Li Hongzhang, and Zuo Zongtang to consolidate local militias built on local allegiances into larger regional armies built on personalistic ties and granted them regional fiscal and administrative authority to support such forces. Once these regional armies suppressed the rebellion, they were not disbanded, and instead became political and military bases of power in the hands of regional leaders at the expense of central authority. From that perspective, the Tongzhi Restoration was a failure insofar as it never truly reconstituted central authority. Instead, the devolution of power into regional hands crippled the ability of the capital to respond to the mounting challenges of the Western powers and Japan, hastening the collapse of the imperial order thereafter, and setting the stage for the military regionalism of the early Republican era.[39]

---

[39] Franz Michael, "Military Organization and Power Structure of China During the Taiping Rebellion," *Pacific Historical Review*, vol. 17 (1949), 469–483, and "Introduction: Regionalism in Nineteenth-Century China," in Stanley Spector, *Li Hung-chang and the Huai Army: A Study in Nineteenth-Century Chinese Regionalism* (Seattle: University of Washington Press, 1964), xxi–xliii. Fritz Mote reminds me that historians of modern China have so far largely overlooked the study of comparable trends of military regionalism and devolution of central power in the decline of some previous dynasties, such as the Tang and Yuan. Such study might underscore perennial parallels stemming from the problems of centralized governance of a polity of China's scale, and it may highlight significant differences in the nineteenth-century context, including the cumulative impact of indigenous economic and social change over the preceding three centuries, the influence and impact of Western military organization and technology, and the changed external context presented by the encroaching Western powers. For the Tang, see C. A. Peterson, "Court and Province in the Mid- and Late-T'ang," in *The Cambridge History*

This argument has been criticized usefully from several directions. Liu Kwang-ch'ing, for example, argued that Li Hongzhang and other regional leaders did not actually possess the degree of autonomy implied by the Michael thesis. During his tenure in Tianjin as governor-general of Zhili and commissioner of the northern ports after 1870, Li required imperial court sanction for all of his regionally based "self-strengthening" initiatives and with respect to his use of revenue. Imperial court relationships with regional leaders like Li were therefore not seen as a zero-sum contest for power, but instead as a collaboration between center and region on behalf of larger national purposes.[40]

Scholars of the early twentieth century have also argued that neither the nature of the new military forces established in the Qing "New Reforms" after 1901 nor the roots of warlordism in the early years of the Republic are adequately explained by the growth of regional armies in the nineteenth century. With respect to the former, the force of personalistic ties in the New Armies was not as great as presumed by the Michael argument, and the impact of modern organizational techniques and professional standards has been seen to have been greater. Among a growing body of work on the warlords, a recent study by Edward McCord providing a close examination of warlord politics in Hubei and Hunan reverses the thrust of the Michael thesis, arguing that warlordism emerged not so much because regional military leaders imposed their own ambitions on a weak political order, but because conflicting local political leaderships too readily resorted to military solutions to regional conflicts.[41]

The upshot of such studies significantly modifies the specifics but does not entirely overturn the thrust of the Michael thesis. In providing closer examination of the growth of modern military forces in China in their specific political and social contexts, they suggest that it was the increas-

of China, vol. 3: *Sui and T'ang China, 589–906* (New York: Cambridge University Press, 1979), 464–560; for the decline of the Mongol Yuan dynasty, see Frederick W. Mote, "The Rise of the Ming Dynasty," in *The Cambridge History of China*, vol. 7: *The Ming Dynasty, 1338–1644, Part I* (New York: Cambridge University Press, 1988), 11–57.

[40] Liu Kwang-ching, "Li Hung-chang in Chihli: The Emergence of a Policy, 1870–1875," in Albert Feuerwerker, Rhoads Murphey, and Mary Wright, eds., *Approaches to Modern Chinese History* (Berkeley: University of California Press, 1967), 68–104.

[41] Edward A. McCord, *The Power of the Gun: The Emergence of Modern Chinese Warlordism* (Berkeley: University of California Press, 1993).

ingly modern elements of such forces, not their residual traditionalistic ones, that became significant as time went by. At the same time, they also underscore the scale of the crisis of political authority and of civil-military relations that Michael sought to address and that grew in significance as the twentieth century proceeded.

SO WHAT?

What difference do the changing conclusions of the historiography of the late imperial period sketched above make for those interested in the modern Chinese state, and especially the evolving contemporary state? Why should political scientists and others who seek to understand the state in present-day China spend their time on and turn their attention to the debates and conclusions of the historians of the late imperial era? The main reason is that the new historiography presents the possibility of a change in the fundamental framework through which the roots of the modern Chinese state are understood.

What has been sketched in this chapter as the standard picture of the late imperial state (perhaps somewhat unfairly insofar as it was never embraced universally) had a particular utility for many in helping to explain the 1949 communist revolution and the state it created. According to this understanding, "modern Chinese history" began in 1840 when, with the Opium War, the West presented China with a challenge to which it had to respond. Up to 1840, the principal dynamic of change throughout China's long imperial era proceeded according to the cyclical rise and fall of imperial dynasties. Within this dynastic cycle pattern, change had proceeded mostly within Chinese tradition, and so history before 1840 has been conventionally referred to as "traditional China."

Chinese tradition, however, could not become the basis for and was, in fact, an obstacle to China's effective response to the West because the requirements of modernization ran counter to the priorities of Confucian social and political order. "The failure of the T'ung-chih [Tongzhi] Restoration demonstrated with a rare clarity," Mary Wright asserted with a vigor in 1957 that might surprise today, "that even in the most favorable circumstances there is no way in which an effective modern state can be grafted onto a Confucian society."[42] China's only alternative,

---

[42] Mary C. Wright, *The Last Stand of Chinese Conservatism: The T'ung-chih Restoration, 1862–1874* (Stanford: Stanford University Press, 1957), 300.

therefore, was to reject tradition, which is to say China required a revolutionary response. The 1911 Revolution overthrew the traditional order, but it failed to provide a successful political alternative. The Nationalist regime established in Nanjing in 1928 failed, too, because it actively embraced tradition as a means to establish its rule and failed to wage the social revolution necessary to bring China into the modern era. Only the communists succeeded in presenting a truly revolutionary alternative, harnessing the bulk of China's population (the peasantry) into a new regime that broke the bonds of the past and began the effort to build a truly modern China.

The communist regime turned out not to be truly revolutionary, however; it was also still Chinese. And so in telling ways, the new regime reflected the values and practices of the authoritarian political culture that the state in traditional China had embodied. Mao Zedong ruled as a new emperor. The remainder of the party leadership and state bureaucracy competed for favor at Mao's court. Party cadres and intellectuals recapitulated the roles of the scholar-officials and gentry of the old order. Chinese communism in the "People's Middle Kingdom," Professor Fairbank suggested, amounted to Marxism in a Confucian mold.[43]

This perspective thus found the roots of the communist order – featuring a very strong state reaching deeply into a weak and fragmented society – in the revolutionary transformation of the late imperial order – a powerful traditional state with a capacity to intrude deeply into society. It explained the demise of Confucianism in light of its seeming incompatibility with the demands of modernity, and certainly in the 1950s, when this view was consolidated, no Confucian East Asian society appeared to present a story of successful modernization on that basis. For these and other reasons, this narrative seemed compelling to many, and remains so outside the walled kingdom of late imperial studies. It continues to be the standard narrative employed by many students of contemporary China, as well as specialists in comparative politics from outside the China field.

This longstanding approach does not stand up well in light of the trends of historical scholarship on the late imperial era sketched above. The more recent scholarship offers the promise of a very different picture of the transition from the late imperial era into the contemporary period. Such a picture would emphasize the discontinuities between the late

---

[43] John King Fairbank, "The People's Middle Kingdom," *Foreign Affairs*, vol. 44, no. 4 (July 1966), 574–586.

imperial state and the communist one. It would break out of the cyclical pattern that the older state-centered narrative carries from the dynastic past into the current era. It would provide an evolutionary, society-centered picture of the breakdown of a limited imperial state through economic and social change and the concurrent creation of the foundations of a far more intrusive modern state in the twentieth century. In place of the key dates of the older picture – 1840 and 1949 – a new narrative would focus on different turning points – perhaps 1550, marking the onset of a new (or resumed) commercial revolution with attendant economic and social changes, and the other perhaps 1860, marking the decline of central authority in the face of local elite activism and state-building in the wake of the Taiping rebellion.

The result would be an appreciation of the contemporary communist regime as the outcome of emergent modernity in China, reflecting the impact of combined evolutionary domestic factors and the Western encounter. Presumed analogical continuities between Chinese Communist politics and the dynastic politics of the late imperial period would give way to more compelling linkages rooted in the changing social, economic, and cultural realities of the twentieth century. Within the longer perspective of this framework, the Maoist era will appear as a horrific aberration and the Deng reform period as marking a resumption of the longer strands of economic, social, and state-building evolution of the previous centuries. The cities and towns, not the countryside, will likely be the focus of such a framework, as they have served as the primary engine of change over this long span. Such an evolutionary approach may better explain the persisting authoritarianism of Chinese politics until contemporary times. But such an approach also offers a better perspective from which to judge prospects for political pluralism and liberalism in China.

Construction of such an approach will require late imperial historians and political scientists who focus on the contemporary period increasingly to study each other's work. Franz Michael, who held concurrent posts as professor of history and government, surely would have encouraged such a collaboration.

2

The Chinese State
during the Republican Era

RAMON H. MYERS

AFTER 1900 Qing government leaders launched a series of reforms aimed at strengthening China so that it could contain foreign encroachment and enrich society as well as preserve Manchu monarchical power.[1] Within a decade a new Ministry of Education had begun educational reforms and recruiting talented civil servants for government; a flood of imperial edicts established new ministries of trade, police, foreign affairs, and army; and former offices including the Court of Sacrificial Worship, the Banqueting Court, and the Court of State Ceremonial were annexed to the Ministry of Rites. As new central administrative organs such as the Ministry of Posts and Communications and the Ministry of Justice were set up, they each had only one head instead of one Manchu and one Chinese as in the past. Various committees drafted a constitution and rules for electing provincial, national, and local self-governing assemblies, and another compiled a new criminal code, along with commercial and civil codes. These reforms – designed to save the Qing dynasty and protect the powers of provincial governors and gentry elites – restructured the state and delegated more power to the provinces and the people.

The Qing rulers and their supporters continually had to confront the problem – I will call it the Machiavelli problem – of persuading those who benefited from the old order not to oppose their innovations and convincing those who might benefit but were too timid to support reform

The author gratefully acknowledges the assistance of Linda Chao, a research fellow of the Hoover Institution, and comments by the editor and outside readers who reviewed this essay in manuscript form.

[1] This paragraph is based on Chuzo Ichiko, "Political and Institutional Reform, 1901–11," in John K. Fairbank and Kwang-ching Liu, eds., *The Cambridge History of China*, volume 2: *Late Ch'ing, 1800–1911, Part 2* (Cambridge: Cambridge University Press, 1980), pp. 375–415.

to do so.[2] On the one hand, former Manchu officials and displaced central bureaucrats, military officers, and conservative gentry did not welcome these political reforms and feared their loss of power and privilege. Many of these elites resisted and opposed Qing reforms. On the other hand, the new military officers, technocratic professionals, and modern educators who stood to gain from reform were poorly organized and unable to agree on how to support the monarchical-constitutional government being cobbled together by the Manchu regent, Prince Chun, and a few court insiders.

Without the power to implement its reforms, crush those who opposed it, and mobilize elite and popular support, the enfeebled Qing government risked being derailed in its reform efforts. And fail it did, because the Qing was swept from power in October 1911 by a coalition of anti-Qing opponents led by alienated elites and intellectuals who did not perceive the Qing reforms as going far enough or fast enough. Their voice expressed a revolutionary vision for state-building that clashed with a cautionary voice endorsing the Manchu-Chinese reforms.

CLASHING VISIONS OF A CHINESE STATE

Before 1911 a fierce debate had raged in elite circles about how to establish a democratic, constitutional republic with which to replace the Qing imperial state. Sun Zhongshan (Sun Yat-sen) and others argued for violent political revolution to extirpate the "morally bankrupt" Manchu state and create a republic defined by Sun's three guiding principles: (1) to unify China and free it from foreign oppression

---

[2] See Quentin Skinner and Russell Price, eds., *Machiavelli: The Prince* (Cambridge: Cambridge University Press, 1988), pp. 20–21. The Machiavelli problem is stated as follows. "The difficulties encountered in attaining power arise partly from the new institutions and laws they are forced to introduce in order to establish their power and make it secure. And it should be realized that taking the initiative in introducing a new form of government is very difficult and dangerous, and unlikely to succeed. The reason is that all those who profit from the old order will be opposed to the innovator, whereas all those who might benefit from the new order are, at best, tepid supporters of him. This lukewarmness arises partly from fear of their adversaries, who have the laws on their side, partly from the sceptical temper of men, who do not really believe in new things unless they have been seen to work well. The result is that whenever those who are opposed to change have the chance to attack the innovator, they do it with much vigor, whereas his supporters act only half-heartedly; so that the innovator and his supporters find themselves in great danger." These conditions characterized the final moments of Regent Chun and his reform followers.

(*minzuzhuyi*, the principle of nationalism), (2) to empower the people to elect their leaders and representatives (*minchuanzhuyi*, the principle of people's rights), and (3) to design state policies to guide capital investment and allow private capital to accumulate freely to improve people's welfare (*minzhengzhuyi*, the principle of people's welfare).[3]

Sun called for a political revolution to remove Manchu power, establish a new government by military law, and then adopt a government structure established by a provisional constitution. That would be done by lifting military law in every district and returning self-government to the local people, who would elect their officials and councils but retain a military government operating according to a provisional constitution. Within six years a new constitution would be drafted to replace the provisional constitution, thus annulling the military and administrative powers of the military government. At the same time, the people would elect a president and members of parliament to carry out the provisions of the constitution. Much depended on the capabilities and success of the "ever-faithful military government" to implement this three-stage transition to a democratic constitutional polity.[4]

Sun's follower Wang Zhaoming (Wang Jingwei) believed that the Chinese people were ready for radical change and would support Sun's program of state-building:

> Only our people can carry out the political revolution in a responsible way. Only our people possess the capability of shouldering this responsibility. The political revolutionaries will be those who overthrow the autocracy and establish a constitution. If we can use the power of the people to achieve the goal of political revolution, then, in the end we can create a people's democratic, constitutional system [*minzhu lixian zhengti*].[5]

Wang went on to claim that the Chinese people "already possess the qualifications for establishing the Republic of China [ROC]."[6]

---

[3] Julie Wei, Ramon H. Myers, and Donald G. Gillin, eds., *Prescriptions for Saving China: Selected Writings of Sun Yat-sen* (Stanford, Calif.: Hoover Institution Press, 1994), pp. 41–50.

[4] Ssu-yü Teng and John K. Fairbank, *China's Response to the West: A Documentary Survey, 1839–1923* (Cambridge, Mass.: Harvard University Press, 1979), p. 229.

[5] Guoshiguan (National Archives), *Geming kaiguo wenxuan* (Historical materials related to revolution and constructing the nation-state) (Taipei: Guoshiguan, 1995), vol. 1, p. 727.

[6] Ibid., p. 663.

Liang Qichao and other elites disagreed with Sun's and Wang's prescriptions. Liang feared that a violent political revolution would destroy the Qing monarchy and so weaken China that foreigners would enter and partition the nation.[7] Liang also worried that revolution would "unleash popular passions and generate too much empty theorizing."[8] Finally, Liang argued that the Chinese people were insufficiently informed and educated and thus could not establish effective central and local governance. Therefore, China at first must be governed by an "enlightened autocracy" (*kaiming zhuanzhi*) that would educate, inform, and enable the people to appreciate a "constitutional monarchy [that] could cultivate the true power of the citizenry," thus enabling "the citizens to be able to check and balance the state's power."[9]

The Sun and Liang prescriptions for modern state-building embody two ideal types of political thinking and behavior that Thomas A. Metzger has conceptualized as "transformative" and "accommodative,"[10] explaining how China's Confucian leaders and elites over the ages have envisioned creating an unselfish society of high moral values. The transformative mode of statecraft embraces radical means to reorganize the polity and economy to realize the "good" society, whereas the accommodative mode projects pragmatic, gradual means for the polity to attain the same end. The revolutionaries who joined the United League (*Tongmenghui*) in Tokyo led disgruntled military officers, gentry, students, and others in rejecting Liang's accommodative vision in favor of Sun's transformative one. Political revolution, not the reform initiated by the Qing, destroyed the 267-year-old Qing dynasty.

THE MILITARY BEIYANG REGIME

The coalition of victorious revolutionaries did not have the organizational capabilities to forge a new and lasting republic based on Sun's political designs. After discussions among China's top leaders, the Legislative Assembly elected General Yuan Shikai to be the president of the first constitutional Republic of China. The constitutional principles promulgated in 1908 were revised in 1911 to include nineteen articles of a new constitution, which General Yuan used to force the Manchus to abdi-

---

[7] Ibid., p. 594.   [8] Ibid., p. 633.   [9] Ibid., pp. 628–629.
[10] See Thomas A. Metzger, *Escape from Predicament: Neo-Confucianism and China's Evolving Political Center* (New York: Columbia University Press, 1977), pp. 178–190.

cate and win the backing of the revolutionaries.[11] Political parties began forming in preparation for the upcoming elections for the National Assembly (*Guohui*), or parliament, consisting of a Senate and a House of Representatives. China's politics now turned tumultuous.

President Yuan had been responsible for implementing the old Qing government reforms. Although he favored a modern state staffed by educated professionals and bureaucratic discipline, as a pragmatic politician, Yuan wooed the *Tongmenghui* revolutionaries rather than confronting them. By early 1913, however, China's politicians had divided into factions, arguing over whether the government should be monarchical or republican and whether the polity should be federal or unitary.[12] Yuan believed that China must become a unitary, centralized national political structure if it were to become powerful and independent of the foreign powers and that revising the constitution to establish a strong state under a "supreme president" (*da zongtong*) was the only way to achieve that goal.

His wish "to see a strong China, united under himself, was the essence of his patriotism or nationalism. But he was a nationalist only in this sense."[13] By the spring of 1913 Yuan had decided to end the political gridlock between his presidency and the National Assembly by launching what Ernest P. Young has called Republican China's "second revolution."[14] Deploying his 80,000 military troops, he destroyed renegade Guomindang (GMD) forces, crushed pockets of resistance in Shanghai, Nanking, and Kiangsi, dismissed provincial officials who opposed him, and won at least the temporary support of most provincial powerholders. Within two months he had consolidated his power while thousands

---

[11] Ch'ien Tuan-sheng, *The Government and Politics of China* (Stanford, Calif.: Stanford University Press, 1950), p. 53. It must be made clear that the many constitutions drafted during the Republican period were merely drafts compiled by committees of experts and never approved by elected representatives of the people until 1947, when elections were conducted throughout China in 1946 for representatives to the National Assembly. On December 25, 1946, the National Assembly approved the Republic of China's constitution, which was subsequently taken to Taiwan and preserved, although with amended articles, until today.

[12] These comments are based on Ernest P. Young, "Politics in the Aftermath of Revolution: The Era of Yuan Shih-k'ai, 1912–16," in John K. Fairbank, ed., *The Cambridge History of China*, volume 12: *Republican China, 1912–1949, Part 1* (Cambridge: Cambridge University Press, 1983), pp. 209–258. See p. 227 for the two issues that confronted Yuan and other politicians in 1913.

[13] Jerome Ch'en, *Yuan Shih-k'ai*, 2nd ed. (Stanford, Calif.: Stanford University Press, 1972), p. 207.

[14] Young, "Politics," pp. 228–236.

of people perished. Yuan now set about to establish the Beiyang (Northern) regime, with its capital in Beiping, which would consist of military autocrats like himself who governed by a constitution in an embryonic modern state.[15]

President Yuan appointed scholar-officials (*jinshi*), high-ranking military officers, and leaders of local secret societies, many of whom he knew and trusted, thereby gaining power in the provinces. He also appointed his military colleagues, who governed their provinces not only to "satisfy personal ambitions but to feed, clothe, and shelter their soldiers."[16] Yuan then revamped his presidency and the government. After suspending the National Assembly on January 10, 1914, he mandated a Political Council (*Zhengyi huiyi*) to establish an elected Constitutional Council (*Yuefa huiyi*) composed of members having a degree "higher than that of the *zhuren* (a high Qing educational degree) or possessed of education of an equivalent standard";[17] the Constitutional Council amended the "draft" constitution, which had been promulgated on May 1, 1914, to give the supreme president enormous power. Another presidential decree created a law to elect a legislature (*Lifa yuan*), which rubber-stamped the laws drafted by the supreme president.[18] By these manipulations Supreme President Yuan guaranteed his reelection; the elected strongmen who followed – Li Yuanhong, Feng Guozhang, Xü Shichang, Cao Kun, Duan Qirui, and Zhang Zuolin – governed in the same manipulative, autocratic way.

Members of the Political Council, National Assembly (when convened), and legislature were handpicked by Supreme President Yuan, thus ensuring that his office controlled the law-making process, constitutional revision, cabinet appointment, and policy-making processes. The Yuan-governed regime became unstable because of its insipid militarism. President Li Yuanhong and General Duan Qirui, his prime minister, fell out over whether China should participate in the European war, with Duan arguing in favor of participation in the Allied cause.[19] Parliament

---

[15] The Beiyang regime or clique (Beiyang xi) literally means the "northern faction" and was created by leaders of the modern New Army units after 1903.

[16] Ch'en, *Yuan Shih-k'ai*, p. 208.

[17] H. T. Montague Bell and H. G. W. Woodhead, *China Year Book, 1916* (London: George Routledge and Sons, 1916), pp. 438–439. See also Qian Shifu, ed., *Beiyang zhengfu shidai de zhengzhi zhidu* (The period of the Beiyang government political system) (Beijing: Zhonghua shuju, 1984), vol. 1, pp. 60–66.   [18] Ibid., vol. 1, pp. 46–48.

[19] These events are set forth in James E. Sheridan, "The Warlord Era: Policies and Militarism under the Peking Government, 1916–28," in *The Cambridge History of China*, volume 12: *Republican China, 1912–1949, Part 1*, pp. 308–309.

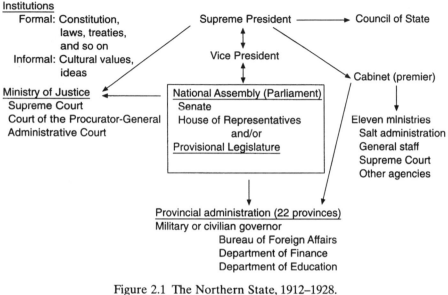

Figure 2.1 The Northern State, 1912–1928.
Source: Based on 1912–1928 editions of *China Year Book* and Qian Shifu,
ed., *Beiyang zhengfu shidai de zhengshi zhidu*, vol. 1–2.

resisted; provincial militarists demanded that Li dissolve parliament, and Li then sacked Duan. These events culminated in Duan calling on the military governors to support him; eight did so and broke with Li, which encouraged Zhang Xun to intermediate and try to restore the Manchu emperor to the throne. General Duan opposed this by mounting a military campaign that set the stage for different military-political cliques to wage war over which clique would control the Zhili region between 1917 and 1928.

After Yuan's attempt to crown himself emperor in 1916 had failed, he died shortly afterward. Various military strongmen tried to govern the Northern State during these years until their defeat in 1927–28 by a coalition of military forces from the south, led by Chiang Kai-shek. The generic structure of the Northern State created by those military strongmen is depicted in Figure 2.1.

Chinese reformers like Sun had conceived the National Assembly as being the nation's highest governing body, with elected representatives empowered to elect a president and vice president, remove them if they performed inadequately, and ensure that the state bureaucracy served the people. Besides representing the new spirit of the republic and pur-portedly drawing from all provinces the best minds and most virtuous leaders to govern the country, the National Assembly was also to revise the constitution, pass laws, and approve treaties. The formal rules adopted by that body (see Fig. 2.1) regulated the behavior of govern-ment, including that of its elected representatives and appointed officials. But the first elected National Assembly – convened in Beiping from April 29, 1912, to November 15, 1912 – was not reconvened in 1913 because of Yuan's "second revolution." And then after 1913 those formal rules were ignored or manipulated by military strongmen like Yuan Shikai, who had reverted to behaving like an autocrat. Those who followed Yuan behaved in the same way.

Dictatorial, Confucian, and conservative, the Beiyang strongmen selec-tively chose only those assembly representatives and high officers willing to do their bidding. They used their military power, patron–client relations, and personalistic rather than impersonal – legal or rule-conforming – means to build a state bureaucracy and military force to enhance and impose their power. Although their outlook included a real-istic appreciation of the advantages of a Western-style state bureaucracy, these military strongmen soon divided into military-regional factions and competed for control over the wealthy east-central and northern provinces.[20] They disliked sharing power and the checks and balances embodied in Western constitutions. They also feared that revolutionaries reorganizing their political parties and social unrest might eject them from office. Yet they wanted a centralized state governed by a powerful leader free of critics and without political gridlock. Their ability to obtain foreign loans temporarily strengthened their power, but in the end their military struggles to control Beiping gravely weakened the Beiyang regime, ultimately destroying it, while exhibiting certain tendencies toward modernization. These impulses for modernization gave the Beiyang regime a longer life than expected and were accepted by its leaders because these reforms elicited economic and military aid from the foreign powers for personal use and also the modest modernization of the Northern State.

Those modernizing tendencies included adhering to a provisional con-stitution that proved advantageous for the Northern State for several

---

[20] See the four maps depicting the distribution of regional warlord power in Sheridan, "The Warlord Era," pp. 298–301.

reasons.[21] First, when bargaining with foreign powers to obtain loans, the Beiyang leaders could cite their commitment to a constitutionalism that decreed that national sovereignty was vested in the people (article 2), not the monarch; accorded certain rights to the people (articles 6–12); and limited their taxes, military service, and obeisance to state laws (articles 13–15), thus constantly reminding liberal elites to champion human rights and guarantee civil liberties. Those vital loans enabled the Beiyang leaders to upgrade the economy, strengthen the military, and improve the state bureaucracy. Thus by retaining constitutional rules the Beiyang leaders could assure the foreign powers that the Chinese government would gradually improve government performance, expand education, and promote economic development.[22] Government officials and personnel, realizing that their careers depended on the state's survival and the goodwill of foreign powers, had an incentive to support the northern military regime.

Second, by accepting constitutionalism, President Yuan Shikai continued the judicial reforms launched before 1911 by promulgating a Provisional New Criminal Code.[23] This was followed by the government's enacting the Organic Law of Judicial Courts, which tried to insulate the independent judiciary from political parties. In March 1914 President Yuan ruled that judges could not join political parties; in 1915 this ruling was extended to include county magistrates. The new Ministry of Justice (see Fig. 2.1) ruled that lawyers, judges, and other legal personnel could not, within three years of leaving office, practice in those areas where they had exercised legal jurisdiction, thus giving China a judicial rule of avoidance. The ministry also depended on lawyers and judges trained in Japan, who insisted on the independence of the judiciary. Thus the new Ministry of Justice represented the rule of law beginning to take root in China.

Another example of bureaucratic modernization encouraged by the regime was the establishment of a modern, but Chinese-style, police system in Beiping, whose exemplary behavior impressed many foreigners. By the late 1910s Beiping's police numbered almost 10,000 uni-

---

[21] Andrew J. Nathan, "A Constitutional Republic: The Peking Government, 1916–28," in John K. Fairbank, ed., *The Cambridge History of China*, volume 12: *Republican China, 1912–1949, Part 1*, p. 264.

[22] See H. G. W. Woodhead, ed., *China Year Book, 1926* (Tientsin: Tientsin Press, 1927), pp. 1222–48.

[23] Xu Xiaoqun, "The Fate of Judicial Independence in Republican China, 1912–37," *The China Quarterly*, no. 149 (March 1997), pp. 4–6.

formed men, or about twelve policemen for every thousand residents, which was a ratio higher than that for London, Paris, and Berlin.[24] The city's police budget was "on a par with a regular national ministry in the 1920s."[25] Beijing's police were not only well paid, trained, and disciplined, but they operated to preserve the peace and social harmony and to win the respect and praise of the capital's citizens.

One state agency to benefit from modernization was the Salt Administration, which the Reorganization Loan dictated be reorganized to increase salt tax collection and thus service that loan's repayment.[26] The government agreed to continue staffing the Salt Administration with foreign and Chinese personnel, paid them higher salaries than other officials, carefully recruited personnel, promoted only on the basis of merit, and tightly monitored for corruption. These reforms increased salt tax revenues from $11 million in 1913 to $85 million in 1923, thus providing the government with enough revenue to service the Reorganization Loan and fund other state activities.

Again, it was President Yuan who "established a new system of rank classifications and procedures for promotions in the civil bureaucracy as a whole."[27] He initiated new rules for an open civil service examination, the first of which was held in 1916, roughly a decade after the imperial examination system had been abolished. Those exams, whose purpose was to discover educated personnel with some technical knowledge, supplied personnel to the central government's ministries and agencies.

This was not the case at the subprovincial level of the Beiyang military state. As early as 1908–9 the Qing government had initiated local elections for councils and leaders to manage administrative cities, non-administrative market towns, and rural townships. Yuan Shikai, however, soon abolished this form of local self-government and substituted the appointment of functionaries by the county government over these administrative units. Out of this confusion there emerged different subprovincial governance systems depending on the character of the provincial governor.

In Shansi province, for instance, Governor Yan Xishan in 1917 encouraged districts to appoint headmen as "adjuncts of county government" and local gentry to promote schools, charities, and public works.[28] In most

---

[24] David Strand, *Rickshaw Beijing: City, People, and Politics in the 1920s* (Berkeley: University of California Press, 1989), p. 72.   [25] Ibid.

[26] Julia C. Strauss, "The Evolution of Republican Government," *The China Quarterly*, no. 150 (June 1990), pp. 337–339.   [27] Ibid., p. 336.

[28] Philip A. Kuhn, " The Development of Local Government," in John K. Fairbank and

provinces county officials were appointed by the provincial governor, who in turn depended on traditional organizations like the household collectivities of *baojia* and *lijia* to collect taxes and promote anti-footbinding, anti-opium, public security, and literacy.

Meanwhile, the office of supreme president had little choice but to allow its powerholder clients to innovate so as to preserve the state system created by Yuan Shikai. Essential to this state's survival was that its leaders effectively control the Zhili region – an area embracing Beiping and Tianjin that had convenient access to banks and foreign consortia. Zhili regional commanders Yuan Shikai, Li Yuanhong, Cao Kun, and Wu Peifu went on to become the top leaders in the Beiyang government by virtue of their military commands in the Zhili region.

Just as "draft" constitutional rules and foreign loans helped to shape political incentives, the personalized, authoritarian structure of the Beiyang government allowed for the devolution of power to provincial leaders and their administrative structures. Although various rewrites of the "draft" constitution called for the supreme president and vice-president to share power with parliament and the National Assembly, the Beiyang leaders still controlled membership in the two legislative and elective organs.[29] The cabinet, consisting of eleven ministries and various agencies, operated with some independence but always subject to the authority of the president and vice-president. Although a supreme president like Yuan Shikai exercised personal influence over the governors of the twenty-two provinces, those who followed him were unable to control the ambitious military governors anxious to modernize their provinces and busily building their personal armies.

The regime's weakening political authority thus produced three crucial patterns of political behavior: (1) Personal ties determined how key government leaders interacted with leading representatives of foreign powers and modern banks; (2) personal and patron–client ties grew between leaders and subordinates within the state structure; and (3) maneuvers and realignments by the Zhili faction (which controlled the Beiping government) became frequent to check and balance provincial leaders from expanding their power base.

These patterns of state governance, influenced by the constitution and

Albert Feuerwerker, eds., *The Cambridge History of China*, volume 13: *Republican China, 1912–1949, Part 2* (Cambridge: Cambridge University Press, 1986), pp. 340–344.

[29] Nathan, "Constitutional Republic," p. 265, listing when actions were undertaken by national-level legislative organs between November 1911 and December 1925.

the Chinese political culture shared by northern China's leaders, functionaries, and elites, enabled leading military leaders to form different regional political factions, so that whenever the Beiyang state (see Fig. 2.1) tried to expand its bureaucracy and military power, it was constrained by the regional military-political factions its leaders inadvertently had helped create. An unstable political system, punctuated by wars and intervals of peace and progress, evolved. C. Martin Wilbur refers to this state of affairs as a "military regional system," in which "no one military authority is able to subordinate all rivals and create a unified, centralized, and hierarchical political structure."[30]

Despite periodic local wars, especially the costly ones of 1924, as described by Arthur Waldron, some social and economic progress did occur.[31] Government data for the period report steady socioeconomic advances for not only the Treaty Port cities but inland areas as well.[32] By 1927, however, the northern state, weakened by wars, could no longer sustain its bureaucracy and military power by extracting resources from the growing economy.[33]

Yuan Shikai's personalized state-building efforts never legitimated the Beiyang state but instead militarized China, giving every provincial and regional strongman strong incentives to expand his army. Such reckless militarization strained the Beiyang state's abilities to mobilize resources; the ensuing perceived weakness encouraged local elites to withdraw support from the Beiyang state. It had no support beyond its narrow regional base of Zhili, and the northern market economy, weakened by a depression in 1924–25, was unable to help. In addition, the many provincial political leaders and elites repeatedly switched

---

[30] C. Martin Wilbur, "Military Separatism and the Process of Reunification under the Nationalist Regime, 1922–1937," in Ho Ping-ti and Tang Tsou, eds., *China's Heritage and the Communist Political System* (Chicago: University of Chicago Press, 1968), vol. 1, book 1, p. 203.

[31] Arthur Waldron, *From War to Nationalism: China's Turning Point, 1924–1925* (Cambridge: Cambridge University Press, 1995), chap. 1.

[32] Ibid.

[33] Statistics for this period are notoriously inaccurate. The Beiping government prepared five budgets after 1911: one for 1912, one for 1914, two for 1916, and another for 1919–20, and these merely represent the government's intentions and hopes. Even so, these budgets reflect the perceptions of government policymakers and leaders of objective tendencies in society that were at odds with government aims. Between 1913 and 1914 expenditures for war were high and rising until 1920. For July 1919 to June 1920 the projected budget for military spending (including ordinary and extraordinary expenditures) amounted to 42 percent of the budget compared to 25 percent in July 1913–June 1914. See *China Yearbook, 1925*, p. 708.

their factional loyalties. After 1924, then, the Beiyang state found it increasingly hard to obtain financial support from foreign powers, particularly Japan, whose domestic troubles were increasing. As political decay set in, the Beiyang state's days were numbered.

THE PARTY-DOMINATED SOUTHERN STATE

By June 1928, Chiang Kai-shek, the GMD's party chairman and the military leader of the National Revolutionary Forces, had defeated the northern, military-dominated state. But no sooner had Chiang proclaimed China unified under the Nationalist Republic of China, with its capital at Nanjing, then regional uprisings erupted in 1930 in Henan, imperial Japan sliced Manchuria from Republic of China rule in September 1931, and more disturbances broke out in Guangdong, Fujian, and other provinces in 1932 and 1933. During those same years the Nationalist government waged relentless military campaigns against communist guerrillas in southeast China and, failing to exterminate them, forced them to relocate in the northwest in 1935–36. The militarization of society and the state continued even as the Nanjing government tried to impose its power over China's provinces.

The Nationalist State, 1928–1937

Unlike the Beiyang state, a political party called the GMD governed the Nanjing state that formed on October 10, 1928. This party of 427,000 members advertised the ideology of Sun Yat-sen.[34] Its leader, Chiang Kai-shek, who had emerged from the civil wars as China's most powerful military leader, now tried to build a new state to unify, strengthen, and modernize China to free it from foreign controls and gain the respect of other nations. The Nationalist state's structure and functions differed because its leaders represented a new political party and ideology, unlike the Beiyang regime, but similar political institutions concentrated power in the hands of powerful leaders, their clients, and their factions, whose ideas and beliefs favored the expansion of state military and bureaucratic power.

---

[34] George E. Sokolsky, "The Kuomintang," in H. G. W. Woodhead, ed., *China Yearbook, 1929–30* (Tientsin: Tientsin Press, 1930), p. 1199. In October 1952 the GMD's membership reached 270,000, more than half the GMD's 1930 membership.

State Organizational Structure

The Nationalist state's power center at first consisted of party-military leaders, dominated by Chiang Kai-shek, who appointed and removed personnel, initiated the drafting of laws, and made policy. At first, a dozen or so GMD leaders of the party's Central Executive Committee dominated the People's Consultative Council, which directed the state's formation and evolving administrative structure. Increasingly, however, military demands to strengthen and modernize brought military leaders of the Military Affairs Commission into state policymaking, and they, along with Chiang, ultimately dominated by the time war broke out with imperial Japan. The dominating presence of these military leaders meant that state power had shifted away from party leaders and favored the development of the Southern State's military power.[35]

Three documents – the October 3, 1928 program of political tutelage; the October 4, 1928 Organic Law of the Nationalist government; and the June 1, 1931 provisional constitution of the period of political tutelage – initially provided the formal rules' structure, or institutions, with Sunist doctrine also providing some guidelines. But as party and state politics became contentious and the Machiavelli problem of how to create a new order resurfaced, personalized relationships, patron–client ties, and factions quickly prevailed over formal rules in political life.

A bird's eye view of the state's administrative structure shows that traditional political culture (informal rules) governed behavior, whereas the GMD political party, two government offices (the Central Political Council and the Military Affairs Commission), and the Office of the President constituted the state's institutional power center (see Fig. 2.2). This power center decided personnel appointments, policies, and laws.

According to Sun's theory, a five-sector government possessed enough checks to balance state power, generate efficiency, and be responsive to popular demands. In an ideal sense, the Nanjing state's Executive Yuan (cabinet and state bureaucracy) was supposed to formulate laws and policies, and the Legislative Yuan to approve laws and review and approve the budget. The Judicial Yuan would adjudicate laws and interpret the constitution. The Control Yuan would provide financial and

---

[35] See Hans van de Ven, "The Military in the Republic," *The China Quarterly*, no. 150 (June 1997), pp. 367–374. For still another perspective on emerging militarism in early twentieth-century China, see Edward Allen McCord, *The Power of the Gun: The Emergence of Modern Chinese Warlordism* (Berkeley: University of California Press, 1993).

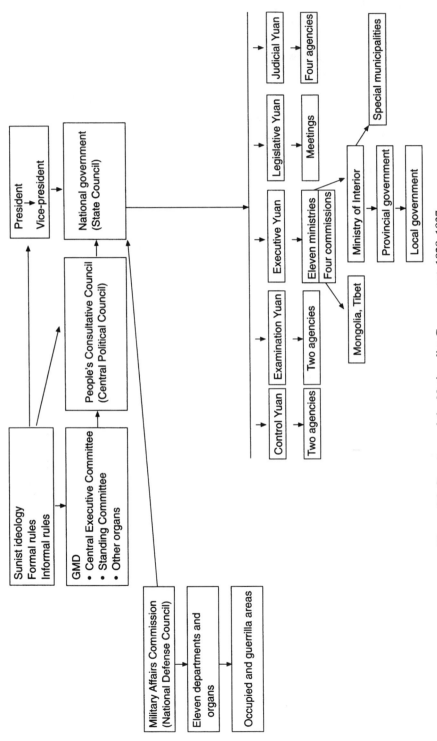

Figure 2.2 Structure of the Nationalist Government, 1928–1937.

personnel oversight. Finally, the Examination Yuan set standards for government personnel and examined those applying for government service.

The Executive Yuan, the largest sector of government, supervised eleven ministries and four commissions; its Ministry of Interior administered special municipalities, provincial and local governments, and Mongolia and Tibet. The state's power center, however, not the Executive Yuan, actually decided policies and appointed, promoted, and demoted top officials.[36] Middle-range and lower officials were selected by the Examination Yuan, which, although small in size (between 200 and 400 officials), soon tested and selected government officials by new criteria.[37] The power center never relinquished power to other state organs as Sun's governing blueprint dictated and constantly interfered in their activities.

Patterns of State Political Behavior

Sunist ideology as well as the formal rules embodied in party-government-drafted documents and the informal rules derived from Chinese political culture dictated that political power be held by only a few powerful individuals, who struggled for predominant power. Sunist ideology argued for concentrating power in the party's Central Executive Committee because Sun believed that the GMD must control the political center and decide affairs of state until a mature local governance system converged with a nationally elected National Assembly based on a new constitution.

But GMD leaders disagreed on how to interpret Sun's prescriptions. Hu Hanmin argued for immediately initiating local governance and preparing a constitution. Chiang, in contrast, believed that China required political tutelage until national reconstruction was well advanced and the nation militarily strong. Their debate ended when Chiang ordered Hu's house arrest on March 2, 1931,[38] an action that split

---

[36] Ch'ien Tuan-sheng, *The Government and Politics of China, 1912–1949*, chap. 11.

[37] Julia C. Strauss, *Strong Institutions in Weak Polities: State Building in Republican China, 1927–40* (Oxford: Clarendon Press, 1998), chap. 2. See also Strauss, "The Evolution of Republican Government," pp. 342–346.

[38] Sidney H. Chang and Ramon H. Myers, eds., *The Storm Clouds Clear over China: The Memoir of Ch'en Li-fu, 1900–1993* (Stanford, Calif.: Hoover Institution Press, 1994), pp. 102–106. See also Strauss, "The Evolution of Republican Government," pp. 342–346.

the party's top leadership, inspired Guangdong province to rebel, and ensured Chiang's dictatorship of the new state.

Various party-state committees now drafted a provisional constitution and other documents that vested great power in the president and the Central Political Council, already dominated by the GMD's Central Executive Committee of top leaders and later by military commanders close to Chiang. Chinese political culture came into play when the state's top leaders selected individuals on the basis of close personal ties, thus promoting patron-clientelism throughout the state structure.[39] Several top GMD leaders like Wang Jingwei were unhappy with Chiang's decisions and policies and engaged Chiang in endless power struggles to impose their agendas, arguments, and courses of action. Their subordinates and clients followed suit. As a consequence of party-state leadership rivalry, political factions – the Western Hills Group, Organizational Clique, Whampoa Clique, Blue Shirts Society, and Political Study Clique – quickly formed.[40] Individuals who shared educational ties and background, originated from the same locale, or were bound by family and friendship also joined these factions and worked for their goals.

Patron-client relations and competing factions, however, did not necessarily make for the weak political foundations and ineffectual administration that weakened the state at its outset, for such behavior had characterized the Beiyang government as well as the old imperial state, yet those states had endured for long periods. A more important factor dictating the Nanjing state's survival capabilities was the power center's strategic and managerial decisions relevant to popular support, performance, and the balance between state bureaucratic expansion and available resources. The efficacy of these decisions depended on the vision shared by the state's leaders and whether that vision could be translated into actions that tried to achieve the following three imperatives necessary for a modern state's survival:

- Optimize spending for national security to guarantee peaceful coexistence with other states while avoiding militarizing society and the state;
- Create a bureaucracy based on instrumentally rational behavior rather than value-rational behavior while obtaining sufficient resources to govern without undermining popular support;

---

[39] For the best study of this argument, see Lloyd E. Eastman, *The Abortive Revolution: China under Nationalist Rule, 1927–1937* (Cambridge, Mass.: Harvard University Press, 1974), chap. 7.

[40] Hung-mao Tien, *Government and Politics in Kuomintang China, 1927–1937* (Stanford, Calif.: Stanford University Press, 1972), chap. 3.

- Establish the rule of law and effective governance rules while maintaining technocratically efficient administrative hierarchies to satisfy society's needs and demands.

The history of those evolving, modern nation-states that replaced empires or loose personal-style governing structures since the sixteenth century strongly suggests that these three behavioral patterns must evolve to ensure the development of any modern state.[41]

The early absolutist states that acquired these three behavioral patterns gradually evolved into a variety of state forms, ranging from democratic monarchies and republics to "hard" and "soft" authoritarian regimes, with short-lived communist states in between.[42] Just as these different kinds of states had failed to survive because of their failure to satisfy all of the above three criteria for successful modern state-building, so too would the Nanjing state's leaders fail. This process of failure had the following features.

Sunist ideology and Confucian values now became melded in the person of Chiang Kai-shek, who was enamored of a transformative vision for China's future and its radical means to realize that vision. For example, Chiang Kai-shek envisaged a unified China free of foreign imperialism with virtuous leaders empowered to govern according to Sun's Three Principles of the People. Realizing the enormity of the obstacles preventing him from realizing his ideal China – the unequal treaties

---

[41] For a discussion of the monarchical states of the sixteenth century that tried to develop these three behavioral patterns and had enormous difficulty in doing so until the nineteenth and twentieth centuries, see J. H. Elliott, *Europe Divided, 1599–1598* (New York: Harper and Row, 1968), chap. 3. States and empires existed in this age; see John B. Wolf, *The Emergence of the Great Powers, 1685–1715* (New York: Harper and Row, 1951), p. 107; Penfield Roberts, *The Quest for Security, 1715–1740* (New York: Harper and Row, 1947), chap. 3; Walter L. Dorn, *Competition for Empire, 1740–1763* (New York: Harper and Row, 1963), chaps. 1–2: "In 1749 the states of Europe still exhibited the characteristic features of the old feudal society" (p. 3). The nobility had lost power, but state laws protected its privileges; see Albert Sorel, *Europe and the French Revolution: The Political Traditions of the Old Regime* (New York: Anchor Books, 1971), for how the political habits of earlier times shaped the behavior of emerging modern states.

[42] For a good account of the characteristics of the fascist and communist totalitarian states that violated these behavioral imperatives, see Elizabeth Wiskemann, *Europe of the Dictators, 1919–1945* (New York: Harper and Row, 1966); Mikhail Heller and Aleksander M. Nekrich, *Utopia in Power: The History of the Soviet Union from 1917 to the Present* (New York: Summit Books, 1986). For a different approach of how the state is the product of the interaction of challenges and state response to those challenges, see Bertrant Badie and Pierre Birnbaum, *The Sociology of the States* (Chicago: University of Chicago Press, 1983); and Charles Tilly, *The Formation of National States in Western Europe* (Princeton, N.J.: Princeton University Press, 1975).

that gave foreign powers a strong foothold in China; the selfish military leaders and politicians who abounded and opposed the Nanjing government; his weak, poorly organized GMD; and his enfeebled military forces, not to mention the nation's poverty and backwardness – Chiang opted for a transformative approach like Sun and other revolutionaries before him to overcome these obstacles to realize his ideal China. According to Chiang's way of thinking, the agency of change and reform could be only the state, and behind the state, a powerful military force, modern and equipped to crush opponents. Chiang therefore introduced reforms and national programs that could help him mobilize society and at the same time enhance state power to build his ideal China.

In 1934 Chiang launched the New Life Movement to promote Confucian virtues and energize society, but within a few months it fizzled out. At the same time, he secretly organized quasifascist associations in the government as an endeavor to mobilize tireless, young, indoctrinated functionaries to energize the government.[43] In 1935 Chiang called for a national economic reconstruction movement. To direct this movement, he established the National Resources Commission (*Ziyuan weiyuanhui*), thus creating a bureaucratic monstrosity of planners and technicians who wasted vast resources building inefficient state-owned and -managed factories, many of which were put out of business after Japan's invasion of China in 1937.[44] By 1936 the state was attempting to control the country's railroads, money supply and banks, mines and industries, foreign trade, and so on.[45]

The Nanjing state rejected Sun's concept of local administration (subcounty elections and self-governance) and tried to impose its bureaucratic power over the small towns and villages of every county under its control.[46] On May 11, 1929, the Legislative Yuan passed a law giving power to the county magistrate in all matters related to local self-governance. But after 1932 a trend set in whereby administrative bureaus began proliferating at the county level to manage the police (who

---

[43] Frederic Wakeman, Jr., "A Revisionist View of the Nanjing Decade: Confucian Fascism," *The China Quarterly*, no. 150 (June 1997), pp. 394–432, for right-wing, fascist-inspired factions to form within the GMD.

[44] Parks M. Coble, Jr., *The Shanghai Capitalists and the Nationalist Government, 1927–1937* (Cambridge, Mass.: Council on East Asian Studies, Harvard University, 1980), pp. 236–240.

[45] Fang Xiangting, "Shina ni okeru tosei keizai" (The system of economic control in China), Tatssumi Iwao, trans., *Mantetsu chôsa geppô* 17:1 (January 1937): 185–206.

[46] Kuhn, "The Development of Local Government," p. 345. Kuhn's account is still the best describing how local governance evolved during the Republican era.

were responsible to the national police administration organ), educational bodies, public health, and so on. These bureaus weakened the authority of the county magistrate and strengthened the central bureaucracy's control over counties. But such development occurred only in the few provinces in which Nanjing state power penetrated outside the provincial capital. The state also tried to establish experimental counties to promote "rural reconstruction," a reform touted to educate the rural people in modern-style schools, the first having been introduced in Ding County of Hebei Province as early as 1902–3. In reality, the Nanjing state's control rarely extended to the county level, except in those provinces where the communist Red Army forces had been driven out and restored to Nationalist rule and in areas – for example, outside Nanjing – designated as model administrative sites. Local governance continued to be a patchwork of Qing and modern-style organizations to preserve order, collect taxes, provide security, and supply public goods.

The Nanjing state had first tried to expand its tax base by taxing commerce and still relying on the imperial state's tax-collecting system, in which as much as a quarter or more of China's cultivated land was untaxed. In 1928 the Nanjing authorities tried to survey Zhejiang province as a pilot project to reform the nation's land tax system, but, as Governor Huang Shaohong admitted in his memoir, "the land survey teams had neither training nor experience. Most landowners refused to report their landholdings or had supplied misleading information. Therefore, even though the government had vigorously tried to increase taxes, it could not mobilize any additional tax revenue."[47] Failing to clarify land property rights, readjust the land tax, or distribute property rights to landless and tenant households (carrying out institutional reform), the Nanjing government neglected one of Sun's most important projects – land reform – a blunder that discredited the government in the eyes of many.

Forever short of funds and unable to meet the military's urgent demand for more funds, the state coopted Chinese banks to buy high-yielding state bonds,[48] which soaked up the available credit in financial

---

[47] Quoted in Ramon H. Myers, *The Chinese Economy, Past and Present* (Belmont, Calif.: Wadsworth, 1980), p. 164.

[48] See Doi Akira, "Shina ni okeru seisaku tenkan to yûkyû shihon ni yoru keizai teki henka" (Economic transformation by a public debt policy in China to convert idle capital), *Mantetsu chôsa geppô* 16:1 (October 1936): 1–44.

centers such as Shanghai, making it difficult for small and medium-size firms to obtain their needed credit. The government soon lost the support of many Shanghai capitalists.[49]

In March 1935, desperate for funds to modernize the military and expand the state, Chiang Kai-shek nationalized the Bank of China and other banks, thus acquiring the power to print the money the state needed for expansion (half the state budget already supported the military). At first the Nanjing state controlled only Zhejiang and Jiangsu provinces, but, with more resources flowing to the military, the Nanjing state, advised by German military experts,[50] extended its control over eight more provinces by 1937: Anhui, Jiangxi, Hubei, Henan, Hunan, Fujian, and, to a lesser degree, Gansu and Shanxi.[51] But even in the provinces the Nanjing state controlled, it never penetrated into the districts or villages as would the communist state that replaced it. And where it did try to extrude into county life by increasing the salt gabelle and other taxes to finance the state's modernizing programs, its functionaries outraged villagers and townspeople, inciting many to organize and resist state tax-increasing efforts.[52]

Some state spending laid the foundation for future agricultural development, which would benefit from later investments in improved seed varieties resistant to disease and drought. The Nanjing government established agricultural colleges, expanded farm extension services, and founded farmers' cooperatives. Along with building roads, constructing railway lines, and expanding telecommunications services, a new infrastructure developed within and around the coastal cities that facilitated the spread of commercialization. Educational institutions, hospitals, and urban services were also expanded.[53] Meanwhile, the private economic sector slowly expanded, fueled by the peace and order the Nanjing state had brought to east-central

---

[49] Coble, *Shanghai Capitalists and the Nationalist Government*, chap. 9.

[50] William C. Kirby, *Germany and Republican China* (Stanford, Calif.: Stanford University Press, 1984).

[51] Tien, *Government and Politics in Kuomintang China, 1927–1937*, p. 180.

[52] See Ralph A. Thaxton, Jr., *Salt of the Earth: The Political Origins of Peasant Protest and Communist Revolution in China* (Berkeley: University of California Press, 1997), chaps. 1 and 7.

[53] For a discussion of such projects, though not in a critical, balanced way, see Paul K. T. Sih, ed., *The Strenuous Decade: China's Nation-Building Efforts, 1927–1937* (New York: St. John's University Press, 1970).

China. Even the country's industrialization had begun to revive by the mid-1930s.[54] Equally important, the state's international credit rating had improved by 1936, an achievement that owed much to the Nationalist government's American financial advisors.[55]

The Nanjing government also prepared a new constitution, promulgated in 1936, calling for the election of a national assembly in 1937 that would choose the nation's president and vice-president and approve the formation of a new constitutional government.[56] Chiang Kai-shek, however, had made certain that the committee drafters had prepared a cabinet-type constitution that would give the president additional powers.

By early 1937, then, the state had exhibited some tangible progress and slightly enhanced its legitimacy. With the exception of Japan, which refused to relinquish its imperial privileges in Chinese territory, the Nanjing state had obtained the foreign powers' consent to abolish the unequal treaties. Having rebounded from the depression of the early 1930s, many regions prospered. But Nanjing's leaders, too weak to impose great power, were compelled to make bargains with the regional commanders, allowing them independent control of their economies in exchange for their loyalty and support. The communist guerrillas had been driven into the poverty-stricken northwest and were trying to regroup. In the major cities along the coast a civil society with new political parties and associations representing many groups in society was emerging.

Yet there were signs that the state's foundations were weak. Its bureaucracy, despite being strengthened and upgraded, was overextended and underfunded, nor did it have the fiscal organs to increase tax

---

[54] For the best study of industrialization by new capital formation between 1914–18 and 1931–36 and the expansion of gross domestic product by between 1.0 and 2.1 percent, see Thomas G. Rawski, *Economic Growth in Prewar China* (Berkeley: University of California Press, 1989), pp. 330–331.

[55] Arthur N. Young, *Cycle of Cathay: An Historical Perspective* (Vista, Calif.: Ibis Publishing Company, 1997), pp. 104–107.

[56] The May 5, 1936, constitution contained 148 articles in eight sections and can be found in the *China Yearbook, 1939*, pp. 218–223. For a good account of the factional struggles as to whether this constitution should be designed to promote a presidential- or cabinet-type governance system, see Suisheng Zhao, *Power by Design: Constitution-Making in Nationalist China* (Honolulu: University of Hawaii Press, 1996).

revenue.[57] Its tax system, singularly inefficient and providing the wrong incentives for economic development, imposed an excessive tax burden on commerce and industry while lightly taxing rich landowners and consumers. Corruption had begun to pervade the state bureaucracy, and party-state factional struggles demoralized its civil servants. In 1930 a few GMD leaders were sharing power, but by 1937 Chiang Kai-shek had concentrated power in himself. The country's huge rural population, uneducated and without local elections, remained outside the state's influence. According to historian Paul Linebarger, the nation had around "two million armed men with nonproductive occupations," a great burden on society and the state.[58] Moreover, this phase of the GMD party-state was militarized, without a rule of law, and struggling to administer a huge society with insufficient resources. The GMD's early penetration by the state had progressively weakened, and by 1936 party leaders exerted little influence on Chiang, his military officers, and security and intelligence units.

Even if Japan had not invaded China in 1937 and the two nations had agreed to a détente, the embryonic state's future would still have been uncertain. Its fate depended on the Nanjing state's ability to create the three conditions mentioned above. But was that inevitable? It had begun to experiment with constitutional governance and to tolerate criticism. Yet the Nanjing state's commitment to making China free of foreign intervention – based on Chiang's strategy of negotiating with Japan while pacifying the nation and preparing for armed struggle with Japan[59] – was increasingly unpopular with the students, intellectuals, and some political elites, who demanded that Japan's creeping aggression be opposed with force. Political opposition to the state still persisted, and provincial strongmen operated independently of Nanjing. The Nanjing state still lacked the military and economic power and social support to unify China and remove

---

[57] The Nanjing state, too weak to reform the fiscal system, had to rely on the old imperial state's policy of assigning a tax quota for each province to collect according to its sources of power and send that to the state. For a good discussion of the weaknesses of the Nanjing state's fiscal system, see Morita Kazuo, "Shina no zaisei kikô to sono unei no tokushokushô" (The special characteristics of China's fiscal organs and their administration), *Mantetsu chôsa geppô* 17:4 (April 1937): 31–75; 17:6 (June 1937): 105–55.

[58] Paul Myron Anthony Linebarger, *Government in Republican China* (New York: McGraw-Hill, 1938), p. 112.

[59] See Parks M. Coble, *Facing Japan: Chinese Politics and Japanese Imperialism, 1931–1937* (Cambridge, Mass.: Council on East Asian Studies, Harvard University, 1991).

Japan's imperial presence from the country. Therefore, when Japan invaded China, a burst of nationalist fervor produced great popular support for the Nanjing state and Chiang's leadership, but this lasted only for a year or two.

Japan's invasion resulted in the Nanjing state's scorched-earth policy and a retreat to the southwest provinces of Yunnan, Guizhou, and Sichuan, with the new capital located in Chongqing, Sichuan province. Until 1945, this beleaguered state, referred to below as the Chongqing state, perhaps could have become stronger had it adopted different strategies, but instead it became engulfed in a process of political decay.

Rather than using police and militia power to collect a land tax in kind, and brutally conscript labor for military and construction purposes, this state could have provided new incentives to mobilize the people to support its goals on a voluntary basis. By adopting a strategy of expanded guerrilla warfare, the state could have reduced the burden on the people of waging a costly conventional warfare. Instead, the Chongqing state opted for maximum conventional warfare, intensified its extraction of physical and human resources to support its large bureaucracy and military, and failed to win the strong support of the local elites and ordinary people for its goals.

A strategy of institutional reform like that used by the GMD on Taiwan during the 1950s might have aroused the patriotic fervor of the populace and mobilized resources for war with Japan if reforms had been introduced that could have motivated rural and urban people alike to raise production. A land survey and land tax adjustment, followed by affirming property rights and redistributing public lands to landless farmers, might have mobilized rural support for the state. Introducing technology and improving land use were introduced and helped to increase farm production, but too many citizens perceived the burden of supporting the military to fall on them and refused to comply. Encouraging private enterprise by reducing taxes could have enhanced the region's capacity to wage a resistance war. The Chongqing state, however, refused to downsize its large bureaucracy, which had to tax and cooperate with unpopular regional powerholders to extract the resources it required. Meanwhile, state military leaders discouraged the GMD from interfering with the bureaucracy or trying to build grassroots organizations.[60] Rebuffed, the party became moribund.

To protect its personnel from inflation, the state indexed officials' salaries for price increases and then printed the money needed to pay this bureaucracy and its armed forces. The severe inflation that ensued redistributed income from business people, workers, and rural people to the public sector, thus imposing great hardships on the wage and salary recipients who made up at least half of the region's work force. Increasing the land tax in kind and indiscriminately conscripting rural labor enabled the Chongqing state to increase its grain extraction between 1941 and 1942 and maintain high grain deliveries in 1943–45,[61] even though farm production in this region, as well as elsewhere in the country, stagnated during the 1938–45 period.[62] But these harsh practices caused the loss of popular support, so that when the communist forces invaded in mid-1949, the local elites and people refused to respond to the Nationalist government's call for local resistance.

These actions flowed from the state's power center (Fig. 2.3) whose autocratic leaders embraced the ideology of nationalism and Chinese political culture and used personal relationships, patron-client ties, and factions to project their power. By 1938 Chiang Kai-shek and a few close subordinates alone decided state policies. The Chongqing state's success at waging large-scale conventional war, extracting enough resources to support a huge military, and maintaining the state's legitimacy, especially toward the outside world, was achieved by ignoring the decay of its foundations: the GMD-managed organizations and the gentry-led organizations made up of elites and ordinary people, who consistently withdrew their support from the state.

Sunist doctrine no longer exerted any influence; state leaders could appeal only to nationalism and patriotism to justify their strategies, embodied in state edicts and laws. The political behavior of this state, which depended on the old informal patron-client relations based on

---

[60] Hsi-sheng Ch'i, *Nationalist China at War: Military Defeats and Political Collapse, 1937–45* (Ann Arbor: University of Michigan Press, 1982), chap. 5, for a devastating account of why the GMD declined during the war years.

[61] Ch'i, *Nationalist China at War*, p. 159.

[62] Lloyd E. Eastman, *Seeds of Destruction: Nationalist China in War and Revolution, 1937–1949* (Stanford, Calif.: Stanford University Press, 1984), p. 47.

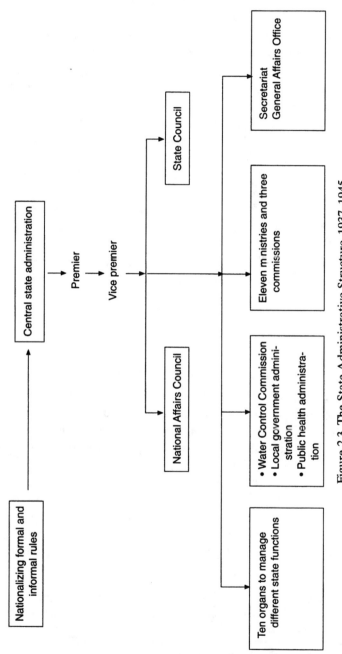

Figure 2.3 The State Administrative Structure, 1937–1945.

Source: Executive Yuan, *Guomin Zhengfu nianjian* (Republic of China Yearbook) (Chongqing: Executive Yuan, 1944), pp. 2–3.

personal ties, produced the inevitable factional struggles that characterized this government until August 1945.[63]

From the outset, Chiang's strategy was to expand the state's conventional military forces, with aid from its new ally, the United States, to
prevent Japan's military advances and to confront the Communist Party,
whose military units had already expanded into northern China. Meanwhile, the Chongqing state used harsh, autocratic methods to silence
critics at home and to maintain its resource extraction. Its policies
managed to work until 1943, when official corruption, ineffectual governance, and popular dislike of the state worsened. By the war's end
Chiang's poor leadership as exhibited in fighting the Japanese and
mounting official corruption and ineptness had come to light in a number
of journalistic accounts.[64] The moment of victory, August 14, 1945, proved
short-lived for the Chongqing state, for the GMD no longer held any
appeal for the young, the urban middle class, or even the rural gentry.
The war-weary officials, eager to return to their homes in the coastal
provinces, were urged to depart by the elites and citizens of the southwest region, who also hoped the Chongqing state would quickly leave for
Nanjing.

The Nanjing State and the Civil War

While relocating to Nanjing in the fall of 1945, the Nanjing state became
engaged in a full-blown civil war with the Chinese Communist Party and
its Red Army. The takeover of Manchuria by the Soviet Union's Red
Army in early August 1945 forced the Nanjing government to negotiate
with the Red Army's military and civilian negotiators, as reported in the
diary of Chang Jiangao, a member of General Xiong Shihui's team sent
to Manchuria in October 1945 to recover the region for the ROC Nationalist government.[65] The Nanjing government's agreeing to a flawed treaty
with the USSR cost it dearly, because the Soviet government used that
treaty to prevent U.S. ships from deploying Nationalist troops in Dalian.

---

[63] For a description of factional struggles of 1944–1945, see ibid., chap. 5.

[64] For two important journalistic reports that greatly influenced public and official opinion
in America, see Theodore H. White and Annalee Jacoby, *Thunder Out of China* (New
York: William Sloane Associates, 1946), and Graham Peck, *Two Kinds of Time* (Boston:
Houghton Mifflin, 1967). This book first appeared in the late 1940s.

[65] See Donald G. Gillin and Ramon H. Myers, eds., *Last Chance in Manchuria: The Diary
of Chang Kia-ngau* (Stanford, Calif.: Hoover Institution Press, 1989).

Meanwhile, Chinese communist forces quickly concentrated in the northeast and within two years had defeated the Nanjing government's best forces.

The central government's bureaucracy never recovered its former power and influence of the Nanjing era. The political decay already evident in the Chongqing state accelerated[66] as officials fled the country or were driven from government by charges of corruption. Official conferences achieved nothing. Laws could not be enforced, and the state had no dependable source of revenue except to print money.

Chiang Kai-shek desperately pressed for national elections for a National Assembly. Although these were limited in terms of voter participation, a National Assembly was elected, which convened in 1946 and approved the revised 1936 draft constitution. Limited national elections the next year selected the first-term National Assembly, which amended the 1946 constitution and elected the ROC government's first-term president and vice-president, who then selected the state leaders. But even these reforms could not arrest the state's declining legitimacy.

According to Chen Lifu's memoir, between August and October 1945 Chiang and his close associates made three strategic errors that sealed the Nanjing state's fate. Chen still believed that the state had a military force strong enough to destroy the Chinese communists and enough credibility and power to reconstruct the country.[67] First, the Nationalist Generals He Yingqin and Chen Cheng blundered by not moving their troops quickly into North China and southern Manchuria, not absorbing the Chinese militia in Japanese-occupied areas, and not reestablishing control over the local governments of these regions. Communist guerrilla forces were able to swiftly form grassroots networks that attacked railroads and communications, further isolating the cities. Generals He and Chen instead positioned their troops in large cities and refused to link up with local elites, embrace friendly guerrilla forces, or use militias that had helped the Japanese. In Manchuria the Red Army gave the communists advanced weapons they later used to defeat the best government military units Chiang sent to the region.

---

[66] For a discussion of this concept, see Samuel P. Huntington, "Political Development and Political Decay," in Ikuo Kabashima and Lynn T. White III, eds., *A World Politics Reader: Political System and Change* (Princeton, N.J.: Princeton University Press, 1986), pp. 95–139.

[67] Chang and Myers, eds., *Storm Clouds Clear over China*, chap. 8.

Second, Chiang allowed T. V. Soong to establish an exchange ratio of one yuan of ROC currency to 200 yuan of the puppet currency used in the Japanese-occupied areas. This ratio gave state employees the ability to buy cheaply and in large quantity the local goods and services priced in the old puppet currency, producing a major transfer of wealth from the local people to the returnees. The worsening inflation was also blamed on the Nanjing state.

Third, Chiang permitted General George C. Marshall to visit China to enforce President Truman's new China policy of insisting on the negotiation of a truce between the Nationalist and communist leaders and their military forces and withholding aid to the Nationalists if they did not negotiate in good faith.[68] Marshall not only infuriated both sides but weakened the Nationalist troops that might have dealt the communist forces a series of devastating blows. After Marshall returned to America, the civil war rapidly spread. U.S. policymakers now completely cut off military and economic aid to the Nanjing government, and Sino-American relations rapidly deteriorated.

These strategic errors by Chiang and his advisors, along with the Nanjing state's weak roots in society and loss of vitality during the Sino-Japanese War, suddenly tipped the military balance in favor of the communists and reduced the Nanjing state's effective governance. Despite the last-minute attempts to establish a constitutional government, Chiang and the Nationalist government had failed to persuade the communists and liberal elites to participate in their constitutional reform. The civil war quickly ground on to its inevitable finale.

CONCLUSION

After 1911, Chinese political leaders and elites drafted constitutions to restore or enhance legitimacy and to salvage or strengthen the state's power. Although those constitutions became dead letters, a persistent constitutional spirit encouraged elites to debate constitutional governance and criticize state leaders for ignoring the rule of law. In some measure, these redrafted constitutions induced state leaders to establish

---

[68] See Ramon H. Myers, "Frustration, Fortitude, and Friendship: Chiang Kai-shek's Reaction to Marshall's Mission," in Larry I. Bland, ed., *George C. Marshall's Mediation to China, 1945–January 1947* (Lexington, Va.: George C. Marshall Foundation, 1998), pp. 149–172.

limited checks and balances in government, which in turn encouraged them to train loyal, skilled, and experienced civil officials to project state power. Through this new power, the state carried out reforms to create a modern judiciary, expand modern education, build a better-educated civil service, improve the market economy, and develop a modern military.

Between 1911 and 1949 state governance was characterized by charismatic strongmen like Yuan Shikai and Chiang Kai-shek. The shared values of nationalism and Chinese political culture persuaded those leaders to opt for military solutions and expand the state bureaucracy. Yuan and those strongmen who followed him repeatedly used state power to crush those regional powerholders who challenged their rule, but with limited success. Yuan's state-modernizing efforts merely extended the reforms of the late Qing monarchy to establish an autocratic regime that manipulated the draft constitution for its particular ends. Chiang Kai-shek, however, was more ambitious in his goals. His transformative efforts expanded the state and military to unify China, eradicate foreign imperialism, and build a new Chinese society.

In theory, state power during the Republican era was vested in the people, who had certain rights and duties; in reality, a few strong leaders and their bureaucratic-military supporters competed to use state power for their purposes. Nationalism and strongman rule, in reality, created the Beiyang state, whereas nationalism, ideology, and strongman rule strongly influenced the design of the Nanjing state. Personal ties, patron-client ties, and factionalism constrained the Beiyang cabinet's powers, particularly the five-*yuan* structure of the Nanjing state.

State leaders tried to expand the state's influence and legitimacy throughout China, but deep suspicions and hatreds made cooperation between state and provincial leaders short-lived. The leaders of both states failed to establish forms of self-governance in rural and urban communities that might have encouraged more citizens to support them.

Even so, the evolution of the embryonic modern state after 1900 was an event of momentous importance in Chinese political history. Certain parts of that state received strong foreign influence: Japanese law faculties contributed to the development of a new judicial system; German military officers trained Nationalist armed forces after 1930; American universities educated the Chinese for the fields of education, public health, medicine, and engineering.[69] Some state ministries and agencies acquired many educated, disciplined, and cosmopolitan personnel. For better or worse, a mixture of modern and traditional bureaucratic habits helped to project this state's power and influence onto Chinese society.

As both states tried to expand and project their power, their leaders never solved the Machiavelli problem: They failed to acquire the financial resources and popular support that could sustain their growth and complete their leaders' reforms. State leaders mainly relied on building a modern military force to defeat their military opponents. Paradoxically, the personal connections of the powerful, patron-clientelism, and factional competition prevented both states from losing popular support more rapidly than they otherwise might have. Within only a few years, however, the rapid bureaucratic and military expansion of both states, mistaken leadership policies, and the worst habits of Chinese political culture produced only political decay and ultimate collapse.

[69] For transfer of American science, see Peter Buck, *American Science and Modern China, 1876–1936* (Cambridge: Cambridge University Press, 1980); for adoption of American medicine, Mary Brown Bullock, *An American Transplant* (Berkeley: University of California Press, 1980); and for educational developments, see Yeh Wen-hsin, *The Alienated Academy* (Cambridge, Mass.: Council on East Asian Studies, Harvard University, 1990).

3

The Evolution of the State in the Republic of China on Taiwan

BRUCE J. DICKSON

FROM the vantage point of 2000, Taiwan is widely seen as a text-book case of successful economic development and of peaceful transformation from authoritarian rule to democracy. It has drawn the attention of scholars and politicians who see it as a potential model for other developing countries, not least of all the People's Republic of China (PRC). But this was not always so. After Chiang Kai-shek moved the Nationalist government to Taiwan in 1949, he created a strong authoritarian state which repressed domestic aspirations for political change. Although Taiwan's rapid economic modernization began in the late 1950s, its notable economic success was matched by its continued authoritarian political system and the deterioration of its international standing. Until a decade ago, most observers saw little hope of its political transformation or its renaissance as an inter-national player. Indeed, it has only been in the past ten years that one could describe Taiwan as a model of political development and be taken seriously.

The evolution of the state on Taiwan has been shaped by an uneasy amalgam of traditions from imperial China, legacies of the Nationalist era, distinctive qualities of Taiwan's political economy and social struc-ture, and the consequences of development itself. The relative impor-tance of each of these factors has varied over time, but each has made an impact on the structure of the state, its goals, and its performance. Over time, the legacies of the past diminished in importance, and the issues of the present began to dominate. Indeed, it was the willingness of the Guomindang (GMD) to shed its traditional orientations that

The author thanks Ralph Clough and Ramon Myers for their comments and suggestions on this chapter.

allowed it to adapt to the changing domestic and international environments it faced.

This chapter attempts to make sense of this evolution. I begin by describing the mainland influences that shaped the initial period of GMD rule on Taiwan, both the institutions it created and the policies it pursued. I then assess the role of the state in initiating first economic modernization and then political democratization, and the interaction between those two related but quite distinct phenomena. Finally, I explore the implications of these developments for the nature of the state in the contemporary Republic of China on Taiwan.

THE INHERITANCE FROM THE MAINLAND

Understanding the state on Taiwan begins with one simple fact: for most of the past century, Taiwan was ruled by outsiders. Between 1895 and 1945, Taiwan was a colony of Japan. Although Japan built schools and basic infrastructure, and introduced the ways and means of a modern economy, the immediate benefits of development were highly skewed in favor of the Japanese. Taiwanese were not allowed to pursue education beyond the eighth grade (except in medicine or education), to use their own language in schools or work, to own or invest in the modern sectors of the economy, or to govern their own affairs.

At the end of World War II, when Taiwan was returned to Chinese sovereignty, many Taiwanese had high expectations for increased autonomy. The Nationalist government initially seemed supportive of these aspirations, but relations between local Taiwanese and mainlanders sent to govern the island rapidly soured. The mainlanders moved into buildings formerly occupied by the Japanese, rather than returning them to their previous owners. Relations were further strained by the paradoxical attitudes of mainlanders toward Taiwanese: They viewed those who collaborated with the Japanese as traitors and those who resisted the Japanese as potential troublemakers.[1] Tensions between mainland officials and Taiwanese society culminated in the incident of February 28, 1947. A confrontation between a street vendor and police triggered antigovernment demonstrations, which were followed by weeks of reprisals during which virtually every member of Taiwan's elite was imprisoned, executed, or simply disappeared. Although the true costs of this incident

---

[1] Alan M. Wachman, *Taiwan: National Identity and Democratization* (Armonk, N.Y.: M. E. Sharpe, 1994).

and its aftermath are still not known and remain the source of great controversy in Taiwan, the victims numbered in the thousands and perhaps tens of thousands and cast a pall over relations between state and society for decades to come.

As the Chinese civil war neared its end in 1949, the GMD moved its seat of operations to Taiwan. Faced with the challenges of governing the hostile territory that was now its home and of regrouping its forces to retake the mainland, its state building efforts in these early years were heavily influenced by the inherited traditions and institutions from the mainland and had little to do with Taiwan per se.

The Structure of Government

Taiwan's central level government institutions were directly transported from the mainland. The Republic of China (ROC) government apparatus consists of the National Assembly and five *yuan*, or branches: Legislative, Executive, Control, Examination, and Judicial. The National Assembly originally had the power to elect the president and amend the constitution; with the holding of the first direct presidential election in 1996, it now has only the latter responsibility. The Legislative Yuan is the top law-making institution and has oversight over the government's budget and operations. The Executive Yuan consists of the permanent government bureaucracy, including the prime minister's office and other cabinet ministries. For most of the post-1949 period, it was the most powerful branch of government; as a consequence of the past decade's democratization, the Legislative Yuan has taken a more assertive role in daily governance. These three branches of government were modeled on the experience of modern Western states, and had no corollaries in Imperial China. The Control Yuan investigates and occasionally punishes official misconduct, primarily corruption. It is the rough equivalent of the imperial censorate, which similarly was tasked with exposing improper behavior, including that of the emperor. The Examination Yuan is charged with testing and approving civil servants. It has its origins in the imperial examination system, which was the screening process for those interested in official careers. Whereas the imperial examination system tested a candidate's knowledge of the Confucian classics, the Examination Yuan tests a person's professional competence for a particular post, thereby creating Taiwan's meritocratic civil service. The Judicial Yuan is the top judicial organ, with jurisdiction over judges at all levels and the authority to interpret the constitutionality of laws.

These central organs were originally designed with all of China in mind, but after the GMD's retreat to Taiwan they were superimposed on a provincial level of government that covered primarily the same geographic space,[2] leading to redundancy in the two levels. The two levels of government were maintained to preserve the fiction that the ROC government had sovereignty over all of China, not simply the island of Taiwan. Under Lee Teng-hui's tenure as president, however, the territory over which the ROC claims sovereignty has been limited to only the island of Taiwan and the islands off the shore of the Chinese mainland that it currently controls. In 1997, the ROC government announced that the provincial level of government would be dramatically downsized. Thus, an important symbol of the ROC state's commitment to national unification, that is, the maintenance of the provincial government on Taiwan, is now losing its status.

In addition to these structural features, two other political institutions were inherited from the mainland. The constitution adopted in 1946 continues to govern Taiwan, but for much of the post-1949 period it was suspended. Between 1948 and 1991, the constitution was superceded by temporary provisions (more formally, the Provisional Amendments for the Period of Mobilization for the Suppression of the Communist Rebellion), and in May 1949 the GMD imposed martial law on the territories under its control at that time, including Taiwan and the offshore islands. To enforce the temporary provisions and martial law on Taiwan, the GMD relied on the military wing of the state. The temporary provisions gave the president virtually unlimited powers to "take emergency measures to avert an imminent danger to the security of the state or of the people – without being subject to the provisional restrictions prescribed in . . . the constitution."[3] This gave tremendous power to the president and the agencies under the presidential office. In 1967, Chiang Kai-shek ordered the creation of the National Security Council (NSC) to advise him on matters of national security. In the context of the times, virtually any issue could be deemed a national security issue and fall under the rubric of the temporary provisions and the NSC. Over time, the institutional apparatus that grew up around the NSC included not only mili-

---

[2] The province of Taiwan consists of the island proper; several offshore islands near the mainland coast are also part of the territory claimed by the ROC on Taiwan and are occupied by the ROC, but are administratively part of Fujian province.

[3] Article one of the temporary provisions, quoted in Hung-mao Tien, *The Great Transition: Political and Social Change in the Republic of China* (Stanford: Hoover Institution Press, 1989), p. 109.

tary and intelligence matters, but financial, economic, and cultural affairs as well. The Taiwan Garrison Command, established in 1950, enforced martial law on Taiwan. It had authority to approve travel abroad by Taiwan citizens and visits to Taiwan of foreigners; to approve meetings and rallies; to preview and censor newspapers, magazines, and books; and to try in military court civilians charged with a host of criminal offenses, even though this was prohibited by the constitution. In 1970, the Garrison Command's powers were extended to include restricting the privacy of personal correspondence, freedom of speech and assembly, religious worship, and other civil liberties.[4] These extraconstitutional provisions allowed the state to intervene in virtually every aspect of the private lives of Taiwan's citizens and were deeply unpopular at home and the cause for intense criticism of Taiwan's political system abroad.[5] In July 1987, then President Chiang Ching-kuo lifted martial law, signifying the democratic breakthrough, and in May 1991, President Lee Teng-hui announced the end of the period of communist rebellion and drafted new constitutional amendments to replace the emergency regulations previously in effect.

The other inherited political institution was the 1947 mainland elections for the National Assembly and the Legislative Yuan. With the constitution suspended and the "period of communist rebellion on the mainland" in effect, it was not possible to hold new elections for these representative bodies. Those elected in 1947 did not have to stand for reelection, not even before the voters of Taiwan. Beginning in the late 1960s, supplemental elections began to be held to fill seats left vacant by the deaths of incumbents and to address the rising demands for greater representation, but the majority of seats were still held by individuals elected on the mainland before the GMD's retreat to Taiwan. Because these parliamentarians were primarily GMD members or members of "fraternal" parties, the government faced little opposition or scrutiny from the legislature. Lee Teng-hui's annulment of the temporary provisions was followed by the Council of Grand Justices' decision to order all incumbent representatives to resign by the end of 1991. The decisions cleared the way for new elections for the National Assembly in 1991 and the Legislative Yuan in 1992, the first time all seats in these bodies were

---

[4] Tien, *The Great Transition*, pp. 110–111.

[5] The National Security Council and the Garrison Command were not the only intelligence agencies involved in enforcing martial law. The GMD, the Ministry of Justice, and the Ministry of Defense also operated their own intelligence bureaus, as did other government offices.

newly elected since 1947. Following the popular elections for governor of Taiwan province and mayors of Taipei and Kaohsiung in 1994 and the 1996 election for president, all of Taiwan's top government officials are now popularly elected, putting Taiwan past one key threshold of democratization.

Along with these national political institutions came the goal of national reunification. For the first two decades after its retreat to Taiwan, party and government officials were not content to be the ruling party of Taiwan but were committed to returning to the mainland, and central policy focused primarily on the goal of reunification. Their concept of the ROC state was continental, not provincial, in scale. Not only was economic and foreign policy predicated on the goal of reunification, but social policy was as well. Mandarin was the official language of Taiwan; even in the schools, students were not allowed to speak their local dialect and the curriculum focused on the history and geography of the mainland at the expense of Taiwan's specific history, geography, and contemporary affairs. These policies contributed to the creation of a Taiwanese national identity.[6]

One Party-State

Also inherited from the mainland was the GMD's status as the ruling party of Taiwan. Moreover, the emergency regulations in effect after 1947 also banned the formation of new parties. The GMD therefore faced no organized opposition until the 1970s, when independent politicians collectively known as the *dangwai* (literally, outside the party) began to actively seek political change. The GMD remains the ruling party of Taiwan, even though it has relinquished its claim to sovereignty over the mainland (but not its ultimate goal of national reunification).

The GMD's defeat in the Chinese civil war was ironically one of the keys to its survival as the ruling party on Taiwan. The lessons of that defeat showed Chiang Kai-shek and other party leaders the weaknesses in their party organization and links with society. According to Chiang's own analysis of the GMD's defeat, it was the organizational prowess of the Chinese Communist Party, not its military strategy or ideological appeal, that led to its victory over the GMD.[7] Consequently, its retreat

---

[6] Wachman, *Taiwan: National Identity and Democratization.*
[7] Lloyd E. Eastman, "Who Lost China? Chiang Kai-shek Testifies," *China Quarterly*, no. 88 (December 1981), pp. 658–668.

to Taiwan gave Chiang and other GMD leaders an opportunity to reform the party's organization, personnel, and links with the government, military, and society, and to implement the types of policies they were unwilling or unable to do on the mainland. The result was the rejuvenation of the Leninist features of the GMD, which had first been initiated by Sun Yat-sen in his reorganization of the party in 1924 but which had atrophied under Chiang Kai-shek's pursuit of military goals after his ascension to party leader following Sun's death. The GMD hoped to mimic the organization style of the Chinese Communist Party, its training methods, even its slogans, in order to compete against it and ultimately defeat it. It failed in this pursuit, but these same attributes allowed it to preside over an authoritarian regime without significant opposition for decades afterward.

Between 1950 and 1952, the GMD underwent a thorough reorganization.[8] To accomplish its ultimate goal of national reunification and its immediate need to govern the citizens of Taiwan, with whom it had hostile relations, the GMD needed a well-organized party apparatus and disciplined party members. Chiang Kai-shek had sought these qualities on the mainland, but opposing factions within the party and government and the weakness of the party itself as an organization prevented him from obtaining them. During the period of reorganization, the party eliminated the factions among its central leadership that had weakened the party during its mainland days.[9] It created a network of party cells throughout the government to monitor its compliance with party policy. It established a school to train middle and high-ranking cadres in party ideology and the current party line. In the military, it formed a political commissar system (under the leadership of Chiang Ching-kuo) to assert the primacy of the party (and Chiang Kai-shek personally) over the military. To sink roots on Taiwan, it undertook a recruitment campaign to expand the social classes represented in the party, in particular targeting farmers and workers, groups the GMD had not targeted on the mainland, and to have candidates for elected office.

During this same time, although not a part of the formal reorganization of the party, the GMD coopted local factions into the party in order to expand its authority at the local level. These local factions competed

---

[8] Bruce J. Dickson, *Democratization in China and Taiwan: The Adaptability of Leninist Parties* (Oxford: Oxford University Press, 1997), chap. 2.

[9] Some of the factions continued to exist in the Legislative Yuan, but because the legislature was weak in these early days, they did not pose a threat to the party.

against one another in local elections, even though they all ostensibly belonged to the GMD. Elections at this time were not democratic because they did not allow for contestation between competing parties or participation in the policy process. Opposition parties were banned and local elected leaders had little influence over major policies, which were decided by the central government. But elections were a significant means of extending GMD control. They were a vehicle for patronage between the GMD and its local factions, and in turn between the factions and their supporters. As economic reconstruction and then modernization began, the winners of elections controlled the spoils of development, and the competition between factions was intense even though the outcomes of elections were generally controlled by the GMD.

Local elections also provided limited opportunities for independent candidates to run for office, and many of these independents later formed the *dangwai*. Even during the most authoritarian phase of the GMD's rule on Taiwan, non-GMD politicians enjoyed some success at winning popular elections. For instance, Henry Kao (Kao Yu-shu) was twice elected mayor of the capital city Taipei during the 1960s; non-GMD candidates also won mayoral elections in Keelung and Tainan in 1964. To preserve direct GMD control over the capital (and to prevent the embarrassment of GMD critics winning popular elections), Taipei was made a "Special Municipality" in 1967 and its mayor was directly appointed by the central government.[10] To further consolidate its political control, the GMD also created professional associations for farmers, workers, and businessmen; the leaders of these associations were usually hand-picked by the GMD and their budgets and activities were closely monitored by the GMD in a classic state corporatist arrangement.[11]

The American influence on Taiwan was also quite prominent, directly and indirectly. The United States provided copious amounts of foreign aid, advisors, and military support. American pressure was partially responsible for the state's economic policy, including the land reform policies of the early 1950s and the commitment to a market-oriented economy. American aid and advisors were not always well received by

---

[10] In a clever move to limit popular protest against this move, however, the first person appointed mayor was Henry Kao! As often happened with successful independent politicians, Kao was coopted by the state and later given a cabinet post. The southern city of Kaohsiung, an important port and political center, was also made a special municipality. Direct elections for the mayors of these cities were not resumed until 1994.

[11] Tien, *The Great Transition*, pp. 45–54.

ROC officials, who resented their dependency on the United States for national security and economic and technical aid. Given the national security threat from the mainland and the need to promote economic development in Taiwan, however, the ROC had little alternative but to rely on the United States.[12] In addition, many party and government elites had received advanced education in American universities, where they not only received technical training but also were exposed to American political values, which in the long run influenced Taiwan's political development.

These initial state-building efforts yielded long-term consequences. First, the political institutions transported along with the GMD to Taiwan shaped the structure of the state, and many have survived to the present day. The most important political institution is the GMD itself; under its sponsorship came first the miracle of rapid economic growth combined with a high degree of equity, and later the incremental and comparatively peaceful transformation of Taiwan's Leninist state into a nascent democracy.

Second, along with mainland institutions came mainlanders, who dominated the political system at all levels. With few exceptions, Taiwanese were excluded from decision-making positions, even at the local level. Instead, Taiwanese typically directed their energies and ambitions into economic pursuits. One of the distinctive aspects of Taiwan's political economy was the separation of political power, generally controlled by mainlanders, and economic power, generally controlled by Taiwanese. This bifurcation originated in these initial years and survived until the Taiwanization of the GMD, begun under Chiang Ching-kuo, but fully realized only during the tenure of Lee Teng-hui.

Finally, as a result of the repression of political and social elites following the February 28, 1947, incident, the elimination of the landed elite following land reform, and the reorganization of the party in 1950–52, the GMD became a strong political machine without a viable organized opposition. Because it did not have links with economic elites, who might distort state economic policy in rent-seeking activities, the GMD state enjoyed a high degree of autonomy from domestic forces. It embarked

---

[12] See Richard E. Barrett, "Autonomy and Diversity in the American State on Taiwan," and Denis Fred Simon, "External Incorporation and Internal Reform," in Edwin A. Winckler and Susan Greenhalgh, eds., *Contending Approaches to the Political Economy of Taiwan* (Armonk, N.Y.: M. E. Sharpe, 1988).

on economic programs, often without initial popular support, to promote Taiwan's modernization.

THE STATE'S ROLE AS THE ENGINE OF GROWTH

The story of Taiwan's rapid economic growth is now a familiar and famous one. Between 1952 and 1994, per capita GNP grew by an average 8.7 percent per year, rising from $196 to $11,604. The volume of total foreign trade rose from $303 million in 1952 to over $1.78 billion in 1994; in per capita terms, foreign trade rose from $38 to $8,481; and as a percentage of GNP, foreign trade rose from 18.1 to 73 percent. By the end of 1994, it had foreign exchange holdings of over $92 billion.[13] Because these numbers have been repeated so often and for so long, they no longer hold the element of surprise and wonder that they first elicited. But more important than what happened in the "Taiwan miracle" is *how* it happened.

Competing explanations for the Taiwan miracle center on two viewpoints: the free market explanation and the developmental state explanation. The free market explanation, favored by most economists, focuses on the terms of trade. According to this explanation, Taiwan prospered because the prices for its goods reflected relative scarcities, and as its economy was increasingly opened to the global market its domestic prices closely approximated prices on the international market. It focused on goods and industries in which it had a comparative advantage: first light industry and assembly, and as the level of education in the population rose, technology-intensive industries, such as computer chips. The state contributed generous funding for education and infrastructure investment (roads, ports, telecommunications, etc.). Thus, according to the neoclassical explanation, Taiwan's development was a testament to the virtues of market forces and international competition.[14]

The alternative explanation, favored mostly by political scientists and sociologists, centers on the role of the state in promoting development. The developmental state model focuses not on prices and comparative advantage but on the political calculus of economic policy and the insti-

[13] *Taiwan Statistical Data Book, 1995.*

[14] Walter Galenson, ed., *Economic Growth and Structural Change in Taiwan: The Postwar Experience of the Republic of China* (Ithaca: Cornell University Press, 1979); Shirley Kuo, *The Taiwan Economy in Transition* (Boulder: Westview, 1983).

tutional framework of policy implementation. As developed by Chalmers Johnson, the developmental state model has four structural components.[15] First, stable rule by an autonomous state able to resist political demands that would slow growth (such as demands for higher wages or protection from competition). Second, cooperation between the public and private sectors of the economy, but under the overall guidance of a economic planning agency. Third, a policy commitment to equitable distribution of wealth and large-scale and long-term investment in public education, available on a universal basis, to ensure equal access to jobs. And fourth, government intervention in the economy, but intervention based on the price mechanism.[16] As a consequence of these four factors, the developmental state is usually an authoritarian one, willing to trade civil liberties and political freedoms for the sake of growth and equity.

In Taiwan's case the gap between the free market and developmental explanations is not as broad as for Japan or South Korea, the two other states with which Taiwan is often compared and on which the developmental state model is based. The peculiar aspects of Taiwan's political economy prevented the state from intervening as directly or as forcefully as in Japan and South Korea. The ethnic tensions between the mainlander political elites and the Taiwanese economic elites left the state unable to build a government–business consensus, as in Japan, and unwilling to use coercion to enforce economic decisions, as in South Korea. Unlike the large integrated firms in Japan and South Korea, Taiwan's economy was dominated by small- and medium-scale enterprises, making it difficult for the firms to organize collective action toward the state or for the state to exercise direct control over

[15] Chalmers Johnson, "Political Institutions and Economic Performance: The Government-Business Relationship in Japan, South Korea, and Taiwan," in Frederic C. Deyo, ed., *The Political Economy of the New Asian Industrialism* (Ithaca: Cornell University Press, 1987).

[16] Other variations on the developmental state model as applied to Taiwan include Robert Wade, *Governing the Market: Economic Theory and the Role of Government in East Asian Industrialization* (Princeton: Princeton University Press, 1990); Tun-jen Cheng, "Political Regimes and Development Strategies: South Korea and Taiwan," in Gary Gereffi and Donald L. Wyman, eds., *Manufacturing Miracles: Paths of Industrialization in Latin America and East Asia* (Princeton: Princeton University Press, 1990); Stephan Haggard and Tun-jen Cheng, "State and Foreign Capital in the East Asian NICs," in Deyo, ed. *The Political Economy of the New Asian Industrialism*; Thomas B. Gold, *State and Society in the Taiwan Miracle* (Armonk, N.Y.: M. E. Sharpe, 1986); Alice Amsden, "The State and Taiwan's Economic Development," in Peter B. Evans et al., eds., *Bringing the State Back In* (Chicago: University of Chicago, 1985).

them.[17] The GMD state was autonomous from Taiwan's society: the 1947 repression and land reform of the early 1950s broke the political and economic power of the local elites, the GMD's own enterprises gave it the financial resources it needed without having to rely on contributions from private business, and businessmen were not represented in the top GMD organs.[18] But although the state was autonomous, it was not unitary. The decentralized nature of the government meant that economic planners had little influence over finance officials, who favored conservative monetary policies and opposed market distorting policies. As a consequence of these factors, the state relied upon indirect measures, such as tax breaks, loan incentives, licensing agreements, support for research and development, foreign trade promotion, and infrastructural development, rather than more direct means of intervention. The state did not "pick winners," as was common in Japan and South Korea; instead, its incentives were made available on a nearly universal basis to a wide array of firms. Thus, state intervention in the economy was a prominent part of Taiwan's economic success, but these actions were generally market conforming, rather than market distorting. The state may have led the market, but it did not supplant the market.[19]

Like most late developers, state intervention to boost economic development was necessary in Taiwan.[20] During the period of Japanese control, Taiwanese were excluded from the modern sectors of the economy and were therefore not experienced in managing a firm, much less engaging in entrepreneurship. In contrast, mainland officials newly arrived on Taiwan were experienced in running a continent-sized economy and eager to put their skills to the task of modernization on Taiwan (they were yet another inheritance from the mainland). The nature of Taiwan's political economy also contributed to the need for the state to play a leading role in economic development. Because the small scale of Taiwan's enterprises at that time prevented them from raising

---

[17] Cheng, "Political Regimes and Development Strategies"; Yun-han Chu, "The State and the Development of the Automobile Industry in South Korea and Taiwan," in Joel D. Aberbach et al., eds., *The Role of the State in Taiwan's Development* (Armonk, N.Y.: M. E. Sharpe, 1994).

[18] Chu, "The State and the Development of the Automobile Industry."

[19] Wade, *Governing the Market*.

[20] The classic statement on the role of the state in promoting economic development in late developing states is Alexander Gershenkron, *Economic Backwardness in Historical Perspective* (Cambridge: Harvard University Press, 1962).

sufficient amounts of capital, the state relied upon public enterprises in capital- and energy-intensive industries, such as steel, shipbuilding, and petrochemicals. Taiwan's business class was not only capital poor but risk averse, reluctant to venture into new industries or product lines without state support. These factors required the state to provide initial investments in new industries, often selling off firms or shares of them after the initial push. In addition, Taiwan's economic planners had the advantage of the Japanese model, which relied on foreign trade and investment to rapidly expand production once the domestic market was saturated. The example of Japan's success with outward-oriented growth minimized both the domestic debate over proper economic policy and the costs associated with trial and error. By relying on the Japanese model, capital accumulation by the state, wise investments in new industries, and tax and lending incentives available to the private sector, the state on Taiwan was able to overcome its initial economic backwardness in a remarkably short period of time.

To boost economic modernization, the state provided ample funding for education, research and development, foreign trade promotion, and finding foreign partners for joint ventures. All this is consistent with the free market explanation. But the state did much more than this, repeatedly leading the way into new industries. Taiwan's small- and medium-sized enterprises excelled at finding niches with low barriers to entry (especially low capital requirements). This allowed rapid readjustment and flexible response to changing market demands and easy accommodation of technological change. But given their small scale and low level of capitalization, these firms were also risk averse and reluctant to venture into new areas. As a result, the state took the lead in moving into new industries. When the state wanted to develop an electronics industry, it had to convince reluctant skeptical firms that integrated circuits were a good investment. It created the publicly owned Electronic Research and Service Organization to research and develop the technology, found foreign partners to develop commercial applications, and established a joint venture of public and private enterprises to manufacture and market integrated circuits. Technology and trained personnel were transferred to the private sector, allowing it to develop without shouldering all the risk.[21] Similarly, in textiles, computers, plastics,

---

[21] Wade, *Governing the Market*; Constance Squires Meaney, "State Policy and the Development of Taiwan's Semiconductor Industry," in Aberbach et al., eds. *The Role of the State in Taiwan's Development*.

machine tools, automobile parts, and information-intensive technology, the state played the leading role in mapping out strategy and providing the necessary resources to make the strategy work and to draw private firms in. These indirect means of intervention created new forms of comparative advantage and allowed Taiwan to move out of the light industry and simple assembly sectors. When the state tried more direct means of intervention, as in the creation of an automobile manufacturing plant, it generally failed.[22]

In these important economic sectors, the market alone was inadequate to achieve the state's economic goals. State intervention, indirect and generally market-conforming, was necessary to kick start the economy and push business into new sectors. After giving business a push, however, the state withdrew, selling (or simply transferring) its share in joint ventures to the private sector. The state knew when to get in, but it also knew when to get out. This, too, is a characteristic of successful late developers. In more recent years, political pressures resulting from democratization have also led the state to withdraw further from intervention in the economy; this trend will be discussed in the final section.

Talented personnel, wise policies, and autonomy from those seeking preferential policies that would retard or distort growth were key elements of Taiwan's success and provide lessons for other countries to draw upon. But Taiwan's rapid development, like that of the rest of East Asia, was also due to situational factors that are not transportable to other countries and may not be replicated in the future. The Japanese colonial legacy; infusion of copious U.S. aid up through 1965; the expanding postwar economy, which created demand for the types of goods and services produced in Taiwan and allowed the state's policy of export orientation to succeed; the cold war environment, in which the anti-communist posture of the state gave it foreign support; and its position in the East Asian regional economy are situational factors – accidents of history if you will – rather than learned attributes and for that reason may be difficult for other countries to follow.[23]

---

[22] Wade, *Governing the Market*; Chu, "The State and the Development of the Automobile Industry."

[23] Bruce Cumings, "The Origins and Development of the Northeast Asian Political Economy: Industrial Sectors, Product Cycles, and Political Consequences," in Deyo, ed., *The Political Economy of the New Asian Industrialism*; Gold, *State and Society in the Taiwan Miracle*; Ezra Vogel, *The Four Little Dragons* (Cambridge: Harvard University Press, 1991).

EVOLUTION OF THE POLITICAL SYSTEM

The state built by the GMD during the early decades of the ROC on Taiwan is best described as a strong state, autonomous from social pressure and zealous in its defense of its political monopoly. It did not allow opposition voices to be heard or political parties to be formed. The first attempt to create a new party in 1960 (ironically led by a mainlander) was stopped and its leaders charged and convicted of conspiring with "communist agents." An early attempt by Peng Ming-min – later a leader of the Democratic Progressive Party (DPP) and its presidential candidate in 1996 – to advocate Taiwan independence was similarly suppressed.[24] These actions reflected Chiang Kai-shek's concern that local affairs not be allowed to interfere with the more important task of retaking the mainland.

Beginning in the early 1970s, as the transition from Chiang Kai-shek to his son Chiang Ching-kuo began, the GMD initiated limited liberalization of the political system, and especially of the party system itself.[25] Just as the state was not a unitary actor in the setting and implementation of economic policy, so too was the party not unified behind the ways and means of liberalization. Chiang Ching-kuo had trusted advisors on both the left and the right. As advocates of liberalization competed with hard-line defenders of the status quo for influence within the party, the political system as a whole fluctuated between phases of hard and soft authoritarianism.[26] In hindsight, these initial efforts at liberalization facilitated the later democratization of Taiwan's political system, but the two processes deserve to be understood separately.

Recognizing that the GMD was still dominated by mainlanders, even at the local level, and that its reputation for unresponsiveness to local concerns was creating renewed popular pressure for political reform, Chiang Ching-kuo sponsored a series of measures to improve popular support for the GMD. These steps were triggered by the sudden decline

---

[24] The planned dissemination of these materials was revealed to the Garrison Command by the printer. Peng Ming-min later wrote that "paradoxically, we had been trapped by our own underestimation of the police-state organization under which we lived and against which we were in protest. . . . Every petty informer knew he would be rewarded" (quoted in Wachman, *Taiwan: National Identity and Democratization*, p. 133). The KMT's ability to create mistrust among members of society hampered collective political action.

[25] This discussion of liberalization and democratization draws on Dickson, *Democratization in China and Taiwan*, part 2.

[26] Edwin A. Winckler, "Institutionalization and Participation on Taiwan: From Hard to Soft Authoritarianism?," *China Quarterly*, no. 99 (September 1984), pp. 481–499.

of the ROC's diplomatic standing. Japan and Canada led the wave of countries that broke diplomatic ties with the ROC to establish formal links with the PRC, the ROC lost its seat in the United Nations, and the Nixon visit to China in 1972 signaled to Taiwan's leaders that its relations with its primary benefactor were about to change for the worse. These foreign shocks led to popular demands for political change, led by some of Taiwan's most respected intellectuals.[27] Many of these intellectuals had links with advocates of reform within the GMD, suggesting that these demands were at least partially orchestrated by those within the state who favored liberalization in order to further their cause.

The hallmark of early liberalization was the "Taiwanization" (in Chinese *bentuhua*, or indigenization) of the GMD. This program had two elements: first, Taiwanese began to be appointed to top positions in the local party bureaucracy to make the party appear more responsive to local society; second, second-generation mainlanders[28] were appointed to central party and government posts. This latter dimension of Taiwanization was done as part of Chiang Ching-kuo's succession strategy to replace the older generation of mainlanders, with whom he had tenuous ties, with a younger generation that would be loyal to him.[29] At the elite level, increasing numbers of Taiwanese were added to the Central Standing Committee (the GMD's equivalent of the Politburo). To minimize the opposition of mainlanders who might feel they were being squeezed out, the number of seats on the Central Standing Committee was enlarged to accommodate the newly appointed Taiwanese members.

These personnel changes had important implications for the party's adaptability. First, this younger generation had little or no experience on the mainland, and made national reunification less of a priority relative to the development of Taiwan itself and by extension the party's own popularity on Taiwan. Second, unlike the technocrats in the government,

---

[27] Mab Huang, *Intellectual Ferment for Political Reforms in Taiwan, 1971–73* (Ann Arbor: Center for Chinese Studies, University of Michigan, 1975).

[28] This included both those who were born on the mainland but lived most of their lives on Taiwan as well as those born on Taiwan to mainlander parents. Only those whose families were already on Taiwan prior to the Japanese colonization are defined as Taiwanese. In fact, until recently identification cards included the holder's "home province" (either Taiwan or a mainland province), regardless of where they were actually born.

[29] Despite being Chiang Kai-shek's son, Chiang Ching-kuo did not enjoy the loyalty of his father's followers. They suspected he was not sufficiently anti-communist, due to the long period of time he spent in the Soviet Union (when he joined a branch of the Communist Youth League) and his marriage to a Russian woman.

most top party officials had social science and humanities backgrounds. This gave them a stronger orientation to the political implications of party and state goals and a greater willingness to use political strategies other than traditional party propaganda to mobilize GMD supporters. Most important, more sophisticated means of nominating and campaigning for candidates for elected office began to be used, and elections themselves were taken seriously as a feedback mechanism on the party's performance. Third, this new generation had extensive exposure to foreign influences, primarily received through higher education in Western schools. In fact, as part of Taiwanization, the GMD gave scholarships for foreign education to entice young college graduates to join the party. As a result, many of Taiwan's young political elites came into direct contact with political systems and political values quite different from Taiwan's. Together, these factors made the second generation of leaders on Taiwan less beholden to party traditions, especially the mainland orientation, and more concerned with preserving the GMD's status as the ruling party of Taiwan. The mainland legacy began to be replaced by concern for Taiwan's present and future.

Supplemental elections for the National Assembly and the Legislative Yuan provided a partial opening of the political system. These elections were important for both the GMD and the opposition. For the GMD, they became a very visible referendum on the party's performance, and the party attempted to adapt its policies and to select its candidates in light of this feedback. In supplemental elections as well as local ones, the GMD no longer relied on the support of local factions alone in the selection of candidates but nominated those who were younger, better educated, experienced, and attractive to burnish its reputation. For the opposition, elections became an institutionalized and legitimate vehicle for bringing alternative viewpoints – particularly the Taiwanese viewpoint – into the political system. Although the opposition was not allowed to organize itself, the *dangwai* (literally those "outside the party") gradually developed a shared identity and a loyal following among Taiwan's voters.

These initial and partial liberalizations did not lead directly or immediately to the democratic breakthrough of the mid-1980s. Opposition to these reforms within the party was intense, and hard-liners took advantage of subsequent developments to slow or even reverse the trends. In 1977, a large protest broke out in the Taipei suburb of Chungli against alleged election fraud by the GMD. This was the first anti-government demonstration since 1947, and convinced hard-liners that the costs of liberalization (in terms of potential political instability) outweighed its benefits. Following the announcement of the normalization of U.S.-China relations in December 1978, the GMD canceled local elections scheduled for the following year. As the hard-liners were gaining ascendance within the GMD, activists were becoming more influential within the *dangwai*. Using their journal *Meilidao* (*Formosa*) as cover, they opened offices around the island to coordinate political activities and held a number of rallies, culminating in a large-scale demonstration in Kaohsiung, ostensibly to promote human rights. This demonstration turned unexpectedly violent, and dozens of police and demonstrators were injured. Within days, the GMD arrested many of the top *dangwai* leaders and soon tried and convicted them. The GMD had to stem the popularity of the *dangwai* by portraying them as violent radicals, but, instead, jailing the *dangwai* leaders only bolstered their support. In the 1980 elections, their relatives and lawyers ran as proxies for the imprisoned leaders, and the *dangwai* achieved its highest share of the vote to that date.

During the 1980s, the *dangwai* became increasingly institutionalized. Although the GMD enforced the ban on the formation of new parties, the *dangwai* organized public policy research centers to publicize its views on various political issues and crafted platforms for *dangwai* candidates to run jointly on. In 1986, shortly before Chiang Ching-kuo announced his plans to lift martial law, the *dangwai* formally organized itself as the Democratic Progressive Party. Although the GMD declared this move illegal, it took no steps to enforce the law.

Although the *dangwai* was ironically helped by the GMD's hard-line tactics before the lifting of martial law, it was simultaneously hampered by internal squabbling. From the outset, and up to the present, the opposition to the GMD has been divided on its strategy and tactics: should it focus on promoting democratic values and practices and practical issues affecting society and the economy, or should it focus on nationalistic aspirations and, above all, Taiwan independence? Those who held elected offices, such as Kang Ning-hsiang, tended to be more moderate and tried to work for political change from within the existing political system. Others, primarily journalists and intellectuals in the Meilidao movement, wanted to use public demonstrations and confrontational politics to discredit the GMD and gain public support for Taiwanese aspirations. Election results indicate that the *dangwai* and later the DPP did best when they focused on social and economic issues but lost voter support when they emphasized the independence issue. During the mid-1980s, moderates held the most influence within the *dangwai*, but the issue of national identity, and in particular whether Taiwan is an integral part of China or an independent nation, has been at the heart of Taiwan's politics throughout the post-1949 era and remains the most divisive issue today.

The period of hard authoritarianism continued until the mid-1980s, when a series of scandals discredited the GMD hard-liners in the GMD. Wang Sheng, the leader of the Political Warfare faction and an ally of Chiang Ching-kuo as far back as their mainland days,[30] was exiled as ambassador to Paraguay after creating a secretive office to approve party decisions, in effect usurping the authority of the Central Standing Committee. The military intelligence organs were implicated in the murder of Henry Liu, a Taiwan-born U.S. citizen who wrote an unflattering biography of Chiang Ching-kuo and was murdered outside his California home by members of the Bamboo Gang. This murder on U.S. soil revealed the close connections between the state security apparatus and organized crime and brought renewed scrutiny of Taiwan's political system at home and abroad, including hearings in the U.S. Congress. Military intelligence chief Wang Hsi-ling and two leaders of the Bamboo Gang were convicted of Liu's murder and sentenced to life in prison (although Wang was quietly released from jail several years later). In addition, Chiang Ching-kuo transferred his son Chiang Hsiao-wu to Taiwan's trade office in Singapore. This step was interpreted as punishment for his son's involvement in the murder and a signal that the successor to Chiang Ching-kuo would come from outside the family. A series of financial scandals in the early 1980s led to the resignations of cabinet ministers and the GMD's general secretary. These events created a common perception that the GMD had been in power for too long and was increasingly out of touch with society, leading to public demands for further political reform and greater accountability of party and government officials.

By the mid-1980s, the path of previous events created a situation ideal for the transformation mode of democratization: advocates of reform in the GMD had eclipsed their hard-line opponents, the GMD remained stronger than the *dangwai* (even though the *dangwai* was gaining organizational strength and popular appeal), and moderates were

---

[30] Edwin A. Winckler, "Elite Political Struggle," in Edwin A. Winckler and Susan Greenhalgh, eds., *Contending Approaches to the Political Economy of Taiwan* (Armonk, N.Y.: M. E. Sharpe, 1988).

stronger than extremists within the *dangwai*.[31] Each of these three conditions was necessary for Taiwan's democratization to unfold as it did.

The democratic breakthrough in Taiwan is best understood as a path-dependent process, with the political events and decisions by multiple actors of one period shaping subsequent developments. It was not simply the result of economic modernization. Reaching a certain standard of living does not by itself trigger democratization; in each country, democratization is a political process driven by ambitions to share or retain power.[32] Nor was democratization solely the result of one man's decision; Chiang Ching-kuo's decision to lift martial law was a key turning point in the political evolution of Taiwan, but the decision came only after the hard-liners among his advisors had been replaced by advocates of reform. There has been much speculation about Chiang Ching-kuo's motivations: was he concerned about his historical legacy? Did he have a change of heart after seeing Wang Sheng's usurpation of power and the murder of Henry Liu? Did he have democratic inclinations for years but strategically hide them until a propitious time? Was he the captive of his advisors? We simply do not know, and we may never know.[33] The written record does not reveal much about his motivations and his closest advisors have promoted his democratic image without providing much evidence. Although he is now viewed as the sponsor of Taiwan's democratization, he counted both advocates of political reform and hard-liners among his protégés. Nor was democratization simply the passive response of the state to popular demands for democracy.

---

[31] In the transformation mode of democratization, the state initiates democratization, remains in control of the process, and survives relatively intact into the democratic era. Alternative modes of democratization include replacement, in which the opposition initiates the process which brings down the authoritarian regime and creates a new democratic one in its place, and transplacement, in which the authoritarian state and its political opposition initiate democratization together. For details, see Samuel P. Huntington, *The Third Wave: Democratization in the Late Twentieth Century* (Norman: University of Oklahoma Press, 1991), esp. chap. 3; see also Guillermo O'Donnell and Philippe C. Schmitter, *Transitions from Authoritarian Rule: Tentative Conclusions about Uncertain Democracies* (Baltimore: Johns Hopkins University Press, 1986).

[32] Huntington, *The Third Wave*.

[33] For differing viewpoints on Chiang's personal role in Taiwan's democratization, see Andrew J. Nathan and Helen V. S. Ho, "Chiang Ching-kuo's Decision for Political Reform," in Shao-chuan Leng, ed., *Chiang Ching-kuo's Leadership in the Development of the Republic of China on Taiwan* (Lanham, Md.: University Press of America, 1993), and Linda Chao and Ramon H. Myers, *The First Chinese Democracy: Political Life in the Republic of China on Taiwan* (Baltimore: Johns Hopkins University Press, 1997).

Although the *dangwai* was increasingly well organized, the GMD was still able to determine the timing of the democratic opening and maintain control of the process of change as it unfolded. It responded to its environment, but its response was not automatic or deterministic. Instead, it was the result of prolonged and often intense intraparty debate.

The changing perception of the threat from China was also integral to the timing of the democratic breakthrough. The suspension of the constitution and the enforcement of martial law were predicated on the threat of imminent invasion from the mainland, and this threat had justified the maintenance of the authoritarian nature of the state. But by the mid-1980s, GMD leaders were confident that China's moderate leaders were committed to economic reform and political liberalization and were unlikely to undertake risky military adventures. In addition, they believed that they could preserve stability during democratization and therefore not elicit a threatening response from the mainland.[34] Without this perception of a diminished threat from China, the timing and mode of democratization may have been quite different. By the mid-1980s, both the domestic and international environments faced by the GMD had changed to facilitate the peaceful democratization of Taiwan.

Taiwan's democratization continued after Chiang Ching-kuo's death and the succession of Lee Teng-hui. In May 1991, Lee declared the end of the "Period of National Mobilization for the Suppression of the Communist Rebellion," voided the temporary provisions, and reinstated the constitution.[35] This cleared the way for new elections for the elected representative institutions: the National Assembly, the Legislative Yuan, and the Control Yuan. The members of these bodies are now directly elected by the voters of Taiwan (with a few seats reserved to represent overseas Chinese). This has made the Legislative Yuan the focal point of political debate. DPP legislators chair several important legislative committees,

---

[34] This portrayal of the GMD's perception of a reduced threat from the mainland is based on interviews conducted in fall 1991 with GMD leaders and aides to Chiang Ching-kuo. For more details, see Dickson, *Democratization in China and Taiwan*, esp. chap. 6.

[35] The constitution has been amended to reflect changing political developments on Taiwan, particularly the end of martial law and the changing role of national security organs. For an assessment of constitutional revisions, see Hung-dah Chiu, *Constitutional Development and Reform in the Republic of China on Taiwan*, Occasional Papers/Reprint Series, Contemporary Asian Studies, no. 2 (Baltimore: University of Maryland School of Law, 1993).

including foreign affairs, and are able to exercise greater scrutiny over the government by calling cabinet officials to testify before the committees. In addition, the National Assembly in 1994 amended the constitution to give the president the authority to appoint cabinet ministers without the approval of the prime minister. Thus, one of the consequences of democratization has been the reallocation of power among the state institutions, to the advantage of the legislature and the presidency and the detriment of the executive. To further consolidate the formal aspects of democratization, Lee promoted constitutional amendments allowing direct elections for the previously appointed posts of governor and mayors of Taipei and Kaohsiung and (over the objections of many within the GMD) direct elections for president. Lee deepened the Taiwanization of the GMD and government bureaucracies, symbolized by his appointment of Lien Chan as premier in 1992, the first time both president and premier were Taiwanese.

Lee also redefined the ROC's sovereignty: it no longer claims to be the legitimate government of all China, but simply the territories currently under its control, namely the island of Taiwan and the offshore islands. Lee has repeatedly stated his support for eventual reunification with the mainland and his opposition to Taiwan independence, but at the same time has advocated a separate Taiwan. This rhetorical sleight of hand has confused rather than clarified his position, and created criticism both within his party and from China. Within this framework of the "Republic of China on Taiwan," he has embarked on "flexible diplomacy" to break Taiwan out of its isolation, and has asserted that negotiations with the mainland should be handled on a "special state-to-state" basis. It actively seeks to maintain and reopen diplomatic ties with foreign countries, particularly poor countries of Africa, Latin America, and the Caribbean. In addition, Lee and other top leaders have traveled abroad in a variety of official and unofficial capacities, and have been formally received by leaders of foreign governments, especially in Southeast Asia. It has bid to join or rejoin a host of international organizations, most notably the United Nations and the World Trade Organization. In these ways, Lee has tried to claim some of the recognition and respect he feels Taiwan deserves given its record of political, economic, and social accomplishments.

The GMD has not benefited from its actions to sponsor and consolidate democratization. Its share of the popular vote has declined steadily since the early 1970s. Even though Lee won a decisive victory in his 1996 presidential election with a 54 percent majority, the party as a whole has done much worse in recent elections. The GMD's share of the vote in the Legislative Yuan elections fell from 60.5 percent in the 1992 elections to 46.1 percent in 1998, and in the National Assembly elections from over 70 percent in 1991 to 49.7 percent in 1996. The GMD no longer controls the three-quarters majority in the National Assembly necessary to pass constitutional amendments, and between 1995 and 1998 did not even have a simple majority in the Legislative Yuan. However, after the 1998 elections, it now controls nearly 55 percent of the seats in the legislature. Its performance in local elections has been even worse. In the county-level elections of 1993, the GMD won only 47 percent of the vote, the first time the GMD had received less than a majority in any election (although it still won 15 of the 23 elections for mayors and county magistrates). In the 1997 county elections, it suffered its worse performance ever; it polled only 42.1 percent of the vote, second to the DPP's 43.3 percent, and won only eight of the twenty-three executive posts. As a result, the DPP now governs over 70 percent of Taiwan's population at the local level. Despite its contributions to Taiwan's economic and political development, the GMD's reputation for corruption, links with organized crime, and slow response to social issues is weakening its support.

The party is now divided into "mainstream" and "nonmainstream" factions (supporters and opponents of Lee Teng-hui, respectively). The nonmainstream faction is primarily made up of first- and second-generation mainlanders who are now the minority voice in government affairs, after being the dominant voice for decades. They see Lee's actions as a betrayal of the state's commitment to national reunification and the party's traditional ideals. On a more personal level, they also see little opportunity for their own political advancement, given the emphasis on Taiwanization and despite their experience and ability. In 1993, some of the GMD's most popular politicians split off to form the New Party, ostensibly to promote the issue of clean government but also to reclaim the commitment to reunification they felt Lee had abandoned. In the 1996 presidential election, two GMD veterans (Lin Yang-kang and Hau Pei-tsun) ran as independent candidates to represent the "true GMD" against Lee and the mainstream faction, and also campaigned actively for New Party candidates in the 1995 legislative elections; for these actions, they were both expelled from the GMD. The New Party endorsed the Lin-Hau ticket rather than nominate its own candidates. It placed a distant third behind Lee and the DPP's Peng Ming-min, receiving only 15 percent of the vote.

Not only is the party divided into mainstream and nonmainstream factions, but individual legislators frequently vote against the party leadership. Consequently, it must work to maintain the support of its own members and elicit enough support from the opposition to get its bills passed. The GMD's declining popular support and weak party discipline may ironically benefit the consolidation of Taiwan's democracy. The DPP is not stuck in a permanent minority status. With skillful coalition building and negotiations it can shape legislative outcomes. As Tien and Chu note, "this will, in turn, provide incentives for competing elite groups to accept the values of democratic institutions and avoid confrontational strategies."[36] Taiwan's legislature remains among the most lively in the world, but the changing alignment of Taiwan's party system may now facilitate democratic consolidation.

The nature of Taiwan's party system is still in flux. In the space of just one decade, the party system moved from a one-party authoritarian system to a one-party dominant system to an unstable one-and-a-half party system. A true multiparty system may be emerging, but each of Taiwan's parties now faces tremendous challenges. The GMD must stem the deterioration of popular support. Because its positions on most key domestic and foreign policies have come to resemble those of the DPP, it must also show that it can offer distinctive viewpoints on public policy positions. If it loses its status as a ruling party, the fractious groups within the party will make it even harder for the GMD to reach a consensus on electoral strategy and other policy issues. The DPP must show that it will act responsibly with the reins of power at the national level, in particular that it will find a way to balance its commitment to Taiwan independence with the needs of daily governance and will not take provocative actions that would elicit a military reaction from the mainland. At the same time, it must resolve the internal debates on what priority to make of the goal of Taiwan independence. Some of the strongest proponents left the DPP after the 1996 presidential elections to form the Taiwan Independence Party, but that did not end the matter. The DPP's internal debate on electoral strategy and policy agendas will continue. The New Party must demonstrate that it can attract enough voters to remain viable in the long run. It is unequivocally in favor of national reunification, and for that reason its popular appeal is limited. To broaden its appeal, it has emphasized domestic issues of social and economic justice and opposi-

---

[36] Hung-mao Tien and Yun-han Chu, "Building Democracy in Taiwan," in David Shambaugh, ed., *Contemporary Taiwan* (Oxford: Clarendon Press, 1998), pp. 97–126.

tion to money politics and the influence of organized crime over the government, issues also adopted by the DPP. It won 13 percent of the vote in the 1995 Legislative Yuan elections, which was more surprising than the GMD's poor performance in that election. The New Party may never gain enough support to be the ruling party, but if it survives with more than 10 percent of the seats in the Legislative Yuan, it may play the role of king-maker between the DPP and GMD. But in the 1997 county level elections, it won only a negligible 1.4 percent of the vote, suggesting its performance in the 1995 national elections will not be repeated at the local level. Like the other parties, it also has been plagued with internal divisions which have reduced its popular appeal.

Recent constitutional reforms will take the ROC state on Taiwan farther from its mainland traditions. In July 1997, the National Assembly approved constitutional amendments that reformed the central and local governments. The president will now have the authority to nominate the Prime Minister without the approval of the Legislative Yuan, the Legislative Yuan will be able to issue a vote of "no confidence" in the Prime Minister and his cabinet, requiring a new cabinet be formed, and the president will be able dissolve the Legislative Yuan. The provincial level government will be severely reduced, with most of its budget split between the central and county levels. The governor will no longer be directly elected, but appointed by the central government, and the provincial assembly will similarly be appointed by the government and its functions downgraded from legislative to merely consultative. As a result of these reforms, the traditional five-branch central government is maintained, but distribution of power among the branches of government is sharply reallocated in favor of the legislature, and the power of the president is also enhanced.[37] The reform of the provincial government has been more controversial; although it will reduce redundancy in government functions and the potential for conflict between future gov-

---

[37] These reforms were the result of agreements between the GMD and DPP and approved by the National Development Conference in December 1997. This conference called for other measures which have not yet been formally adopted as constitutional amendments, such as transferring the Control Yuan's authority to impeach the president and to audit the government's budget to the Legislative Yuan and ending direct elections to the National Assembly. Plans to eliminate direct elections for township chiefs and councils in favor of appointments by the county governments remain under discussion between the GMD and DPP. The GMD dominates this level of government, but it is also the level at which corruption and links with organized crime are most apparent and therefore most damaging to the GMD's reputation.

ernors and presidents (even though it created public animosity between the incumbent governor James Soong and his former ally Lee Teng-hui), it also gives the appearance of reducing the ROC's claim that Taiwan is but one province and not an independent country. For that reason, New Party members walked out of the National Assembly in protest before the votes on amending the constitution were taken.

The evolution of Taiwan's political system was abetted by the GMD's policy of inclusion. Parties with inclusive recruitment policies tend to adapt more easily to changes in their environments, and this is borne out by the GMD's experience. As demands for greater participation rose, it incorporated new voices into the leadership at all levels. The cooptation of new members with high levels of education and exposure to the international community brought advocates of political reform into the party to match the rising demands outside the party. The Taiwanization of the party and government transformed the state from a collection of mainland émigrés with little interest in or understanding of Taiwan's affairs to an entity more consonant with the ethnic makeup and political sensibility of Taiwan's population as a whole. As the party adopted a more inclusive recruitment policy, it also allowed for the limited liberalization of the political system as a whole. Over time, the opening of the political system continued in fits and starts, culminating in the lifting of martial law and the formation of new parties and continuing with the Lee Teng-hui reforms. The gradual opening of the political system allowed democratization to proceed gradually and generally peacefully, with minimal instability.

THE IMPLICATIONS OF ECONOMIC AND POLITICAL CHANGE

Decades of economic and political change have transformed the state on Taiwan. The imperial and mainland influences have gradually withered, replaced by the concerns of Taiwan and the consequences of modernization itself. Taiwan remains a distinctly Chinese environment, but one more preoccupied with enhancing the benefits of the present than preserving the legacies of the past.

Although economic development did not have a direct impact on democratization, democratization has had direct and immediate consequences for the economy. One impact has been the deregulation of the economy, including the privatization of banks and many state-owned enterprises. An ambitious $300 billion, six-year development plan to invest in transportation, telecommunications, and other construction projects announced in 1991 was later scaled back, as problems with land acquisition, corruption, and other policy commitments prevented the state from meeting the plan's goals. The developmental state model is therefore less appropriate for understanding Taiwan's current political economy than it was during the authoritarian period. Popular concerns for the environment and welfare issues have also led to changes in policy. As environmental restrictions on business have increased and wages have risen, Taiwan's businessmen have looked elsewhere – particularly to China – for places to invest in polluting and labor-intensive industries. In addition, democratization has been accompanied by a decline in Taiwan's economic growth rate, although not all the changes in economic policies and the reduction in the growth rates can be attributed to democratization. Taiwan's economy is experiencing structural readjust-ment motivated by competitive pressures (especially from China) and unrelated to domestic political changes under way. In addition, all the countries in the East and Southeast Asian region have experienced eco-nomic difficulties in recent years, and Taiwan's economy has been ham-pered by some of these spillover effects.[38]

The relationship between the state and interest groups has also been transformed. In earlier years this relationship was best described as a state corporatist system, in which the state created the groups, chose their leaders, provided their budget, and used the groups as a means of con-trolling the activities of the groups' members without allowing the groups to influence policy.[39] As a result of political democratization and economic deregulation, the balance of power between the state and the interest groups has shifted in favor of the groups.[40] As the Legislative Yuan became the focal point of political activity and the additional parties were added to the political process, interest groups have been able to lobby for their particular viewpoint and are no longer dependent on the GMD's patronage.

The increased lobbying activity of big business has also created a polit-

---

[38] Christopher Howe, "The Taiwan Economy: The Transition to Maturity and the Political Economy of Its Changing International Status," in Shambaugh, ed., *Contemporary Taiwan*, pp. 127–151.

[39] Tien, *The Great Transition*, pp. 45–54.

[40] Yun-han Chu, *Crafting Democracy in Taiwan* (Taipei: Institute for National Policy Research, 1992); Jonathan Unger and Anita Chan, "Corporatism in China: A Develop-mental State in an East Asian Perspective," in Barrett L. McCormick and Jonathan Unger, eds., *China after Socialism: In the Footsteps of Eastern Europe or East Asia?* (Armonk, N.Y.: M. E. Sharpe, 1995).

ical backlash. The GMD has always expected its candidates to support their own campaigns with very little financial support from the party. As Taiwan adopted a truly competitive election system with multiple parties, the cost of getting elected increased substantially. One result has been closer ties between big business and elected politicians. There is still not a strong institutional link between the GMD and business, especially when compared with Japan or South Korea; the GMD still owns more than sixty companies that provide a strong financial footing. This allows it to maintain a full-time staff of more than 3,000 without relying on contributions from big business. But links between big business and elected officials have grown, leading to intense public dissatisfaction and giving the DPP and the New Party a new issue for attacking the GMD (even though business also donates more secretly to the other parties and independents).[41]

Democratization brought an end to the political institutions that had perpetuated martial law. The Taiwan Garrison Command was disbanded after Lee announced the end of the "Period of National Mobilization for the Suppression of the Communist Rebellion." The National Security Council was transferred from the President's office, where it operated without external oversight, to the Executive Yuan, where it is accountable to the Legislative Yuan.[42] The range of issues over which it has jurisdiction is still broad, but civilian issues such as publishing and travel no longer fall under the rubric of "national security." Like the rest of the state, the military also has been increasingly indigenized. After the presidential elections in 1996, Lee dismissed many mainlander protégés of General Hau Pei-tsun (who opposed Lee in the election) from senior staff positions and replaced them with a younger generation of Taiwanese officers.[43] The historically close link between the GMD and the military has been loosened.[44] For instance, although the political commissar system continues to exist, it now focuses on service functions

---

[41] Tien and Chu, "Building Democracy in Taiwan."

[42] David Shambaugh, "Taiwan's Security: Maintaining Deterrence Amid Political Accountability," in Shambaugh, ed., *Contemporary Taiwan*, pp. 240–274.

[43] Shambaugh, "Taiwan's Security," p. 248.

[44] Cheng Hsiao-shih traces the loosening of the party-military link back to the 1960s, and attributes it to four factors: socioeconomic development and the rising influence of technocrats, the fading of the myth of national reunification through military means, the professionalization of the military, and the increased importance of constitutional procedures. See his *Party-Military Relations in the PRC and Taiwan: Paradoxes of Control* (Boulder: Westview Press, 1990), pp. 126–133.

(such as providing housing and medical care for military personnel) and no longer provides political indoctrination or oversight functions for the GMD. The result has been a professionalization of the military, a healthy sign for the consolidation of Taiwan's democracy. Still, the separation of the GMD from the military has not gone far enough to satisfy the opposition, and it remains to be seen whether the military would follow the command of a DPP president.[45]

The GMD's Leninist nature also changed as a result of democratization. The GMD no longer has a monopoly on political organization, traditional party ideology is less relevant as a guide to policy, party cells in the government and military have been deactivated, and the party no longer directly controls the groups through which it formerly mobilized society on behalf of party goals. As the influence of elected politicians rose in the party relative to first-generation ideologues and second-generation technocrats, both of whom relied on the authoritarian controls of the state to pursue their goals, the advantages of a Leninist party were abandoned for the exigencies of democratic competition. As the party increasingly adapted to popular pressures from Taiwan's society and stopped trying to transform it, the Leninist model was no longer relevant for the GMD, as either an organizing principle or an analytical tool.

What did not change as a result of democratization was the salience of the national identity issue. Lee Teng-hui's efforts to consolidate Taiwan's democracy and strengthen its international posture have tried to address the national identity issue without being able to solve it. Just as divisions arose over previous episodes of liberalization and democratization, Lee's actions have encountered strong opposition within his own party. The issue of national identity remains the central issue of Taiwan's politics, but it has grown more complicated with democratization. Whereas it used to be a partisan issue between the GMD and the opposition, divisions within the GMD and DPP are now greater than the differences between the two parties. Now that Lee has adopted many of the DPP's foreign policy objec-

---

[45] Similarly, it is not clear whether a democratically elected DPP president could work effectively with the Executive Yuan, whose permanent civil service members are mostly GMD members. In each ministry, the ruling party only appoints the minister and the political vice minister, but the administrative vice minister and the rest of the ministry's personnel are members of the permanent civil service.

tives as his own, the main fault line on the national identity issue is no longer between the two parties, but within each party. The GMD's mainstream faction and the DPP's Meilidao faction advocate a gradual approach on the issue, out of deference to both public opinion and China's position.[46] The GMD's nonmainstream faction and most of the New Party remain committed to reunification, but contingent upon future political change on the mainland. The New Tide faction of the DPP and the Taiwan Independence Party (which split off from the DPP in 1996) are committed to the immediate establishment of an independent Taiwan. As a result, the main fault lines on the independence-reunification issue are no longer between the parties but within them.

But the national identity issue is not Taiwan's to solve on its own. Taiwan's precarious international status, shaped by China's opposition to anything resembling independent status for Taiwan, continues to constrain political choices by Taiwan's leaders. They are not free to choose from the full array of policy options, especially on the issues of sovereignty and membership in international organizations. Taiwan cannot join an international organization or increase its level of diplomatic recognition just because its leaders want to or popular opinion demands it. Concern for China's reaction has prevented the GMD's support for drafting a new constitution and holding a public referendum on the independence issue (as the DPP has proposed) and also has dampened popular enthusiasm for independence, at least for the present. One of the requirements of a full-fledged democracy is that the nation not be subject to a veto by external actors,[47] and on this score Taiwan's democracy remains fragile.

Taiwan's democratization amidst the unresolved national identity issue also seems to violate Rustow's contention that democratization is possible only after the definition of the nation, both its geographic and ethnic boundaries, has been agreed on. Indeed, Rustow says this is the

---

[46] The Meilidao faction of the *dangwai*/DPP has evolved considerably over the years. It advocated a radical approach to the independence issue during the 1970s and 1980s, but as the DPP gained electoral support and the chances of becoming the ruling party increased, the Meilidao faction adopted a more moderate position. Those who continue to hold independence as the top priority have formed new factions, or new parties (the Taiwan Independence Party and the National Construction Party).

[47] Terry Lynn Karl and Philippe C. Schmitter, "Modes of Transition in Latin America, Southern and Eastern Europe," *International Social Science Journal*, no. 138 (May 1990), pp. 269–284.

only prerequisite for democratization.[48] The national identity issue is far from being solved in Taiwan, and yet democratization has proceeded. How has this happened? For one thing, the popular consensus, reflected in more than a decade's worth of public opinion polls, is that citizens of Taiwan prefer to defer this issue to the future. While it is a highly partisan issue, it is not one that appeals to many voters. Second, the Taiwanization of the GMD and the government has also reduced the salience of this issue. The state can no longer be described as an external occupying force. It increasingly reflects Taiwan's society, both in appearance and in policy preferences. The GMD is no longer a symbol of mainland hegemony. During the 1998 elections, Lee Teng-hui introduced the concept of the "new Taiwanese," referring to the broad spectrum of people on Taiwan – regardless of whether they come from mainlander or Taiwanese backgrounds – who are committed to maintaining an Independent identity for Taiwan and contributing to Taiwan's future development. Third, the Taiwanization of the state has reduced the partisan split over national identity. What emphasis to place on preserving the status quo, pushing for national reunification, and promoting Taiwan independence (or an independent Taiwan, as Lee Teng-hui characterizes it) has created internal divisions within the GMD and DPP that are more serious than the difference between the two parties. This has made it difficult for the individual parties to manage their own affairs, but also allows coalition building by like-minded members of different parties. This consensual style of politics is quite conducive to the consolidation of democratic values and practices.

The Republic of China on Taiwan remains a distinctly Chinese entity, but the role of the state and the goals it pursues are increasingly derived from the wants and needs of contemporary Taiwan. The traditions of imperial China and the legacies of the Nationalist era on the mainland,

---

[48] Rustow says that national unity "means that the vast majority of citizens in a democracy-to-be must have no doubt or mental reservations as to which political community they belong to." See Dankwart A. Rustow, "Transitions to Democracy: A Dynamic Model," *Comparative Politics*, vol. 2, no. 3 (April 1970), p. 350. This clearly has not yet been achieved on Taiwan. The other aspects of Rustow's model were met in Taiwan's case: Democratization was preceded by a prolonged period of unresolved conflict, after which the political protagonists – the GMD and the *dangwai*/DPP – consciously adopted democratic rules and procedures to institutionalize diversity, and finally a period of habituation ensued, during which parties, politicians, and citizens developed experience with and commitment to democratic institutions. However, Rustow asserts that the background condition of national unity must precede the phases of conflict, decision, and habituation.

both important influences on the initial state-building efforts on Taiwan after 1949, are not as tangible today as in the past. As a result of democratization, and in particular Lee Teng-hui's efforts to indigenize the state and promote an "independent Taiwan" (but not Taiwan independence), the Republic of China on Taiwan is better positioned to champion the aspirations of Taiwan's society for the present and future and less committed to upholding the legacies of the past.

4

The Chinese State
during the Maoist Era

FREDERICK C. TEIWES

When Mao did not personally intervene the system functioned more or less by standard procedures. The government dealt with issues, there were local discussions and feedback to the Center. But whenever Mao intervened this could no longer be sustained, the waters were muddied, and in 1958 there was no planning.[1]

WHILE the subject and focus of this essay is the Maoist state, it cannot be separated from the dynamics of Chinese Communist Party (CCP) elite politics. This is clearly reflected in the above statement by a leading ministerial official from the heavy industry sector in the mid- and late 1950s, someone who thus operated in both the heavily bureaucratic Soviet model period and under the personally driven policies of Mao Zedong during the Great Leap Forward. Simply put, the way in which the state functioned was fundamentally a result of the interactions of a small number of leaders – numbering no more than two dozen – at the apex of the system, with the input of Mao as unchallenged leader crucial whether in allowing other leaders to operate complex bureaucracies or taking the whole process by the scruff of the neck himself. This is by no means to say that Mao and his two dozen colleagues were the be-all and end-all of the Chinese state from 1949 to 1976, but it is to assert that his (and their) role was decisive.[2]

---

[1] Interview with former central level bureaucrat, March 1993.

[2] This is not the place to rehearse in detail the argument of Mao's unchallenged authority with which this writer has been long associated, although it is necessary to draw on the relevant body of work in what follows. For detailed analyses in support of the "unchallenged Mao" thesis, see, for the entire pre-Cultural Revolution period, Frederick C. Teiwes, *Politics and Purges in China: Rectification and the Decline of Party Norms, 1950–1965*, 2nd ed. (Armonk: M.E. Sharpe, 1993); for the early 1950s, Teiwes, *Politics at Mao's Court: Gao Gang and Party Factionalism in the Early 1950s* (Armonk: M.E. Sharpe, 1990); for the mid- and late 1950s, Teiwes with Warren Sun, *China's*

A number of key issues arise about the Maoist state. One concerns the changing role of the many complex bureaucracies of the People's Republic of China (PRC), particularly the relationship of these institutions to the party leadership. Suffice it to say at this point that the above view of the dominance of a small group of leaders is not universally held,[3] and in any case the nature of that dominance has shifted over time. Also of relevance here is the mode of policy implementation which characteristically embraced both bureaucratic and mass campaign methods during the Maoist era. Another set of issues concerns the relationship of the state to society, the extent of the reach of the state and the related question of the capacity of the state to mobilize resources to achieve its goals. Here I will argue, again against some opinion,[4] for a totalistic state, one which may have fallen short of the idealized totalitarian model,[5] but which nevertheless achieved a remarkable degree of penetration of society. Of importance here is the question of the nature of totalistic control, the degree to which such control was based on legitimate authority, and the degree to which it reflected brute force. Other matters to be canvassed are the nature and sources of Chinese Leninism, with attention to both revolutionary traditions and the Stalinist model; the impact of factionalism on the functioning of the state; and the nature of the symbiotic but changing relationship of the party-state and the military.

In addressing these broad issues, I first examine the implications of the CCP's revolutionary experience which so profoundly affected the functioning of the Maoist state. Next, the structure of the state is reviewed, with the roles and interrelations of the major vertically organized insti-

---

Road to Disaster: Mao, Central Politicians, and Provincial Leaders in the Unfolding of the Great Leap Forward, 1955–1959 (Armonk: M.E. Sharpe, 1999); and for the Cultural Revolution through 1971, Teiwes and Warren Sun, *The Tragedy of Lin Biao: Riding the Tiger during the Cultural Revolution, 1966–1971* (London: Hurst and Co., 1996).

[3] The systematic statement of the opposing view of institutional determination of policy is David Bachman, *Bureaucracy, Economy, and Leadership in China: The Institutional Origins of the Great Leap Forward* (New York: Cambridge University Press, 1991).

[4] The classic statement arguing the limited reach of the Maoist state is Vivienne Shue, *The Reach of the State: Sketches of the Chinese Body Politic* (Stanford: Stanford University Press, 1988). For a more recent challenge to the totalistic view, see Elizabeth J. Perry and Li Xun, *Proletarian Power: Shanghai in the Cultural Revolution* (Boulder: Westview Press, 1997).

[5] The classic statement of the model with direct reference to communist systems is Carl J. Friedrich and Zbigniew Brzezinski, *Totalitarian Dictatorship and Autocracy* (New York: Praeger, 1956).

tutions analyzed in broad terms. This is followed by a more detailed discussion of the evolution of the state over key time periods, before a summary assessment of the large issues raised above is offered. A final brief concluding statement highlights the challenges the Maoist state left for its successor.

THE LEGACY OF THE CHINESE REVOLUTION

Unlike the Russian Bolsheviks, the CCP came to power with extensive experience in running substantial quasi-states. Such experience went back more than two decades to the Jinggangshan and other base areas during the southern phase of the revolution, and during the anti-Japanese war involving territories in north and east China populated by upward of 100 million people. While such areas were often tenuously held and subject to significant fluctuations in the extent of control,[6] they nevertheless did provide training in the tasks of government for a substantial corps of cadres who continued in their own areas or were dispatched to other regions with the nationwide takeover in 1949. While most of this took place in rural areas, some urban experience was gained during the civil war after 1945 as the CCP occupied various small cities in the north and northeast.[7] Thus when the CCP entered cities and towns all over the country, it came with at least a core of seasoned officials rather than impractical revolutionaries.

There were aspects of this governing experience larger than simply the accumulation of relevant skills. Perhaps most significant was the fundamental pragmatism of the CCP's approach. While clouded by the party's own subsequent romanticism about its past as well as the Western construct of a voluntaristic "Yan'an syndrome," the basic thrust of Mao's revolutionary policy was to attempt only what was possible, to mobilize the masses behind *achievable* objectives while avoiding reckless adventures in a context where the CCP was the weaker force. Moreover, notwithstanding romantic notions of popular initiative, the essence of the "mass line" during the revolution was calculated, top-down leadership by the party. This approach, in turn, was linked to other aspects of revolu-

[6] See the excellent analysis in Kathleen Hartford, "Repression and Communist Success: The Case of Jin-Cha-Ji, 1938–1943," in Hartford and Steven M. Goldstein, eds., *Single Sparks: China's Rural Revolutions* (Armonk: M.E. Sharpe, 1989).
[7] See Suzanne Pepper, *Civil War in China: The Political Struggle, 1945–1949* (Berkeley: University of California Press, 1978), chap. 8.

tionary practice derived from the party's comparative weakness – the need for allies and decentralized operations. In the former case, the united front became an integral part of the CCP's strategy for success[8] – one of its "three magic weapons" together with party leadership and armed struggle, and aspects of a united front, albeit with great fluctuations, continued to exist throughout the Maoist period and beyond. As for decentralized operations, while this made a virtue of necessity, it was also a hardheaded realization of what became a key if subsequently erratically implemented CCP principle of policy implementation, that political effectiveness required "flexibly adapting policy to suit local conditions" (*yindi zhiyi linghuo yunyong*).[9]

A less well-understood feature of the revolutionary period was the degree to which the Soviet model of both government and the economy was accepted before the PRC was established. While clearly Mao's program included both operational independence and policies adapted to Chinese realities, and various tensions existed between the CCP and Moscow throughout the 1940s, there was never any question that Mao and his colleagues considered themselves part of an international movement headed by Stalin, or that the Soviet model represented the only true path for a communist party in power.[10] There was, in fact, an almost seamless transition from rural revolution to priority to the urban areas. Not only was such a shift of focus endorsed by the Central Committee plenum in March 1949, it was clearly seen as something entirely natural and highly desirable by the communist nationalists who wanted to modernize China as rapidly as feasible. For all the acceptance of the Soviet model, however, there was also pride in Chinese revolutionary traditions, and for all the pragmatism of actual practice, the mass movement pro-

---

[8] See Shum Kui-Kwong, *The Chinese Communists' Road to Power: The Anti-Japanese United Front (1935–45)* (Hong Kong: Oxford University Press, 1988).

[9] On post-1949 difficulties inherent in following this principle once a centralized, social-engineering state was installed, see Frederick C. Teiwes, "Provincial Politics in China: Themes and Variations," in John M. H. Lindbeck, *China: Management of a Revolutionary Society* (Seattle: University of Washington Press, 1971), pp. 125–26.

[10] See Frederick C. Teiwes with the assistance of Warren Sun, *The Formation of the Maoist Leadership: From the Return of Wang Ming to the Seventh Party Congress* (London: Contemporary China Institute Research Notes and Studies no. 10, 1994), pp. 23–34. The degree of CCP orienation toward the Soviet Union at the end of the revolutionary period has long been underestimated in the West; see the insightful review of new archival documentation in Odd Arne Westad, "Brothers: Visions of an Alliance," in Westad, *Brothers in Arms: The Rise and Fall of the Sino-Soviet Alliance, 1945–1963* (Stanford, Calif.: Stanford University Press, 1998).

vided a method of immense emotional appeal but limited practical applicability to the modernizing project.

In addition to the above, the revolutionary period left a critical normative legacy for the Maoist state. Undoubtedly the most crucial was Leninist organization and discipline. While quite able to produce disastrous results, both during the revolution and under the Maoist state, this "organizational weapon" was the bedrock of CCP success. While not fully implanted in the party's early years, the hierarchical organization and demand for absolute obedience once a decision was made gradually transformed the CCP into a "weapon" far more disciplined and effective than the Guomindang, which had its own Leninist pretensions. This organizational weapon was first and foremost the contribution of Comintern agents dispatched by Moscow, but the Leninist approach was eagerly grasped by Mao and elaborated by him and other leaders, notably Liu Shaoqi.[11] While many CCP leaders apart from Mao himself had experience with the Stalinist version of Leninism through study in the Soviet Union, the Chinese Leninism which emerged in key respects was truer to the original Leninist version than its Stalinist corruption.

One aspect of Leninist norms which took hold in the CCP was a significant degree of collective rather than autocratic decision making. This was undoubtedly due as much to political reality, the fact that before the early 1940s Mao's power was insufficient for him to have the final word, as to Leninist norms, but it also reflected Mao's shrewd understanding of the requirements of revolutionary success. These required relatively uninhibited discussion in the making of policy so that all aspects of a problem could be considered before iron discipline took over in implementation. They also mandated party unity in the face of a more powerful enemy, something reflected in both a persuasive approach to party discipline and a subtle handling of factions within the CCP. In the former case the "save the patient" emphasis of party rectification was adopted in conscious rejection of both Stalin's blood purge and the CCP's own earlier sanguinary handling of inner-party disputes, even if excesses occurred during the Yan'an rectification. Even this "persuasion," however, was firmly linked to the need for struggle against erroneous ideologies and the recognition that some genuine enemies had infiltrated the party, but the emphasis was on an inclusive organization.[12] The drive

---

[11] For an analysis refuting claims that Mao and Liu represented conflicting organizational approaches over a long period, see Teiwes, *Politics and Purges*, chap. 1.

[12] See ibid., chap. 3; and Teiwes with Sun, *Formation of the Maoist Leadership*, pp. 52–59.

for unity was also seen in the ban on factions (*zongpai*) as active proponents of policy programs counter to those of the Party Center, but for-
giveness and integration into responsible positions of those guilty of
"erroneous lines" in the past as long as they repented, and in the recognition through appointments to leading posts of members of "factions"
or "mountaintops" (*shantou*) based on particular revolutionary experiences and organizations.[13] Such measures maximized party unity during
the struggle for revolutionary success.

The symbiotic relationship of the party and army was another key
legacy of the revolutionary period. With the CCP prevailing over two
decades of military conflict (the "magic weapon" of armed struggle), the
Red Army, later the People's Liberation Army (PLA), was highly politicized. But while politically more important than the Soviet Red Army
ever became,[14] the PLA nevertheless firmly adhered to the Leninist principle of subordination to the party – in Mao's phrase, "the party controls
the gun." And this was indeed the case throughout the armed struggle,
with the military accepting comparatively low-ranking positions in the
central party bodies elected at the 1945 Party Congress. By the time of
final victory in 1949, however, a subtle change was under way. The heads
of conquering armies assumed key positions in the new regional administrations, the party oversight body for the PLA contained more military
leaders in comparison to civilians than before 1945, and Mao would
shortly reassess contributions to the revolutionary success in a far more
pro-army manner than that implied in the 1945 rankings. While the PLA
emerged from the revolution viewing itself as the party's army, its status
had been enhanced, and "party control of the gun" was rapidly becoming a matter of the generals saluting Mao.[15]

The legacy of the revolution, however, involved more than experience
in governing, a disciplined core organization, and a set of normative principles; it also crucially encompassed success itself. And not just any
success, but success against prohibitive odds which undoubtedly startled
even the most committed CCP members, and which promised a transformative future in terms of both an unquestioned ideological goal and
the restoration of national pride. This had a number of important consequences. First, it made Mao's position impregnable; notwithstanding con-

---

[13] See ibid., pp. 2, 19–23, 34–52.
[14] See Jonathan R. Adelman, *The Revolutionary Armies: The Historical Development of the Soviet and the Chinese People's Liberation Armies* (Westport: Greenwood Press, 1980).
[15] See Teiwes with Sun, *Formation of the Maoist Leadership*, pp. 59–64.

tinuing lip service to collective leadership, he was now in a position to enforce his will whenever he chose. Already declared the "savoir of the Chinese people" in Yan'an, from the heights of the implausible nation-wide victory he was at once the founder of a new dynasty and the father of a successful Marxist revolution.[16] From then on it would be simply a matter of Mao's self-restraint whether the successful patterns of the revo-lutionary struggle would be adhered to or whether he would head off into uncharted waters and drag the party-state with him. Second, a larger group of leaders emerged as the heroes of the revolution, possessing a status that could be challenged only by Mao and which placed them in a relatively clear pecking order vis-à-vis one another. In addition, they were young enough (in their forties for most key central figures and younger still in the provinces) to be around for years to come. This pro-vided the potential for a stable leadership, one that by and large existed up to the Cultural Revolution, Mao's erratic behavior notwithstanding. Finally, these leaders and lower level officials were *revolutionaries*, self-confident in view of their successes, genuinely committed to the broad outlines of Marxism-Leninism, however crudely understood in individ-ual cases, and absolutely convinced of their own right to rule and trans-form China.

The Chinese revolution thus left a diverse legacy for the Maoist state. It included a disciplined party machine with established norms, but also with a charismatic leader with the prestige and authority to alter those norms if he saw fit. It further included a deep commitment to the unity that had been crucial to success, but also an intellectual outlook that vali-dated struggle against unhealthy trends and deviant individuals. The legacy also involved a highly pragmatic and cautious approach to policy, although this was accompanied by faith in the mass movement and a sense of succeeding against the odds. If the outlook on the eve of the PRC was for a continuation of a disciplined CCP, an emphasis on unity, and pragmatic policy, the other factors remained. Apart from possible changes in Mao's future subjective outlook, a crucial change had already occurred with the defeat of the Guomindang enemy. With "all under heaven" except Tibet (delayed until 1951) and Taiwan (still unreclaimed) under CCP control,[17] the discipline of revolutionary struggle which had

---

[16] Note that all leaders of successful independent communist revolutions died in office. Of course, Fidel Castro, whose revolution was not truly Marxist in the first instance, is yet to test the proposition.

[17] This, of course, excludes Hong Kong, "returned to the motherland" in 1997, and Macau, scheduled for return in 1999.

repeatedly forced pragmatic policy adjustments had passed into history. To paraphrase Benjamin Yang, whereas previously Mao's "revolutionary idealism" was controlled by his "political realism," now that constraint was significantly diluted.[18]

THE STRUCTURE OF THE MAOIST STATE

At one level, there was considerable structural continuity thoughout the period of the Maoist state despite drastic changes in political direction and even in the functioning of major institutions. With a few exceptions, there was considerable continuity in intermediate territorial administration from the provincial to county levels which also reflected continuities with the traditional state, although there was much more fluidity at lower levels in response to the CCP's socioeconomic engineering in the countryside.[19] In terms of vertical nationwide organizations, there was little change from the establishment of a long-term state organization in 1954 up to the onset of the Cultural Revolution in 1966, while even with the severe disruptions of that movement by the mid-1970s the three main institutions, the party, government, and army, were all functioning in a manner analogous to their traditional roles. And even during the 1967–69 period when the party as an integrating institution ceased to exist, a notional "Party Center" in theory remained authoritative, second only to the pronouncements of the Great Helmsman himself. Yet there obviously were considerable changes in the roles of these institutions and their relationships from period to period, changes which will be examined in more detail later in this chapter.

Notwithstanding some significant modifications, not to mention periods of strident rejection, in broad outline as well as much detail the structure of the party-state was based on Soviet principles and/or practice. This was nowhere more important than in economic organization (dealt with in Chapter 6), but it extended throughout both state and party bodies, and was infused in the Leninist norm of party leadership over all other institutions. The adherence to and departures from the Soviet model are discussed as I review each of the main verti-

---

[18] Benjamin Yang, *Deng: A Political Biography* (Armonk: M.E. Sharpe, 1998), pp. 136–37.

[19] This spatial dimension of the state is not examined in any detail in this chapter. For a summary of territorial administration from the great region to basic levels as of the eve of the Cultural Revolution, see A. Doak Barnett with a contribution by Ezra Vogel, *Cadres, Bureaucracy, and Political Power in Communist China* (New York: Columbia University Press, 1967), pp. 107–20, 313–24.

cal structures beginning with the three pillars of party, government, and army. In addition, brief special mention must be made of the public security apparatus, which had links to both governmental and military institutions, and has historically played a crucial role in other state socialist systems. Finally, attention is given to the additional organs supported by the Maoist state: the judicial system, the state's representative bodies, united front organizations, and so-called mass organizations. In this discussion the focus is on periods when these institutions functioned more or less "normally"; the peculiarities created by the uniquely Mao-inspired Great Leap and Cultural Revolution are dealt with more fully in the following section on the evolution of the Maoist state.

The Party

Under Leninist principles the party is the ultimate authority of the political system. It sets overall policy, lays down the "political line" which is meant to guide all specific policies, and could and did order all other institutions to do its bidding. In theory authority flowed from the large (about 1,100 to 1,500 delegates), occasionally convened (four times during the Maoist era) national party congresses, themselves formally elected by lower-level party congresses, through the Central Commitee (ranging from 77 to 319 full and alternate members over 1949–76)[20] to the top bodies. In fact, it was a strictly top-down hierarchy. At the top was the Chairman himself, not granted any great powers by the various party constitutions, but fortified by a 1943 decision giving him final say within the Secretariat,[21] and more important by his enormous prestige. There is simply no case of Mao not getting his way when he insisted upon it; to

---

[20] The essentially status-recognition rather than decision-making function of the Central Committee was reflected in its infrequent plenary sessions from late 1959 to early 1969, when it met only three times despite CCP statutes calling for two meetings per year. Even when the Central Committee met more regularly up to 1959, it was usually to endorse decisions already taken elsewhere. However, in some important instances, particularly during the Great Leap Forward, plenums or work conferences with many of the same participants held immediately prior to the formal sessions thrashed out key issues. But the meetings which had a significant influence on policy or politics were occasions either where the agenda was dictated by Mao or, as at the Third Plenum in 1957 or the Lushan gatherings in 1959 and 1970, where sudden changes of course resulted from the unanticipated actions of Mao and/or other top leaders, not because of the notional authority of the Central Committee.

[21] See Teiwes with Sun, *Formation of the Maoist Leadership*, p. 17.

the extent other top leaders exercised influence it was through their various assigned roles in the period up to 1958, or by using opportunities presented by Mao to push a particular advocacy thereafter.[22] In organizational terms, the highest decision-making bodies were the Politburo of twenty-three to twenty-six members, and especially its five- to nine-member Standing Committee, or Secretariat as the equivalent body was known until the 1956 Eighth Party Congress. When these bodies or the more loosely defined Party Center[23] decided something, it was binding on the entire system. These bodies, however, basically ceased functioning during the heyday of the Cultural Revolution from 1967 to 1969, when the Cultural Revolution Group dominated by Mme Mao, Jiang Qing, assumed a leading role in pushing the movement forward, and, more important, vague "supreme directives" from the Chairman himself became the guiding principles of state.

In addition to the policy-determining role of these top bodies, the party was organized as a parallel hierarchy to the government structure, a nationwide set of committees designed to provide overall guidance and leadership to all the other parts of the system. (While the principle of party ledership held, the rather special institutional relationship of party and army is treated separately below.) At the top in Beijing stood various functional departments, most important, organization, propaganda, and united front, to oversee specific areas of work. As in Soviet practice, these organs were gathered under the umbrella of the new central Secretariat formed under Deng Xiaoping at the Eighth Party Congress, until it was disbanded in the Cultural Revolution.[24] The crucial role of the party as an institution, however, came in the various territorial jurisdictions,

---

[22] Of course, the change in 1958 was not absolute, but it was fundamental. See the discussion of different periods, below.

[23] Documents in the name of the Party Center usually implied some assent by Mao himself, particularly after his 1953 criticism of other leaders for issuing documents he had not vetted; see Teiwes, *Politics at Mao's Court*, pp. 42, 181–82. Other leaders particularly prominent in the formulation of Party Center documents up to the Cultural Revolution were Liu Shaoqi as the number two in the party and heir apparent, and Deng Xiaoping as General Secretary from 1956.

[24] While patterned on the Soviet Secretariat in organizational terms, the new CCP Secretariat was politically far less significant. This can be seen in that Stalin as General Secretary had headed the Soviet body, and Khrushchev subsequently used it as a major resource in his bid for power. In China, Deng's position was subordinate not only to Mao, but also to Liu Shaoqi, who was the most authoritative voice at the Party Center after the Chairman. The pre-1956 Secretariat, more analogous to the Soviet body in power terms, was now succeeded by the Politburo Standing Committee, which gave less attention to party administration.

where the party secretaries were unambiguously the most authoritative leaders, and through the system of an interlocking directorate or, more graphically, multiple hats, under which party secretaries concurrently headed all other key institutions.[25]

The dominance of the party organization increased as one went down the administrative ladder, largely because of the decreasing complexity of functions at each lower level. Thus at the central level, with the great complexity and specialization of the government, particularly in the economic sphere, the small functional departments of the Secretariat could hardly provide detailed direction of government activities. Moreover, while government bodies were always led by important party leaders,[26] these figures normally held positions only on CCP decision-making bodies rather than in the party apparatus per se,[27] so that their bureaucratic frame of reference was their state rather than party roles even if, as I argue, this resulted only in limited cooption by those bureaucratic units. At the provincial level, however, at least during the Soviet model period and to a lesser degree in the 1960s before the Cultural Revolution, most of the key modern economic functions were managed directly by central ministries, making it easier for provincial party committees to concentrate control over the "remaining" governmental activities, something even more pronounced at still lower levels. This led to repeated expressions of concern that the party was interfering too much in governmental affairs and demands that it should restrict itself to overall guidance rather than micromanagement, but the essential political equation was clear: Below the center the party organization ruled.[28]

Party dominance was also accomplished through a number of additional devices. The control of appointments in all organizations through the Soviet *nomenklatura* system was crucial; all appointments were

---

[25] See Barnett, *Cadres*, pp. 123, 127–29, 343–45; and Kenneth Lieberthal, *Governing China: From Revolution Through Reform* (New York: W.W. Norton, 1995), p. 212.

[26] In form, particularly in the early years of the regime, many ministerial posts were held by non-CCP figures, but real power resided with their party "subordinates."

[27] For example, State Planning Commission head Li Fuchun and Minister of Finance Li Xiannian, both Politburo members, had no role in the central party organization before 1958 when they were added to the Secretariat under the peculiar conditions of the Great Leap Forward, discussed below. A related factor was the use of party "fractions" or "core groups" (*dangzu*) in the state apparatus to guarantee CCP oversight, but as these groups were led by leading ministerial personnel the same issue of organizational perspective remained; see Barnett, *Cadres*, pp. 23–24.

[28] See the reference to Barnett in n. 25, above.

vetted by the organization departments of party committees with the higher levels controlling key appointments for the next two levels down.[29] A second key element, reflecting the importance of ideology in the system, was firm party control of the media and constant oversight of permissible discussion, plus absolute direction of acceptable discourse in particularly politicized periods. Here party propaganda departments at all levels exercised control (at least before the Cultural Revolution), thus providing with the organization departments a vise-like grip on the key factors of ideology and organization.[30]

Finally, translating this control into dominance in the basic-level official structures and society more generally is the system, again taken over from the Soviet communists, of party branches or cells. Ideally involving a party presence in all organizations (apart from officially sanctioned non-party groups) and nearly all groups in society – albeit ironically having the greatest presence among the oft-maligned intellectuals and the least representation among the peasants who were the backbone of the revolution,[31] the party was deeply embedded in society at the grass roots. With a membership that had built up to 2.5 percent of the population by the early 1960s[32] and which monopolized key positions in the *danwei*, or units,[33] within all urban workplaces, bureaucratic organizations, schools, and residential areas as well as rural production units, a substantial force exposed to systematic indoctrination in official values, and with a sense of its own elite status existed, one which enforced party control through a combination of ideological commitment and self-interest. Indeed, as Andrew Walder's work has demonstrated with special attention to factory organization, the idealized party was in significant measure a patronage network where "active support and loyalty [from party members and non-CCP citizens alike] are exchanged for mobility opportunities, material advantages, and social

---

[29] For an overview, see John P. Burns, "China's *Nomenklatura* System," *Problems of Communism*, September–October 1987.

[30] As reflected in the title of Franz Schurmann's major pre-Cultural Revolution study, which captured one critical essence of the Maoist state, *Ideology and Organization in Communist China* (Berkeley: University of California Press, 1966).

[31] In 1956 the proportion of party membership among key social groups was one-third of intellectuals, 18 percent of workers, and 1.4 percent of peasants.

[32] See John Wilson Lewis, *Leadership in Communist China* (Ithaca: Cornell University Press, 1963), p. 116.

[33] On the *danwei*, see Lieberthal, *Governing China*, pp. 167–68. See also the various articles in Xiaobo Lu and Elizabeth J. Perry, eds., *Danwei: The Changing Chinese Workplace in Historical and Comparative Perspective* (Armonk: M.E. Sharpe, 1997).

status."[34] All of these factors, apart from the Cultural Revolution period when Mao simply brushed the CCP organization aside, meant the party was the central glue and most powerful institution of the Maoist state.

The Government

While the government administrative structure also reached deep into society,[35] for our purposes the focus is on its central organs. The key body was the State Council (or Government Administrative Council before 1954), headed by Premier Zhou Enlai. Although his actual power and influence varied, Zhou as premier throughout the Maoist period up to his death in January 1976 brought considerable prestige to the government apparatus as the number three leader of the regime after Mao and his chosen heirs, Liu Shaoqi (to 1966) and Lin Biao (1966–71), and finally as number two himself after Lin's mysterious death, although never as the designated successor. The inner core of the State Council was its Standing Committee made up of Zhou and ten to sixteen vice-premiers representing the various functional areas, but also importantly reflecting party status.[36] The basic administrative units were the ministries and commissions, as well as the lower-level bureaus directly under the State Council (e.g., the State Statistical Bureau and the New China News Agency). These units covered the whole range of public functions, something that was much more extensive than what the imperial state contemplated or what the Republican state was willing or able to under-

---

[34] *Communist Neo-Traditionalism: Work and Authority in Chinese Industry* (Berkeley: University of California Press, 1986), pp. 246–47. The dominance of the party committee in industry marked a significant adaptation of Soviet practice, specifically the system of one-man management by factory managers, which was replaced by "factory manager responsibility under the leadership of the party committee" in the mid-1950s. See Schurmann, *Ideology and Organization*, chap. 4; and Teiwes, *Politics and Purges*, pp. 153–54.

[35] The lowest formal level of government in the countryside was the administrative township (*xiang*) and, from 1958, the people's commune, although lower level production units (cooperatives and later the various subordinate parts of the people's communes) existed under party direction. In the cities urban districts (*qu*) were the lowest formal governmental level, but their writ extended to the street level through local police stations (*paichusuo*) and through the nonstate residence committees.

[36] Thus the vice premiers elected in 1954 included Lin Biao, a general of enormous prestige but no operational responsibilities due to illness, Deng Zihui, whose primary duties were in the Central Committee's Rural Work Department, and He Long, who held only a minor ministerial post but was also a leading general with a key position in the military.

take. This maximum government thus involved massive organizations, large numbers of bureaucrats, and a substantial array of specialist expertise.

One of the consequences of the broad range of activities was the need to provide coordination, something achieved by organization into so-called functional systems (*xitong*).[37] While these systems were not limited to the government and one (the united front system) was primarily concerned with party affairs, a particularly significant role was to bring together functionally related organs of the government, organs which apparently on their own did not have a great deal of informal interaction during the Maoist period.[38] The relevant *xitong* were agriculture and forestry, industry and communications, finance and trade, culture and education, political and legal affairs, and foreign affairs. Each of these systems, or parts thereof, was coordinated by a State Council staff office headed by a high-ranking leader in the pre-Cultural Revolution period.[39] One of the significant features of the *xitong* was the holding of periodic work conferences of the organs making up the various systems, thus providing forums where detailed policy could be discussed and various organizational interests could be articulated.[40] A rich bureaucratic life could and did unfold within these gatherings, but one which was often overwhelmed in the politics of the Maoist state.

While the governmental (and larger) system "functioned more or less by standard procedures" in the absence of Mao's interference, it was frequently subject to a number of other pressures. One type came in reac-

---

[37] The classic discussion of these systems for the pre-Cultural Revolution period is Barnett, *Cadres*, pp. 6–9, 456–57. For a treatment over a longer period with different delineations, see Lieberthal, *Governing China*, pp. 194–207.

[38] See Frederick C. Teiwes and Warren Sun, eds., *The Politics of Agricultural Cooperativization in China: Mao, Deng Zihui, and the "High Tide" of 1955* (Armonk: M.E. Sharpe, 1993), pp. 18–19.

[39] The six systems listed correspond to the staff offices in existence from 1959 to the Cultural Revolution and more loosely to small groups at the Party Center (there the several economic functions were placed under a single financial and economics small group), while the pre-1959 staff offices were broken down somewhat differently, e.g., into transport and communications, light industry, and heavy industry, construction, and planning. See Donald W. Klein and Anne B. Clark, *Biographic Dictionary of Chinese Communism, 1921–1965* (Cambridge: Harvard University Press, 1971), pp. 1102–3. Note also that the military *xitong*, although apparently not referred to as such in the pre-Cultural Revolution period, had no corresponding government staff office and a special relationship with the party, as discussed below.

[40] See Michel Oksenberg, "Methods of Communication within the Chinese Bureaucracy," *The China Quarterly (CQ)*, no. 57, on such conferences in the context of a discussion of a wider range of meetings.

tion to a number of pathologies of large organizations including red tape, empire building, hoarding of resources, and diminished responsiveness to political direction, and in this respect understandable pressures for greater efficiency and control were magnified by revolutionary traditions such as "crack troops and simplified administration" (*jingbing jianzheng*) and an ideological aversion to "bureaucratism" (*guanliao zhuyi*).[41] A major consequence of this was periodic efforts to retrench personnel and streamline organizations, a process that saw the reduction in number of ministries; at other times, however, new ministries would be added particularly in the economic sphere to attend to functions seemingly short-changed under simplified administration. Thus the numbers varied significantly, with forty-nine ministries in place in 1966 on the eve of the Cultural Revolution, while only twenty-nine were sanctioned at the reorganization of the State Council in 1975 after nearly a decade of antibureaucratic efforts.

Another set of pressures on orderly administration was the CCP's frequent recourse to mass campaigns, another legacy of the revolutionary period. Leaving aside the fundamental assaults on organizational patterns during the Great Leap and Cultural Revolution, which are discussed subsequently, even in less unusual circumstances there was an alternation of bureaucratic and campaign modes of policy implementation. During mobilization phases seeking social, economic, and/or political breakthroughs, organizational routines were disrupted, to the extent that bureaucratic units sometimes were reduced to skeleton staffs while personnel were dispatched to participate in the movement of the moment, and special bodies outside the normal chain of command and higher-level work teams were organized to conduct them. Although priority goals were achieved, the resultant disruption often had significant costs for the regime, resulting in consolidation phases designed to correct imbalances which appeared during the upheavals and to restore regular administration.[42] While the oscillation of campaigns and comparatively

---

[41] On the revolutionary tradition of simplified administration, see Mark Selden, "The Yenan Legacy: The Mass Line," in A. Doak Barnett, ed., *Chinese Communist Politics in Action* (Seattle: University of Washington Press, 1969), pp. 112–16. For a comprehensive analysis of organizational deviations and CCP strategies for dealing with them, see Harry Harding, *Organizing China: The Problem of Bureaucracy, 1949–1976* (Stanford: Stanford University Press, 1981).

[42] See Barnett, *Cadres*, pp. 25, 32–35; and Frederick C. Teiwes, *Elite Discipline in China: Coercive and Persuasive Approaches to Rectification, 1950–1953* (Canberra: Contemporary China Papers no. 12, 1978), pp. 41–42, 129ff, 151–52.

relaxed periods continued throughout the Maoist era, from the time of the Great Leap the more or less planned rhythm of pressing forward and "taking a rest" began to break down as more chaotic events unfolded.[43]

A final source of pressure on administrative arrangements concerned the effort to find the appropriate level of devolution, one that provided sufficient decentralization to tap local initiative without losing overall central control. Here there were shifting emphases on vertical (*tiao*) and horizontal (*kuai*) integration, with the former stressing centralized control by ministries particularly during the Soviet model period before the Leap Forward, and the latter enhancing the role of the party-led provincial authorities to varying degrees from the Leap onward. While the problem was a continuing one producing shifts in emphasis throughout the Maoist period, again it was only with Mao's personally initiated Great Leap and Cultural Revolution that the centralization/decentralization issue became a major disruptive force on government operations.[44]

The Army

Any analysis of the Maoist state must, as David Shambaugh has emphasized,[45] include the army as a major actor. Most fundamentally, as with all previous Chinese states, the military was the ultimate prop of the regime. Moreover, as we have seen, revolutionary history produced an unusually close relationship between party and army, with the PLA remaining extremely politicized throughout the Maoist era and many military men of the earlier period having transferred to civilian duties after 1949. The fact that the revolutionary struggle was a prolonged armed struggle meant that the military heroes of the revolution emerged in 1949 with high status and important positions in the overall party-state;

---

[43] Throughout the 1950s up to the leap there was a rhythm of targeted campaigns such as land reform, the Three- and Five-Anti Campaigns, and agricultural cooperativization where intense pressure was brought to bear for relatively defined goals, and this was followed by deliberate efforts to lower the temperature and integrate an unsettled population into the new framework. The Great Leap and Cultural Revolution, in contrast, lacked careful definition and the subsequent easing of pressure had more to do with coping with crisis situations in ad hoc ways than representing a planned respite.

[44] On the question of vertical and horizontal approaches, see Jonathan Unger, "The Struggle to Dictate China's Administration: The Conflict of Branches vs. Areas vs. Reform," *Australian Journal of Chinese Affairs* (*AJCA*), no. 18 (1987). Cf. Lieberthal, *Governing China*, pp. 169–70.

[45] See David Shambaugh, "Building the Party-State in China, 1949–1965: Bringing the Soldier Back In," in Timothy Cheek and Tony Saich, eds., *New Perspectives on State Socialism in China* (Armonk: M.E. Sharpe, 1997).

indeed, there were echoes of the successful generals of earlier changes of dynasties sharing in the spoils of victory. The army as an institution usually participated in major political movements, and its leaders were required to become involved in any major leadership conflicts. Beyond this, the PLA administered major public works, and its presumed virtues were held up as models throughout the Maoist era, with particular emphasis following the Great Leap and the post-leap crisis. And the visible role of the army in assisting with harvests, disaster relief, and so on contributed to a widely accepted image of a people's army, of "the people and the army are one family" (*min jun yijia*). In institutional terms, moreover, the PLA was both formally under the State Council through the Ministry of Defense,[46] and more crucially under the party through its Military Affairs Committee (MAC). The state chairman was constitutionally commander-in-chief until 1975 (even though the office was empty after 1968), and then the party chairman assumed the role. Yet in crucial respects the army was a quite separate institution.

While the principle of party leadership of the army remained sacrosanct during Mao's lifetime, the late 1940s transformation of the principle into obedience to Mao personally developed rapidly after 1949. To put it another way, it increasingly became a relationship between Mao and his generals, with extremely limited input from the civilian party. This is seen most clearly in the makeup of the MAC. In the immediate post-1949 period this authoritative body included, in addition to Mao as MAC chairman, Vice-Chairmen Liu Shaoqi and Zhou Enlai as the number two and three leaders of the party, with generals Zhu De and Peng Dehuai also as vice-chairmen. Although Zhou had important ties with the army going back to his period as political commissar of the Whampoa Academy in the 1920s, from the late 1930s he had largely performed non-military roles, while Liu's army credentials were modest at best. When the MAC was reorganized in 1954, however, both Liu and Zhou were not reappointed, while the sole civilian apart from Mao to serve among the half-dozen to dozen leading members, in a pattern largely retained until 1975, was Deng Xiaoping.[47] The key army leaders from that time to the early 1970s were the successive Ministers of Defense and ranking MAC

---

[46] While Lieberthal, *Governing China*, p. 205, argues with cause that the ministry "in reality has almost no real power in the military," the Minister of Defense was the ranking military official in real as well as theoretical terms when the position existed during the Maoist era.

[47] Deng, although dismissed during the Cultural Revolution, was reappointed in January 1975. At that time the pattern was partially broken with the appointment of civilian

121

vice chairmen, Marshals Peng Dehuai (1954–59) and Lin Biao (1959–71), with Deng as PLA Chief of Staff and Marshal Ye Jianying as Defense Minister by 1975, most significant during the remainder of the Maoist period.

Deng's role was undoubtedly in significant measure due to the fact that of all CCP leaders he and Lin Biao were Mao's personal favorites, but it also had much to do with the little understood fact that Deng was one of the great military heroes of the revolution, one who would have earned the title of marshal in 1955 when ten top generals were so honored, except for the delicacy of the situation created by his significant civilian positions.[48] Deng, then, had credibility based on achievements in battle which provided a link to the party organization, but overwhelmingly the MAC consisted of men whose primary concern was the army itself. The net effect was to limit severely party and government input into military affairs, although clearly on budgetary matters the decisions of civilian bodies were decisive, at least in the pre-Cultural Revolution period.[49] But on strictly PLA matters, the great figures of the armed revolution set the agenda, subject, of course, to Mao's approval, or (as in the Cultural Revolution) they simply followed in his wake.[50] The military

radicals Zhang Chunqiao and Wang Hongwen to the MAC Standing Committee in what was undoubtedly a balancing effort on Mao's part. The body, however, was still dominated by revolutionary military heroes and serving army leaders. For a breakdown of MAC membership after 1949, see *Zhonghua Renmin Gongheguo dang zheng jun qun lingdao renminglu* (Namelists of PRC Party, Government, Military and Mass Organization Leaders) (Beijing: Zhonggong dangshi chubanshe, 1990), pp. 12–15. See also Shambaugh, "Bringing the Soldier Back In," pp. 137–40.

The definition of military as opposed to civilian in this case is complicated, and cases could be made for (particularly) Chen Yi, He Long, and Nie Rongzhen, all vice premiers and holders of operational government posts, as partial civilians. However, the criteria used here are, first, the historic roles of each of these marshals as leading commanders during the revolution, and, second, primary concern with military functions as was certainly the case with He, but less clearly with Nie.

[48] For a typical view largely ignoring Deng's revolutionary military credentials, see June Teufel Dreyer, "Deng Xiaoping: The Soldier," *CQ*, no. 135 (1993). For more appropriate assessments, see David S. G. Goodman, *Deng Xiaoping and the Chinese Revolution* (London: Routledge, 1994), chap. 3 and pp. 117–19; and Yang, *Deng*, chap. 9.

[49] See, for example, the discussion of the failed effort to increase the military budget in 1956, in Roderick MacFarquhar, *The Origins of the Cultural Revolution 1: Contradictions among the People 1956–1957* (New York: Columbia University Press, 1974), pp. 69–74, 135–38.

[50] Lin Biao's 1969 statement that "In our work, we do no more than follow in [Chairman Mao's] wake" (see Teiwes and Sun, *The Tragedy of Lin Biao*, p. 1) had a broader application, but it ironically summed up the situation of the PLA's then institutionally preeminent role.

policy sphere itself had been largely quarantined from all except Mao and the generals, although during the Cultural Revolution Zhou Enlai – as Mao's trusted assistant, not as premier – again emerged to play a major role in army affairs.[51]

If the civilians largely kept out of PLA matters, conversely before the Cultural Revolution the army had a limited role in civilian politics as such. While top military figures had great status, making up about 40 percent of the full Politburo members selected in 1956 and both more and less later,[52] and clearly such status gave them the right to comment on the full range of CCP affairs, there is little to indicate that army leaders played a key role in shaping the major pre-1966 political or economic policies of the party and government. A case in point is the Great Leap and the terrible famine that occurred in its aftermath. While foreign scholarship has hypothesized that the PLA was a force for curbing the leap based on its peasant-conscript constituency and other organizational interests such as avoiding alienation of the Soviet Union,[53] in fact there is little indication of PLA involvement in the policy process which saw first the intensification and then the "cooling down" of the movement. Indeed, while Peng Dehuai spoke out against leap excesses at the watershed 1959 Lushan conference, he did not even wish to attend the meeting, and among his harshest critics once Mao turned on him were leaders of the military establishment itself.[54] The later, active PLA involvement in politics during the Cultural Revolution, as we shall see, was thrust upon the army, and in fundamental ways did not reflect its interests.

In addition to the high-level relations of the PLA and the civilian party-state, the organizational separateness of the army was ironically reflected in its political control system. The point is that this intricate system involving party committees and branches, political commissars,

---

[51] While this point is still being researched, interviews suggest that Zhou's intense involvement in PLA matters was such that he might be considered to have been actually running the daily affairs of the military. I am indebted to Warren Sun on this point. Cf. Thomas W. Robinson, "Chou En-lai and the Cultural Revolution in China," in Robinson, ed., *The Cultural Revolution in China* (Berkeley: University of California Press, 1971), pp. 227ff; and John Wilson Lewis and Xue Litai, *China's Strategic Seapower: The Politics of Modernization in the Nuclear Age* (Stanford: Stanford University Press, 1994), pp. 40ff, 239.

[52] Just over half of the 1969 Politburo at the height of military institutional influence, and about 30 percent of the 1973 body following the death and disgrace of Lin Biao. In addition, the military was heavily represented as vice premiers before 1966 with about 40 percent of that group, but usually without major civilian portfolios.

[53] See, e.g., Parris H. Chang, *Power and Policy in China* (University Park: Pennsylvania State University Press, 1975), pp. 110–14.

[54] See Teiwes with Sun, *China's Road to Disaster*, pp. 198–99, 205, 212.

and discipline inspection commissions[55] was virtually self-contained within the military itself – another departure from Soviet practice. Despite some formal links, it was the PLA's General Political Department, not the Central Committee's Propaganda and Organization Departments, which set the ideological agenda and assigned personnel, while the army's party committee system, although notionally under the CCP Central Committee, was staffed entirely by military personnel. Similarly, when rectification movements were held, the army frequently had its own focus as well as its own machinery, and the severity of the campaigns was normally more restrained than in civilian institutions.[56] Perhaps the greatest civilian intrusion in formal structural terms occurred at the territorial level below the center where, during the pre-Cultural Revolution decade, provincial party first secretaries served as ranking political commissars in the provincial military districts and in nine of thirteen large military regions spanning one to four provinces. This undoubtedly was symbolic of civilian control of the gun, but one must be skeptical concerning how active such party secretaries were in this role. More broadly, personnel evidence suggests the party and army organizations in the localities were largely distinct.[57]

Paradoxically, the PLA, while completely loyal to the party, linked to it through a myriad of personal relationships and shared revolutionary experiences, thus being "inextricably intertwined with the party/state,"[58] in key respects led a quite separate institutional life, "virtually a state-within-the-state"[59] The military was preoccupied for much of the Maoist period with its own professional interests on the one hand and its revolutionary traditions on the other, leaving the larger affairs of state to the civilians. This would change dramatically during the Cultural Revolution,

---

[55] For a detailed overview, see David Shambaugh, "The Soldier and the State: The Political Work System in the People's Liberation Army," *CQ*, no. 127 (1991). See also Ellis Joffe, *Party and Army: Professionalism and Political Control in the Chinese Officer Corps, 1949–1964* (Cambridge: Harvard East Asian Monographs, 1965); and Fang Zhu, "Political Work in the Military from the Viewpoint of the Beijing Garrison Command," in Carol Lee Hamrin and Suisheng Zhao, eds., *Decision-Making in Deng's China: Perspectives from Insiders* (Armonk: M.E. Sharpe, 1995).

[56] See Teiwes, *Politics and Purges*, pp. 293–96; Teiwes, "A Case Study of Rectification: The 1958 *Cheng-feng Cheng-kai* Campaign in Hui-tung County," *Papers on Far Eastern History*, March 1973, p. 73; and Fang Zhu, "Political Work," pp. 125–26.

[57] See Frederick C. Teiwes, *Provincial Party Personnel in Mainland China, 1956–1966* (New York: Occasional Papers of the East Asian Institute, Columbia University, 1967), pp. 46–48. Cf. Shambaugh, "The Soldier and the State," p. 548.

[58] Shambaugh, "The Soldier and the State," p. 532.

[59] Lieberthal, *Governing China*, p. 205.

but it was not a situation of the army's own making. And, as argued earlier, both in periods of concentration on its military functions and when deeply embroiled in internal politics, for the PLA party control fundamentally meant the generals obeying Mao.

Other State-Supported Institutions

In addition to the three pillars of the Maoist order, an array of other organs existed, some official state institutions, others not so categorized but depending on the state for their political and financial support. One critical structure linked to all three pillars was the public security apparatus. Public security or police organs in several guises existed during the Maoist period, not only falling under the Ministry of Public Security, but also involving armed units under the PLA chain of command. Most important, however, was the regime's determination that party control would apply to the police, something achieved both by placing apparatus under the Party Center's political and legal *xitong* and by enforcing dual control involving territorial party committees as well as the ministry. The key here was a conscious decision to prevent Stalin's perversion of the Leninist model which saw, instead of real party leadership, a system where the dictator played off largely separate party and government institutions, and crucially directed an independent secret police organization that physically decimated the higher-ranking institutions of the Soviet state during the Great Purge of the 1930s. Nothing quite like this happened during the Maoist era, even in the Cultural Revolution when brutal police methods were used against disgraced leaders of the Chinese party-state. Indeed, in this period the public security apparatus itself suffered sweeping purges and severe organizational disruption, with its functions being taken over by the PLA.[60]

The public security apparatus, of course, has long been a key element of a repressive state and, in addition to strictly policing functions, has run the vast system of labor camps with important economic as well as penal functions. It was also the senior partner in the judicial system during the Maoist era. A nationwide system of courts and procuracies feeding into the Supreme People's Court and the Supreme People's Procuracy in Beijing purportedly dispensed justice, but the reality was anyone charged with a crime by the police almost invariably was found guilty.

[60] See ibid., pp. 199–201; Barnett, *Cadres*, pp. 219–27; and Ralph L. Powell and Chong-Kun Yoon, "Public Security and the PLA," *Asian Survey*, December 1972.

There were brief efforts in the 1950s to develop legal codes, profession-alize the administration of justice, and establish the principle of judicial independence, but these were swept away with the Anti-Rightist Campaign of 1957 and the Great Leap, well before even more chaotic developments during the Cultural Revolution which affected the public security apparatus itself.[61]

Apart from state administrative organs, another major official struc-ture was the state's representative bodies. Set up in 1954, this system of people's congresses existed from the urban district and administrative village (*xiang*) – later commune – levels to the National People's Con-gress (NPC) in Beijing, theoretically the highest organ of state power. Undoubtedly the most fundamental reason for this system, beyond mere copying from the Soviet example or as an elaboration of similar struc-tures from the CCP's own revolutionary period, is that a regime claim-ing to represent the "people," less the 5 percent or so of the population declared "enemies" of the state, had to have bodies symbolically repre-senting that "people." This system was selected in carefully controlled elections from the bottom up, with NPC delegates chosen by the provin-cial congresses, and it had no independent power. As with representative bodies within the CCP itself, whether the congresses even met depended on political trends, with the regular pattern of the pre-Cultural Revolu-tion period giving way to complete disruption until 1975. Also, their very size and infrequency of meeting – the NPC with roughly 3,000 members met only once a year even in the regularized 1950s – clearly limited any decision-making function.[62] The fundamental political impotence of the representative structure was further reflected in the highest position constitutionally in its power to give – the state chairmanship. With Mao hostile to the position, undoubtedly because Liu Shaoqi had held it from 1959, it simply ceased to exist over the last decade of the Maoist era.

Its political weakness notwithstanding, the representative system nevertheless had several significant functions besides its legitimizing role.

---

[61] See Jerome Alan Cohen, *The Criminal Process in the People's Republic of China, 1949–1963: An Introduction* (Cambridge: Harvard University Press, 1968), passim.

[62] For an overview of the representative system, see Harold C. Hinton, *An Introduction to Chinese Politics* (New York: Praeger, 1973), pp. 164–68. When the congresses were not in session, their functions were exercised by standing committees that in theory super-vised state affairs. While the NPC Standing Committee of about 200 members included some very powerful leaders, these were bound by party discipline and in any case held other positions of much greater significance.

One was a communications and propaganda function. NPC sessions were occasions on which the party line could be spelled out in a blaze of maximum publicity; moreover, the delegates, who held influential positions throughout society, would go back to their work units and convey the leadership's intentions. The same function marked the closely controlled popular elections of the lowest-level congresses, something that occurred six times before the Cultural Revolution.[63] Another function, peculiar to consolidation phases, was interest articulation. Particularly in the mid-1950s when Mao declared large-scale class struggle a thing of the past, forums such as the NPC provided occasions when legitimate claims by bureaucratic units or provinces could be and were made in speeches to plenary sessions or small group meetings, on the proviso that no fundamental party policy was challenged.[64] Related to this was a united front function, also found in consolidation phases, when the party leadership felt a particular need to appeal to social groups who were disaffected and/or whose skills were required. Perhaps the classic case of this occurred during the post-Great Leap crisis when not only were the representatives of such groups urged to speak up at congress sessions, but there was a significant effort to organize inspections by NPC members to help deal with the accumulated problems of the period.[65]

Apart from being a role of the representative system, this latter function was also carried out by united front organizations. Designed to bring together prominent people and organizations outside the CCP, these bodies have been guided by the party's united front *xitong* and reflect the importance of the united front during the revolution. The umbrella organization for the united front was and remains the Chinese People's Political Consultative Conference (CPPCC), a body designed as the direct successor to the Political Consultative Conference of the Guomindang regime, and a body which performed the overall representative function prior to the setting up of the NPC. The CPPCC drew in the so-called democratic parties, the small, middle-class, and intelligentsia-based parties which had made a futile attempt to become a third force between the Guomindang regime and the CCP, as well prominent unaffiliated "democratic personages." The relevance of the CPPCC and the democratic parties

[63] See James R. Townsend, *Political Participation in Communist China* (Berkeley: University of California Press, 1967), chap. 5.
[64] For details on an analogous situation at the 1956 Eighth Party Congress, see MacFarquhar's discussion of provincial economic demands on the center, *Origins 1*, pp. 130–33.
[65] See Teiwes, *Politics and Purges*, p. 372.

was clearly greatest in the immediate post-1949 period when the CCP sought to reassure the population while it built up its organizational strength, a process which even saw non-party people assigned nearly half of the ministerial posts in the initial government. With the passage of time this particular aspect withered away, but the united front function remained and even waxed in particular consolidation periods – notably in the mid-1950s when the party briefly sought to place intellectuals at the center of modernization efforts, and, similar to the NPC, in the post-leap crisis. In such periods, the democratic parties were encouraged to strengthen their organizations and recruit new members, and to provide input into the policy process under the slogan of "long term coexistence and mutual supervision" (*changqi gongcun, huxiang jiandu*). Democratic parties remained cautious, however, and in any case were brushed aside or worse whenever the CCP turned to the left.[66]

Finally, the state supported a range of mass organizations, bodies once again coordinated by the CCP through the united front *xitong*. Unlike the small, bourgeois, and intellectual-based democratic parties, the most significant of these mass organizations encompassed large numbers of people belonging to major social groups.[67] These have involved workers through the trade unions, students, youth,[68] and women. The fundamental purpose of these bodies is to penetrate society, to bring vast sections of the population further into the party's net. The effort, however, has been skewed, with coverage much more extensive in urban areas, as seen in the fact that peasant associations existed only sporadically. While these organs acted as another means of bringing the CCP's message to the grass roots, other functions existed as well, seen perhaps most clearly in the case of trade unions. The unions not only had specific administrative functions concerning welfare in the factories, but also had an interest-articulation and representative function for the workers. This, however, waxed and waned according to party policy, fluctuating between periods when the CCP encouraged such a role and more politicized situations

[66] See ibid., pp. 173–75, 237–38, 348–49, 370, 372; and Frederick C. Teiwes, "The Establishment and Consolidation of the New Regime, 1949–57," in Roderick MacFarquhar, ed., *The Politics of China: The Eras of Mao and Deng*, 2nd ed. (New York: Cambridge University Press, 1997), pp. 26–28.

[67] Mass organizations, however, also include small professional associations and so-called friendship associations with foreign countries. For an overview, see Townsend, *Political Participation*, pp. 150–58.

[68] While the Communist Youth League is different in that it has been selective and designed to act as a feeder for the CCP itself, it is classified as a mass organization.

where too much expression of worker interests was denounced as "economism." Fundamentally, for all the CCP rhetoric concerning the "mass line," the unions and other mass organizations functioned more as Stalinist "transmission belts" in laying down the party line and extending the reach of the state.[69]

THE EVOLUTION OF THE MAOIST STATE

The Chinese state during the Maoist period continually evolved, a process involving adaptation to unfolding conditions, comparatively gradual and subtle changes in relations among the major pillars of the regime, and drastic, Mao-induced disruptions of the system's organizational patterns. While any periodization is to some extent arbitrary, the following distinct phases of the Maoist state will be reviewed: (1) the consolidation of power, 1949–54; (2) the heyday of the Soviet model, 1954–57; (3) the Great Leap Forward, 1958–60; (4) the post-leap recovery, 1960–66; (5) the active stage of the Cultural Revolution and the height of military dominance, 1966–71; and (6) the twilight of the Maoist state, 1972–76.

The Consolidation of Power, 1949–1954

The major features of this initial period of CCP rule were pragmatism, regional, military-based administration evolving toward centralized and civilian forms, the extension of totalitarian rule, and party unity marred by a single major instance of elite factionalism. Pragmatism was first and foremost reflected in the leadership's understanding of the magnitude of the tasks faced, the limits of the party's own resources, the need to reassure a war-weary population, and the fact that revolutionary social-engineering goals, while the long-term objective, could be realized only gradually. Thus, from the outset, major emphasis was placed on the united front with nearly half the ministers selected at the founding of the PRC nonparty people. At the same time, "retained personnel" from the previous state were kept in official positions, including sensitive areas such as the police, so that government administration could function while the CCP, which went from regional movement to national ruler in an unanticipatedly short time, built up its own cadre force. Moreover, a conscious decision was made, based on Liu Shaoqi's spring 1949 Tianjin investiga-

[69] See Paul Harper, "The Party and the Unions in Communist China," *CQ*, no. 37 (1969).

tions and with Mao's full backing, to eschew class mobilization in the cities, while concentrating CCP resources in the crucial modern sector, leaving the traditional sector to its own devices. All of this was linked to a political program in tune with both popular sentiment and Soviet advice: a three-year goal of economic recovery that would restore production to prewar levels, and a fifteen- to twenty-year period of "New Democracy," a program promising a mixed economy and land redistribution to private peasants, as well as only a gradual transition to socialism. Even as projections of the transition shortened due to Mao's impatience in 1952–53, the program remained gradual.[70]

Pragmatism further dictated highly decentralized government, initially in the form of six large regions normally designated as Military-Administrative Committees, and involving party bureaus and military regions on the same territorial basis. As the name indicates, the PLA was very prominent in these bodies, a logical outcome in that the bulk of China was seized by military force and not through social revolution, and due to the unfinished business of mopping up substantial "remnant" Guomindang forces in several areas. Decentralization made sense because of the vastly different conditions throughout the country, ranging from the northern base areas where the CCP had been in control for more than a decade and had instituted various programs of social change to vast areas of the south and northwest where the party had no prior presence and came to the population as an alien armed force. As in the revolutionary period, this required a great variation in approach, and the regional party, administrative, and PLA structures were granted the authority to act accordingly. What is particularly striking, however, was the remarkably smooth transition from military to civilian rule and from decentralized to centralized administration. By 1951 military control commissions, which had initially exercised wide powers over administrative and party organs, were reduced to public security and garrison functions. Moreover, from the outset, the principle of party control of the gun applied in that party men, albeit figures who had served as political commissars during the revolutionary struggle, usually held the most authoritative regional posts as ranking party secretary.[71] Meanwhile, as central government structures developed, regional functions and leading per-

---

[70] See Teiwes, "Establishment," pp. 18–28, 40–41; and Kenneth G. Lieberthal, *Revolution and Tradition in Tientsin, 1949–1952* (Stanford, Calif.: Stanford University Press, 1980), chap. 3.

[71] The exceptional case where a military commander received the top position was in the central-south, where Mao's favorite Lin Biao was appointed.

sonnel were gradually transferred to Beijing, with the six regions abolished in 1954–55 without sign of any major political drama.[72]

But if political realism and orderly administrative development were key features of the period, this was married to a determination to achieve both directed socioeconomic change and the control of society required to make further change possible. The shift from reassuring the population to intense mass movements came in fall 1950, probably earlier than intended at about the time of Chinese involvement in the Korean war, with the intensification of land reform in "newly liberated" areas. By late 1951, in addition to an effort to tap nationalism and mobilize resources for the war effort through an "Aid Korea, Resist America" campaign, a number of movements targeted at specific groups were under way in urban areas: the "Three- and Five-Antis" aimed at the bourgeoisie and officials dealing with the business sector; thought reform focusing on intellectuals, especially those with a Western orientation; and the suppression of counterrevolutionaries, targeting people with close ties to the Guomindang and others judged hostile to the new order. These movements involved intense pressure and in most cases deliberate, if largely surgical, violence, as in land reform where perhaps 1 to 2 million landlords and "local despots" were executed; the stimulation of class tensions, if often with difficulty in the face of particularistic ties in villages and small factories; the recruitment of cadres and party members who became a new elite at the grass roots; the creation of a social support base, particularly in the countryside where poor peasants now received land; and enhanced state capacity both to extract resources and prepare for more socialist forms. But most of all, notwithstanding new efforts from mid-1952 to reassure the population with the winding down of the movements and the start of a consolidation phase, the CCP exposed virtually the entire population to the totalistic objectives of the regime.[73]

Apart from the tensions engendered in society by the rude shock of the various campaigns, conflict existed within the organizations of the party-state, notably among the different types of cadres – especially old revolutionaries from the countryside versus newly recruited urban ele-

---

[72] See Teiwes, "Establishment," pp. 28–32; and Shambaugh, "Bringing the Soldier Back In," pp. 132–34. The "no drama" assertion, while simplifying the situation, is to reject the long-held view that regional "independent kingdoms" were a key facet of the Gao Gang affair (see below). See Teiwes, *Politics and Purges*, pp. 145–50; and Teiwes, *Politics at Mao's Court*, pp. 20–26, 127–28.

[73] See Teiwes, "Establishment," pp. 33–40; and A. Doak Barnett, *Communist China: The Early Years 1949–1955* (New York: Praeger, 1964), chaps. 11 and 12.

ments, and between the "southbound cadres" who had served in the Red Army and northern base areas but now took over the key positions in the "newly liberated" regions on the one hand, and those small guerrilla and underground forces that had maintained themselves in their home areas.[74] While these problems were dealt with by rectification efforts, the higher reaches of the CCP were largely without serious conflict except for the Gao Gang affair, which briefly flared in 1953. This case saw the purge of Gao, the top leader in the northeast and, with the transfer of regional leaders to Beijing, head of the State Planning Commission (SPC), and Rao Shushi, east China leader and new head of the CCP's central Organization Department. This complicated affair, which involved policy differences only in a restricted sense, was fairly quickly disposed of, but while it lasted it not only sent shudders through the top leadership but also revealed basic fault lines in the system – the potential for factionalism and, above all, the vulnerability of party unity to the attitudes of Mao.

Gao Gang's aim was to displace Liu Shaoqi and Zhou Enlai as the number two party leader and premier, respectively, a project that was threatening both to the party unity which had served so well in the revolutionary period, in particular by upsetting the careful distribution of power among various *shantou*, and to the relative status established during the revolution. That this effort created much uncertainty for much of 1953 was in part due to Gao's (apparently false) rumors that Liu was seeking to upset the "factional" balance by favoring underground cadres with connections to himself over military heroes of the revolution, but much more profoundly because of the actions and perceived attitudes of Mao. In this period Mao expressed dissatisfaction with Liu and Zhou over a number of matters, both openly and in private talks with Gao, another personal favorite. Mao's motives can only be speculated about, but a situation was created where, in a classic case of court politics, other leaders, including favorites Lin Biao and Deng Xiaoping, were uncertain of his intentions and temporized. When the Chairman opted for party unity and the status quo at the end of the year, the matter was quickly wound up, even if it had a disconcerting denouement with Gao's suicide in the summer of 1954. Thus while this case differed from subsequent high-level purges in that it had little impact on the policies and regular

[74] See Teiwes, *Politics and Purges*, pp. 98–100; and Ezra F. Vogel, *Canton under Communism: Programs and Politics in a Provincial Capital, 1949–1968* (Cambridge: Harvard University Press, 1969), chap. 3.

functioning of the party-state, the very fact of months of uncertainty due to a lack of clarity about Mao's attitude revealed a structural fault that would have much more disruptive consequences in the future.[75]

The Zenith of the Soviet Model, 1954–1957

Throughout the preceding period, a crucial factor underpinning the relative pragmatism and predictability of the Chinese state was a clear sense of direction – toward urban-centered growth and socialist forms of social organization and governance. This was fundamentally due to the leadership consensus on the model provided by the Soviet Union, something seen in a widespread copying of Soviet methods in a great variety of spheres, propaganda on the need to emulate the Russian "big brother," and Mao's own strong endorsement of this approach. By 1954, however, both the completion of economic recovery and the state's increasing reach created the basis for a fuller implementation of the Soviet model. This, some unique Chinese features notwithstanding,[76] involved the establishment of long-term state institutions on the Soviet pattern with the constitution of 1954 setting up the People's Congresses system, but more important the elaboration of the government administrative structure which had been developing in the preceding years and provided the framework for overseeing the Stalinist model of planned economic development. At the same time, the state's penetration of society was regularized by the establishment of township (*xiang*) governments as the peasant associations which had guided land reform faded away, the articulation of bureaucratic *danwei*, and the systematic development of urban residents' committees.[77]

As the Soviet model came into full play, the most extensively centralized period in the history of the PRC unfolded. This was the high-water mark of vertical rule, with economic ministries having direct control of large industrial enterprises under a strategy giving priority to rapid industrialization. It was also a period of a fairly clear division of labor: The State Council took care of the modern economy under the Soviet-style First Five-Year Plan (FFYP), which formally covered 1953 to 1957; the

---

[75] See Teiwes, *Politics and Purges*, pp. xvi–xxii; and Teiwes, *Politics at Mao's Court*, passim.

[76] Most notably the prominent head of state, a position initially held by Mao until it was assumed by Liu Shaoqi in 1959, as part of Mao's long-term plan to bolster the status of his heir apparent.

[77] See Teiwes, "Establishment," pp. 15–18, 40–45, 50–54.

party – above all its territorial committees – focused on the rural sector, political control, and social change; and the PLA was preoccupied with its own modernization, substantially, but not completely, adopting Soviet methods. While the policies of economic development all went through the Politburo and had Mao's backing, the key policy-makers were figures primarily based in the government, particularly Premier Zhou Enlai and Vice Premier Chen Yun, the architect of both economic recovery and the FFYP. This was truly a case of Mao not personally intervening, at least not to any great extent, in the system, with the result that it functioned more or less by standard procedures. Mao's restraint was undoubtedly in part due to his feeling that he lacked a detailed grasp of economic issues, but it also reflected the norm of collective decision-making that had served the revolution so well. A case in point was the policy of "opposing rash advance" (*fanmaojin*), an effort to wind back unrealistic production targets in 1956–57 led by Zhou and Chen. While in some senses going against his instincts, Mao nevertheless backed the policy and praised Chen's wisdom. Meanwhile, "functioning by standard procedures" encompassed considerable bureaucratic conflict, in this case between economic coordinating agencies such as the SPC responsible for overall plans, and spending ministries and localities pursuing their specific interests.[78]

The situation was dramatically different in the area of "social revolution," most notably the process of collectivizing agriculture. Not only was this the sphere of the party apparatus, it was one where the Soviet model was not slavishly followed, and one where Mao intervened decisively. While collectivization[79] as a social-engineering project was clearly based on the Soviet experience, in terms of both broad objectives and methods it differed markedly. Not only was it more gradualist in implementation and designed to avoid the severe disruption of the Soviet case, although in China too there was considerable peasant resistance and destruction of resources, but for both economic and political reasons it was intended to boost production and living standards through the pooling of resources rather than simply serve as an instrument of extraction as in Stalinist practice.[80] While gradual in comparison with the Soviet experi-

---

[78] See Teiwes with Sun, *China's Road to Disaster*, chap. 1.
[79] Technically the movement mostly dealt with semi-socialist cooperatives rather than full collectives before 1956, but for simplicity I speak of collectivization.
[80] While economically, as in Russia, agricultural surplus was a key input into industrialization under the FFYP, given the much lower level of surplus in the Chinese countryside, it could not be simply extracted without grave rural consequences. Politically, while the

ence, it was a case of implementation by mass movement, with the pace increasing and decreasing over a five-year period after 1951 in response to fears of private agriculture and class polarization on the one hand, and the costs of the disruption of production on the other. The critical point came in spring and summer 1955 when Mao, after strongly advocating retrenchment in support of an emerging consensus early in the year, sharply changed course and demanded a significant acceleration of the process. What is notable is not just that Mao's position virtually single-handedly changed party policy, but that by attacking the previous cautious approach as "right opportunism" he unleashed frenzied activity by local party committees that created collectives in numbers greatly exceeding his own initial demands. This, of course, was proof of what Leninist discipline could accomplish, but at the time it also seemed to prove that Mao had once again been correct and led to "conceit" within the elite as a whole as to what the CCP and mass movements could achieve.[81]

In the eyes of Mao and the party leadership, the "success" of collectivization and the corresponding socialist transformation of industry and commerce in 1956 meant that a new stage had been reached – the basic victory of socialism over capitalism in China. This in turn led to more than a new consolidation phase to deal with the problems of transformation. It meant a fundamentally different situation where, as Mao put it, "large-scale, turbulent class struggle" had basically concluded, and the primary focus was now on economic and cultural development requiring, in the united front tradition, "uniting all forces which can be united." The underlying assumption was that, in the circumstances of the victory of socialism, the vast majority of individuals and groups supported the state, and their grievances were legitimate and "nonantagonistic." This then led to efforts to address those grievances in factories and the countryside, the Hundred Flowers experiment where intellectuals were encouraged to articulate their professional interests, and, most remarkable, flying in the face of Leninist practice, to invite on Mao's initiative non-party people in the spring of 1957 to criticize the party itself. The result was a disaster for all concerned: After much official prodding a

---

CCP's commitment to the peasantry once in power has often been grossly exaggerated, the revolutionary past certainly left a much more positive attitude with the peasants than was the case with the urban Bolsheviks.

[81] See Teiwes, "Establishment," pp. 56–64; and Teiwes and Sun, eds., *The Politics of Agricultural Cooperativization*, editors' introduction.

torrent of criticism developed, albeit one which only rarely challenged the CCP per se, and a harsh party response came in the form of the Anti-Rightist Campaign. While this clampdown was in no way inconsistent with continued adherence to the Soviet model, it created a situation where very real achievements in terms of economic development and deepened social control at the end of the FFYP were partially offset by a political fiasco. Ominously, that fiasco was due to Mao's first major misjudgment of the post-1949 period.[82]

The Great Leap Forward, 1958–1960

While, from a blinkered state socialist perspective, the FFYP period had been a great success, there were a number of pressures for change accumulating by late 1957. A reexamination of the suitability of the Soviet model had been under way in 1956–57, but one which contemplated adjustment only at the margins. After a year and a half of "opposing rash advance," growth had lagged, particularly in the agricultural sector. Political relaxation and attention to social grievances had produced disruptive consequences in the form of worker strikes and peasant withdrawals from the collectives. And the hoped-for central role of intellectuals in economic and cultural development was at least called into question by the Hundred Flowers fiasco. Nevertheless, when the Central Committee met in fall 1957 there was little sign of an impending change of direction; the political tightening and indoctrination efforts accompanying the Anti-Rightist Campaign seemed to represent a sufficient readjustment. Mao, however, suddenly and virtually alone – although there are some indications that the activities of some local leaders at the plenum may have influenced him – now declared the *fanmaojin* program a mistake, and called for a speed-up of economic growth. While as a policy statement this reflected Mao's basic predisposition to rapid growth, his own position in 1956 notwithstanding, it reflected something more that would profoundly alter the functioning of the Chinese state.[83]

This became clear at one of the pivotal turning points of the Maoist state, the January 1958 Nanning conference, when Mao declared *fanmaojin* a mistake of "political line." Apparently unable to face up to his

---

[82] See Teiwes, "Establishment," pp. 67–85; Teiwes, *Politics and Purges*, chaps. 6 and 7; and Roderick MacFarquhar, ed., *The Hundred Flowers* (London: Stevens & Sons, 1960), passim.

[83] See Teiwes, "Establishment," pp. 81–86; and Teiwes with Sun, *China's Road to Disaster*, pp. 66–69.

own miscalculation concerning the Hundred Flowers, Mao proclaimed that the error of "opposing rash advance" had encouraged the "bourgeois rightists" to attack the party. He went on to criticize harshly Zhou Enlai, Chen Yun, and others for their "mistakes," creating a situation "where no one could say anything different." This not only clearly violated the party norm of collective discussion, it also had major personal conse-quences for Zhou, who felt obliged to offer his resignation a little over two months later, and Chen, who lost his key economic decision-making role. Beyond that the pressure was so intense that wild claims of huge production increases and an imminent transition to communism soon became commonplace. The pragmatism of the earlier periods, even with its intimate relationship to social engineering, had given way not simply to revolutionary idealism, but to sheer fantasy.[84]

The impact of these developments had even wider ramifications for the operation of the state. First, Mao now took direct command of the economy. One dramatic result of this was seen over a three week period in June 1958 when the steel target was increased by 2.5 million tons as various leaders trooped to Mao's swimming pool residence and kept raising the ante in response to his pressure. Another feature was policy by ad hoc party conferences such as Nanning, something that continued to and beyond the critical Lushan meeting in summer 1959. Mao com-pletely dominated these sessions, setting the agenda, criticizing col-leagues, and choosing the participants – with provincial party leaders particularly prominent among them. The role of these local leaders, who were favored by Mao as close to the masses, was another major devel-opment; they consistently took a radical position and fed Mao's enthusi-asm during 1958. It is no accident that Mao apparently was considering Shanghai's leftist leader, Ke Qingshi, as a replacement for Zhou Enlai. This, in turn, was linked to Mao's sweeping rejection of the Soviet eco-nomic model as "dogmatism" that relied on specialists and ignored the masses, not to mention that under it the State Council allegedly operated beyond his and the Politburo's control. One of the consequences was a radical, poorly organized decentralization that saw the vertical control of industrial ministries dismembered to a significant degree. And crucially, with party secretaries taking control, the mass movement was extended to the modern sector.[85]

---

[84] See Teiwes with Sun, *China's Road to Disaster*, pp. 73–82, 98–99, 106–108.
[85] See ibid., chap. 3; and Peter N. S. Lee, *Industrial Management and Economic Reform in China, 1949–1984* (Hong Kong: Oxford University Press, 1987), pp. 51–55.

Even this does not fully indicate the impact of the Great Leap on the state. While party committees clearly did gain control over various enterprises that had previously been the sole preserves of central ministries, and the central Secretariat under Deng Xiaoping took a directing role on the economy that formerly belonged to the government, the leap is seen better as profoundly disruptive of organizational roles per se than in terms of a shift in the relative clout of different institutions. For under the demand for ever higher targets from Mao above and the blind promises of provincial party leaders from below, the capacity for economic coordination was lost. Within the government this was seen in a bureaucratic inversion: Whereas under the Soviet model economic coordinating agencies such as the planning committees had the clear upper hand over spending ministries, now they had no choice but to try to satisfy the unrealistic demands of such ministries – particularly where Mao's passions such as steel were involved. The result, as Mao would later complain, was that the planning authorities had abrogated their responsibilities, much as chaotic decentralization prevented nationwide coordination. Meanwhile, although the Secretariat and Deng Xiaoping exercised great power, it was only to place unbearable demands on lower levels, as in Deng's instruction that "even one catty of grain short of the target will not be tolerated," not to advance the organizational interests of the party as such.[86] Similarly, the PLA was simply borne along on Mao's tide, with Peng Dehuai leading attacks on Soviet "dogmatism" as it applied to military affairs, and army resources diverted to building the militias that were set up in the new people's communes in the countryside.[87]

If the Leap Forward created organizational chaos that was only partially corrected in 1959, the whole process was held together by Leninist party discipline. In the circumstances this was tragic, with unrealistic policies continually implemented and driving the country toward famine, as seen in the chilling statement of a county leader that "even if 99 percent die, we still have to hold high the red flag."[88] Another party norm – the

---

[86] See Teiwes with Sun, *China's Road to Disaster*, pp. 111, 114–15, 117–18, 131.

[87] Peng has usually been regarded as a strong proponent of military modernization, but this greatly oversimplifies his position; see Frederick C. Teiwes, "Peng Dehuai and Mao Zedong," *AJCA*, no. 16 (1986), pp. 87–89. On the militias, see John Gittings, *The Role of the Chinese Army* (London: Oxford University Press, 1967), chap. 10.

[88] Quoted in Jasper Becker, *Hungry Ghosts: China's Secret Famine* (London: John Murray, 1996), p. 146. Cf. Thomas P. Bernstein, "Stalinism, Famine, and Chinese Peasants: Grain Procurements during the Great Leap Forward," *Theory and Society*, May 1984.

ban on factions – was also basically honored, at least at higher levels.[89]
While different opinion groups began to emerge during Mao's hesitant
effort to "cool down" the leap from fall 1958, there is no evidence of
cliques of ranking leaders attempting to gain factional advantage over
others in the politicized atmosphere of 1958–60. Where sharp criticism
did occur, as in early 1958 when provincial leaders attacked Zhou Enlai,
Chen Yun, and others, or in the summer of 1959 onslaught against Peng
Dehuai and others at the Lushan conference, it was in response to Mao's
initiative. Rather than factional conflict, the basic impulse was respect
for revolutionary status. Thus Deng Xiaoping played a key role in
defusing the question of Zhou's resignation in 1958, while a range of
leaders at Lushan hoped Mao's rage against Peng would ease short of
the marshal's dismissal. But when Mao insisted they fell in line, with dire
consequences as the resultant radical upsurge greatly intensified the
developing famine which eventually caused 15 to 46 million deaths, if not
more.[90]

The Post-Leap Recovery, 1960–1966

The severity of the situation finally became apparent to Mao in mid-1960,
and a number of measures were instituted from the second half of the
year to redress the situation. Contrary to conventional wisdom, the policies of retreat which unfolded to mid-1962 not only received the bless-
ing of Mao, but his authority was crucial in initiating the process as other
leaders stood paralyzed in the face of horrific conditions until the Chairman began to change his views.[91] By the summer of 1962, however, Mao
determined that the retreat had gone far enough, and under the slogan
"never forget class struggle" moved to strengthen the collective economy
and restore ideological direction. Nothing like the comparatively clear
direction of the pre-leap period could be or was restored, however. While
major elements of the Soviet-style administrative system came back into

---

[89] Factionalism did exist at the lower levels, however, as indicated by purges in twelve
provinces in late 1957 and 1958. See the discussion of factionalism in the concluding
section below.

[90] See Teiwes with Sun, *China's Road to Disaster*, pp. 74, 97, 99, 209–12, and chap. 4 passim.

[91] In addition, other figures sometimes influenced Mao in an orthodox direction, as in the
1961 cases of his secretary Tian Jiaying, a suicide victim at the start of the Cultural Revolution, and Hu Yaobang, the great reformer of the post-Mao period, who both argued
against peasant responsibility systems as weakening the collective economy. See Teiwes
with Sun, *China's Road to Disaster*, epilogue 2.

play, the earlier structure was not fully restored, while the unfolding Sino-Soviet dispute produced a strident rejection of "revisionist" Soviet methods in principle but no clear alternative program. Meanwhile, the degree to which his colleagues were willing to retreat, particularly in the first half of 1962, led to Mao's doubts about them and in particular his heir apparent, Liu Shaoqi, a situation which only deepened as events unfolded over 1962–65. And finally, the severe deprivations of 1959–62 produced a degree of popular alienation that was unprecedented since 1949.[92]

Critical to the functioning of the Chinese state in this period were changes in the *modus operandi* of the top leadership. No longer did Mao seize direct personal control of operations as he did during the Great Leap. Instead, what was now put into effect was the plan for the Chairman's "retreat to the second front," a measure which left his Standing Committee colleagues headed by Liu running the party-state on the "first front."[93] But whereas this plan had been conceived in the 1950s as a way to build the prestige of his associates and guarantee a smooth succession unlike the leadership struggles in the Soviet Union after Stalin, by the early 1960s it had quite a different meaning given Mao's growing disillusionment. What it meant was not simply that Liu et al. would develop policies subject to Mao's approval – something which, after all, was the way Leninist collective decision-making actually worked in the relatively predictable pre-1958 years – but that Mao's views had become so ambiguous and his withdrawal so extensive that other leaders could never be sure what would satisfy the Chairman. A case in point concerned the Third Five-Year Plan (TFYP), something which typically never truly emerged during the period. In preparing a draft plan in 1964, SPC chief Li Fuchun sought to meet Mao's concerns, and after consulting Liu, Zhou Enlai, and Deng Xiaoping, they all concluded the Chairman would be satisfied. To their astonishment, Mao petulantly declared the document an example of "practicing the [Guomindang's] three people's principles" and ordered the setting up of a "small planning commission," which effectively displaced the SPC as the authoritative planning organ. More generally, as Mao's secretary Hu Qiaomu observed,

---

[92] See ibid., pp. 224–29; and Frederick C. Teiwes, *Leadership, Legitimacy, and Conflict in China: From a Charismatic Mao to the Politics of Succession* (Armonk: M.E. Sharpe, 1984), pp. 39–42.

[93] On the early moves to set up the "two fronts," see Teiwes, *Politics at Mao's Court*, pp. 32, 115–18; and MacFarquhar, *Origins 1*, pp. 152–56.

"the Chairman says something today and some other things tomorrow; it is very difficult to fathom him." It was hardly an ideal environment for running the party-state.[94]

Mao's ability to emasculate the top planning body of the state as well as other important organs[95] notwithstanding, the general trend of the period was to restore bureaucratic regularity and greater central coordination. Bureaucratic regularity was seen in the move away from mass mobilization in the modern sector; the measures guiding industry formulated in 1961 placed reliance on specialists and expertise. At the same time, financial control was recentralized in Beijing, various ministries regained many of their powers, and the major administrative development was the creation of six regional CCP bureaus covering roughly the same areas as the 1949–54/55 structures[96] – but now with a centralizing mandate as they coordinated the activities of provinces which had gone their own way during the leap forward. There was no return to the centralized Soviet model, however, as many enterprises were left in the jurisdiction of provincial and local authorities. Moreover, there was considerable experimentation at various levels in the absence of clear direction; thus when Liu Shaoqi promoted "trusts" (*tuolasi*) as a coordinating mechanism in 1964, it involved an across-ministries strategy rather than Soviet-style vertical rule. While the move was away from the mass movement, the shape of the restored bureaucratic structure was far from settled.[97]

While the above trends served to strengthen the government vis-à-vis the party in comparison to the Great Leap, undoubtedly the most novel feature of the period was the increased prominence of the PLA. Although always honored in official propaganda, by 1964 the army became the focus of a "learn from the PLA" campaign, civilian bureaucracies were setting up army-style politcal departments within their orga-

---

[94] See Frederick C. Teiwes, "Mao and His Lieutenants," *AJCA*, nos. 19–20 (1988), pp. 28–29; and Teiwes, *Leadership*, p. 40.

[95] Notably Deng Zihui's Rural Work Department under the Party Center, which Mao disbanded in anger in 1962 due to Deng's advocacy of peasant responsibility systems.

[96] The major difference, apart from overall function, was that in the early period party, administrative, and army organizations coexisted on the same territorial base, whereas now no government administrative structure was created to parallel the party bureaus, and military regions remained on the different territorial bases they had assumed in 1955.

[97] See Unger, "The Struggle to Dictate China's Administration," pp. 21–22; and Kenneth Lieberthal, "The Great Leap Forward and the Split in the Yan'an Leadership, 1958–65," in MacFarquhar, *The Politics of China*, pp. 113–16, 143–44.

nizations, and an indeterminate number of military officers were transferred to civilian duties. While these developments have been interpreted variously as reflecting a completely distinctive army emphasis on ideology as opposed to the managerialism of Liu Shaoqi et al., part of a bid for increased institutional clout or Lin Biao's personal power, or Lin's factional support for Mao against Liu, all of these interpretations are wide of the mark. Not only was Lin, notwithstanding his shameless promotion of Mao's personality cult, profoundly uninterested in power, but the PLA, for all the emphasis on "politics in command" under Lin, actually devoted more time to professional military matters than had been possible under Peng Dehuai during the leap. Moreover, Lin warned against usurping the power of civilian party committees while a civilian[98] proposed "learning from the PLA," and transferred officers seemingly adopted the perspectives of their new organizations. The explanation for the army's enhanced status lies with Mao – his appreciation of the PLA's notional virtues and Lin's promotion of the "Thought of Mao Zedong," and his dark suspicions of his leading civilian colleagues and the drift in national affairs.[99]

If the PLA's increased prominence preceding the Cultural Revolution was a pale precursor to the events after 1966, incipient factionalism also foreshadowed subsequent developments. But this must be understood clearly: whatever differences there were among the top leaders and established party-state officials at the center, there was little indication of divisive factionalism among them. The basic pattern, as already suggested, was for the "first front" leaders (which in reality did not include Lin Biao despite his status, as he both was ill and limited himself to army matters) to determine collectively a position, and then take it to Mao for final decision. Since Mao, despite brooding reservations and occasional temper tantrums as in the case of the TFYP, usually endorsed what was brought to him, political pragmatism reinforced the collective norm. But those more on the margins, notably Kang Sheng, who despite Politburo status had played a limited role after 1949, and Jiang Qing, who for the first time assumed a prominent public role, now fed Mao's suspicions, although the best evidence suggests they had little inkling of what lay ahead. Factionalism was

---

[98] Wang Heshou, the Minister of Metallurgy, proposed the campaign in 1963.

[99] See Teiwes, *Politics and Purges*, pp. 391–93; Teiwes and Sun, *The Tragedy of Lin Biao*, pp. 1–9, 10ff, 56–65, 181–213; and Gittings, *Role of the Chinese Army*, chaps. 11 and 12.

hardly rife, but the access such figures had to Mao bode ill for the future.[100]

While these developments had introduced new tendencies at the center of power, important changes were also taking place in the relationship between state and society. Most significant was the widespread peasant alienation, and even rebellion (in provinces with large national minority populations) that had to be put down by the PLA. Even when the worst had passed by mid-1962, substantial social malaise affected both the population and basic-level cadres whom the regime depended on to enforce its policies. The official response was to tighten controls, and deal with some of the worst problems through a rural Socialist Education Movement over the 1962–66 period. This, however, was neither part of a classic alternation of mobilization and consolidation phases, nor was it traditional social engineering. The basic aim was not some new political or socioeconomic breakthrough, but rather to restore the socialist forms and ideology that had been disrupted by the crisis caused by the post-Leap famine. Moreover, the implementation was both piecemeal, affecting only about one-third of China's villages, and subject to sharp shifts in intensity in response to changing perceptions of rural conditions. As with party policy generally, it was a situation where the leadership was unsure of its direction, where, as Mao put it with regard to economic construction, the CCP had to grope in the dark.[101] This was the scene when the party-state lurched into its second great crisis.

The Active Stage of the Cultural Revolution and the Height of Military Dominance, 1966–1971

The Cultural Revolution, notwithstanding the very real social tensions it tapped, was the individual creation of Mao Zedong. It came as a surprise to virtually all members of the Chinese elite when it began in mid-1966. Equally, the form and duration it took could not be anticipated. As late as the August Central Committee meeting that replaced Liu Shaoqi with Lin Biao as the successor, party committees were still charged with

---

[100] See Teiwes, *Politics and Purges*, pp. xxxvi–xliv, lvi–lxii, 393–94.

[101] See ibid., pp. xli–xlii and chaps. 10 and 11; and Teiwes, *Leadership*, p. 40. Mao's statement was made in 1962, but Zhou Enlai echoed the same view in 1964, commenting on "large unknown areas and a great many unfamiliar phenomena [in socialist construction]."

guiding the movement, and comments by Mao and Zhou Enlai suggested it would be over by the fall. Whatever Mao's motives, which surely involved some combination of distress at the real loss of revolutionary idealism in society, fears of a "Soviet revisionist" future for China, anger at official institutions that he believed to be bureaucracies aloof from the people and unresponsive to his wishes, and warped accumulated resentments at various leaders for imagined slights and disloyalty, he had no strategic plan for the Cultural Revolution. He believed unprecedented measures were called for, that the faults of the system could be revealed only by the "masses" themselves, but once setting the movement in motion he responded to it with tactical adjustments rather than by providing any clear direction. With unprecedented initiative from below, albeit in response to Mao, the movement went through various phases until mid-1968 when Mao ordered an extensive but still incomplete crackdown on "rebel" groups,[102] thus bringing to an end its active stage. The system then notionally shifted to the "construction [which came] after destruction," an effort to build a new order reflecting Cultural Revolution values, and one reflecting the leadership of a cleansed party organization. But the military dominance that emerged during the chaos of 1967 remained, up to the mysterious death of Lin Biao in September 1971.[103]

The Cultural Revolution represented an assault on previously sacred norms and practices in a multitude of ways. In philosophical terms, it rejected the core value of Leninist discipline, attacking obedience to higher level commands as a "slavish mentality" falsely ascribed to Liu Shaoqi, when the proper revolutionary attitude was to question all orders from the point of view of an ill-defined "Thought of Mao Zedong." Nothing could have been more subversive to the party-state; other norms such as collective leadership had either been significantly adapted in practice or honored in the breach, but unquestioning implementation of directives from the top had been the glue of the system. This, of course,

---

[102] The usage of "rebel" groups or organizations here and elsewhere usually refers generically to the mass groups which responded to Mao's call for rebellion and fought one another during the Cultural Revolution, rather than to the "rebel" groups which challenged existing party authority as distinct from "conservative" student Red Guards and others who tended to support such authority. In the event, it was the "rebels" who suffered most from periodic crackdowns.

[103] For an extended overview of the various phases of the active stage of the movement, see Harry Harding, "The Chinese State in Crisis, 1966–9," in MacFarquhar, *The Politics of China*.

was intimately related to a structural revolution: In early 1967 not only did the policy-making Politburo and the central Secretariat cease to function, but the party committees which served as the authoritative integrating bodies disappeared following the "seizure of power" from provincial committees by student Red Guards and "rebel" groups from bureaucratic units and factories. In these developments and throughout the active stage generally, Jiang Qing's Cultural Revolution Group encouraged and manipulated such attacks on the establishment. Meanwhile, as a new power structure, the Revolutionary Committees, was stitched together in territorial designations and work units, these committees were soon dominated by the PLA which by now was the only organization with a functioning nationwide chain of command, and which possessed the coercive means to bring some order out of chaos.[104] Finally, in addition to formal norms and structures, another crucial aspect of the existing system was crudely violated: respect for revolutionary status. With young Red Guards parading heroes of the revolution through the streets, one of the key informal values underpinning the party-state was in jeopardy.

What emerged, then, was something quite unlike the social engineering under the firm grip of the party of the past. Instead, in an inversion of the traditional practice of the "mass line," the movement was more an exercise in consciousness raising, with initiative to come from the masses themselves in response to the Delphic instructions of the Chairman such as "make revolution," "fight self," or "destroy the old and establish the new," rather than by following concrete orders from authoritative bodies on the scene. To be sure, when the "initiative" of the masses became violent to a degree that could not be tolerated, the PLA was authorized to crack down, but never in a manner to eliminate comprehensively "rebel" organizations, even after most Red Guards were dispatched to the countryside from 1968 and harsh penalties, including executions, were sanctioned to curb disruptive behavior. For the remainder of the Maoist period, authoritative institutions, whether Revolutionary Committees, reconstructed party committees from 1969, or the PLA, could never be sure they had carte blanche to suppress the "masses," some horrific crackdowns notwithstanding. In 1966–68, in any case, although manipulated by

---

[104] On the attack on traditional norms, see Teiwes, *Politics and Purges*, pp. 480–87. On the evolution and staffing of the Revolutionary Committees, see Teiwes, *Provincial Leadership in China: The Cultural Revolution and Its Aftermath* (Ithaca: Cornell University East Asian Papers no. 4, 1974), chaps. 1 and 2.

various elite actors from both the center and the localities, "rebel" organizations had their own agendas and were able to negotiate with high
leaders, such as Zhou Enlai, or the local Revolutionary Committees in
quite unprecedented ways.[105]

One result of the masses themselves "making revolution" was that in
some important respects the reach of the state was reduced, ironically at
a time of extensive and bizarre intrusion into extensive aspects of daily
life. Given the urban focus of the Cultural Revolution and the collapse
of higher-level party bodies, the countryside was less than completely
involved, although seemingly more so than previously understood,[106] and
even in the cities sections of the population were able to withdraw from
the movement as it ground on. But for all this, it was paradoxically reflex-
ive obedience, now to the sole authority of Mao, which held things
together. The disrupted and reshaped official organs carried out the
Chairman's orders to the extent they could be interpreted; disgraced
party leaders accepted their fate with only the most limited resistance;
and even "rebel" organizations, for all their pursuit of sectional interests,
justified everything in terms of Mao's ideology and almost never challenged his writ.[107]

In terms of institutions, the new Revolutionary Committees
established at the various territorial levels and in bureaucratic and
economic units combined the functions of party and government, but
crucially had little of the internal discipline of the former party organization. As these new organs of power were established in 1967–68, they

---

[105] On the different factors involved in the agendas of such organizations, see the excellent
study of Perry and Li, *Proletarian Power*, passim. Negotiation, of course, had its own
authoritarian aspects, but leaders such as Zhou often found themselves unable to impose
solutions in meetings with Red Guards, given Mao's endorsement of the mass
movement.

[106] The classic statement of the limited rural impact of the movement is Richard Baum,
"The Cultural Revolution in the Countryside: Anatomy of a Limited Rebellion," in
Robinson, *The Cultural Revolution*. The recent research of Jonathan Unger, "Cultural
Revolution Conflict in the Villages," *CQ*, no. 153 (1998), pp. 84–87, suggests more wide-
spread Cultural Revolution disruption to rural party organizations, and that where these
structures survived, these local organs of the state continued their domination of society.

[107] Party leaders never openly opposed Mao or his policies, but instead adopted various
defensive strategems; see Parris H. Chang, "Provincial Party Leaders' Strategies for Survival during the Cultural Revolution," in Robert A. Scalapino, ed., *Elites in the People's
Republic of China* (Seattle: University of Washington Press, 1972). While a number of
"rebel" groups were sharply critical of Mao's regime as such rather than simply of
selected "capitalist roaders," these seemingly were extremely few and apparently even
they did not attack Mao by name.

implemented the so-called "revolutionary triple alliance" of "rebel" organizations, PLA representatives, and "revolutionary cadres," that is, experienced cadres needed to provide essential administrative skills. Tension between the elements of the old order and the "revolutionary masses" were palpable within these structures, while divisions among various "rebel" organizations were intensified by competition for positions in the committees. Although PLA leaders increasingly took control of the Revolutionary Committees, and subsequently dominated the new "purified" party committees set up in 1969–71, these officers who were used to the most disciplined and professionally oriented setting, "politics in command" notwithstanding, were now faced with challenges to their authority from within and without. They assumed prime responsibility for internal order functions that were secondary to their traditional role, and economic management for which they were ill prepared.[108]

As for the government, although the State Council continued to function, many of its powers were devolved to the provincial Revolutionary Committees, and its central organs were both subject to the challenges of "rebel" organizations from within and the insertion of PLA cadres from without into leading positions in response to Mao's demands to restore order. In the resultant situation, despite the military presence, there was no army takeover as occurred at lower levels. Instead, while PLA representatives played a role, much actual authority was exercised by members of the pre-Cultural Revolution government leadership, even if that leadership had been deeply purged, and the remainder were repeatedly under attack, often having to be rescued by the intervention of Zhou Enlai. The now "dominant" PLA, moreover, was in an unenviable position: forced into roles it did not want, subject to the same type of "rebellion" and factionalism within its ranks as other institutions, having various of its leaders purged, albeit on a lesser scale than their civilian counterparts, and, ironically, for the first time since 1949, exposed to major outside interference in its own affairs. Not only was Zhou playing a major day-to-day role, something which would have been welcomed by the army under the circumstances, but a most unwelcome development was the involvement of Jiang Qing in internal PLA faction-fighting and her attempts to have a say on military matters more generally. This was clearly a major aspect of the so-called conflict of the "two

[108] See Teiwes, *Provincial Leadership*, pp. 18ff, 89–104; and Teiwes and Sun, *The Tragedy of Lin Biao*, pp. 120, 127–33.

cliques," hers and that of Lin Biao, that ultimately led to Lin's death in 1971.[109]

The bizarre demise of Lin Biao reflects the endemic factionalism which had been let loose by the Cultural Revolution, a factionalism affecting official bodies from the center to the grass roots as well as "rebel" organizations that had been enjoined to "fight self" but which engaged in often sanguinary "civil wars" among themselves for narrow advantage. It also, of course, affected the very top leaders of the party-state. The enormous escalation of conflict and reprehensible behavior notwithstanding, however, in this sphere there was an important continuity with the immediate pre-Cultural Revolution period. That is, among the established high-ranking elite itself, whatever settling of past animosities took place, it was in response not only to Mao's unleashing of struggle generally, but usually to his specific targeting of individuals. Much more active were those "marginal" members of the elite, Jiang Qing and the younger party intellectuals in her Cultural Revolution Group, although here the question remains as to their precise initiative independent of Mao. As for Lin Biao and Zhou Enlai, they maintained harmonious relations between themselves, but both tried to protect vulnerable colleagues yet attacked them when Mao demanded, with Zhou more vigorous in both aspects of this paradox. Lin's fall grew out of the most petty concerns within his own camp, where another "marginal" player, Lin's wife, Ye Qun, provoked a conflict with Jiang Qing's camp having little to do with serious policy issues. Once Mao sided with Jiang, matters unfolded to where Lin's group felt it necessary to flee, leaving the successor dead in a plane crash and the party-state's already tarnished credibility in tatters.[110]

The Twilight of the Maoist State, 1972–1976

The "Lin Biao affair" not only left the populace incredulous over claims that Mao's "best student" and successor had attempted to assassinate the

---

[109] See Teiwes and Sun, *The Tragedy of Lin Biao*, pp. 49–55, 117–23; Robinson, "The Cultural Revolution," pp. 213–15; and above, n. 51.

[110] The convoluted story of the "Lin Biao affair" is too complicated to recount here, but is reconstructed in Teiwes and Sun, *The Tragedy of Lin Biao*, pp. 134–60. On factionalism generally during the 1966–71 period, see ibid., passim; and Barbara Barnouin and Yu Changgen, *Ten Years of Turbulence: The Chinese Cultural Revolution* (London: Kegan Paul International, 1993), chaps. 4 and 5. On the Lin-Zhou relationship, see also Robinson, "The Cultural Revolution," pp. 227, 229–30.

Chairman and flee to the "revisionist" Soviet Union, it also left Mao himself seriously demoralized at the same time as his health began to decline precipitously. At Mao's direction, the story of an attempted "military coup" by Lin emerged, a story for which there was only slight evidence at best, since even the leading generals of the "Lin Biao clique" had remained completely loyal to Mao.[111] Meanwhile, for about a year a disoriented Mao allowed Zhou Enlai to institute a series measures aimed at "ultra-left" practices now ascribed to Lin Biao, but without any clear overall political line. By the end of 1972, however, Mao had decided these measures had gone too far and redefined Lin Biao's sins as "ultra-rightist."[112]

From that point to Mao's death a clear-cut division existed in elite politics, between a policy orientation favoring order, restoring various pre-Cultural Revolution procedures and methods, and furthering economic development on the one hand, and an effort to promote Cultural Revolution values and fight "revisionism" on the other. These, in turn, were linked to two relatively well-defined groups at the top, the surviving leaders of the pre-1966 party-state, led by Zhou Enlai and, after his 1973 rehabilitation, Deng Xiaoping, versus the civilian radicals gathered around Jiang Qing. In between, stood a number of regional military commanders and rapidly promoted civilians from the provinces, such as Hua Guofeng, but their basic position leaned heavily toward the old guard. And above all this was an increasingly ill Mao, giving succor to both orientations and both groups. With Zhou Enlai also dying, Mao approved a new set of appointments placing Deng Xiaoping in effective control of the reorganized State Council and the party in 1975, but by the end of the year, having been persuaded by Jiang Qing's group that Deng was seeking to "reverse verdicts" on the Cultural Revolution, he was moving to strip Deng of key powers. The well-known result was to replace Deng with Hua Guofeng as the ranking active figure of the party-state following Zhou's death in early 1976, but the last act would come shortly after Mao's death in the fall when Jiang Qing et al. were arrested, Hua was

---

[111] The only credible possibility, in my view, is that a group of young officers around Lin's son, Lin Liguo, considered such action without Lin Biao's knowledge, but even this is questionable. See Teiwes and Sun, *The Tragedy of Lin Biao*, pp. 152–60. Recent information obtained by Warren Sun suggests that, at most, Lin Liguo canvassed the "option" of killing Mao at the last minute, but this was a panicky reaction to a deteriorating situation, not a concrete plan.

[112] See Roderick MacFarquhar, "The Succession to Mao and the End of Maoism, 1969–82," in MacFarquhar, *The Politics of China*, pp. 275–78, 281–83.

named new CCP Chairman, and the process of negating the Cultural Revolution took its first, tentative steps.[113]

While not involving the same degree of extensive disruption and involvement of "rebel" organizations of 1966–68, these twilight years were marked by considerable continuity with the previous period, not only in factional strife at the top, but also in normative ambiguity, organizational paralysis, and significant social resistance to authority. Despite the reiteration of Leninist discipline in the new 1973 party constitution, the rebellious Cultural Revolution ethos was affirmed at the same time by Mao's latest dictum that "going against the tide is a Marxist-Leninist principle." In addition to the normative confusion, disciplined organizational behavior was undercut both by the ongoing struggles of Cultural Revolution factions in virtually all institutions and by conflicting signals from above. While the old guard gained by far the bulk of leading bureaucratic posts, Jiang Qing's radical group held some key positions,[114] cultivated followers in a wide range of institutions, including the military, established an unsanctioned document reproduction and distribution system to link those followers, and used their extensive (but by no means absolute) control of the media to criticize obliquely both key veteran leaders and official policies. In these circumstances, many cadres reacted with fear and immobility, unsure of which signals to respond to and fearful of being caught on the wrong side. Meanwhile, radical appeals through factional networks and the media to both the remaining "rebel" organizations, which were still quite significant in some areas,[115] and to disaffected social groups resulted in wall-poster attacks on various leaders up to the Politburo level, and widespread strikes, the most notable of which in Hangzhou in 1975 had to be suppressed by military force. Thus clear authority and stable patterns of interaction remained elusive both within official structures and between state and society.[116]

---

[113] For an overview of these developments, see ibid., pp. 278–81, 283–310.

[114] The most notable are the appointments of Wang Hongwen and Zhang Chunqiao as members of the MAC in 1975, when Zhang was also appointed head of the PLA's General Political Department, and Wang's responsibility for party daily work apparently from late 1973 to 1975, when a disappointed Mao replaced him with Deng Xiaoping.

[115] In Zhejiang, "rebel" leaders gained significant official positions in 1974, greatly inhibiting the freedom of action of the provincial leadership. See the excellent study by Keith Forster, *Rebellion and Factionalism in a Chinese Province: Zhejiang, 1966–1976* (Armonk: M.E. Sharpe, 1990), chaps. 7 and 8 and pp. 251–54.

[116] See ibid., chap. 9; and Teiwes, *Politics and Purges*, pp. 484–86.

Despite these difficulties, there were definite if restricted moves to rebuild institutions. The most systematic effort came with the 1975 reorganization of the State Council, a body now dominated by experienced administrators headed by First Vice Premier Deng Xiaoping, and a step linked to a program of limited recentralization, a strengthening of discipline and systems in economic enterprises, and a rectification campaign designed to oust Cultural Revolution activists who were unwilling or unable to implement modernization policies. This development built on earlier measures, particularly the rehabilitation of officials who had been removed during the Cultural Revolution. Such rehabilitations gathered force following Lin Biao's demise, with 90 percent of cadres criticized earlier back at their posts in many organizations in 1972, significant numbers of leaders with pre-1966 local experience appointed to the new provincial party committees, and prominent national-level victims – above all, Deng himself – restored to influential positions.[117]

In the process of institutional rebuilding,[118] a key issue was the role of the party, and especially its relationship to the PLA. Party leadership and CCP control of the gun were especially prominent themes after Lin Biao, but initially no well-articulated central party apparatus existed. Even the traditionally crucial Organization and Propaganda Departments were not reestablished until mid-1975 and fall 1977, respectively.[119] As for control of the gun, Mao entrusted the daily operations of the MAC to Marshal Ye Jianying in the wake of the "Lin Biao affair," and significantly placed Deng Xiaoping in key PLA roles[120] – measures that were clearly more personal than institutional. More strictly institutional measures took place in the localities, with civilians increasingly taking over the leading posts of the party committees, particularly following Mao's

---

[117] See Lowell Dittmer, *China's Continuous Revolution: The Post-Liberation Epoch, 1949–1981* (Berkeley: University of California Press, 1987), pp. 193–94, 200–201; Teiwes, *Provincial Leadership*, chap. 4; and MacFarquhar, "The Succession," pp. 288–96.

[118] Another part of the process was the revival of official mass organizations which had been inactive since 1966, notably the Youth League, trade unions, and women's association. These, however, seemed to reflect radical influence, and thus were not complementary to Deng's efforts. See Dittmer, *China's Continuous Revolution*, p. 195.

[119] While a powerful Central Committee organization and propaganda group existed from late 1970, it was dominated by Jiang Qing's group and thus hardly compatible with institution-rebuilding efforts. At lower levels, the party organization was also restored slowly and unevenly; see Frederick C. Teiwes, "Before and After the Cultural Revolution," *CQ*, no. 58 (1974), pp. 335–36.

[120] As a MAC Vice Chairman and PLA Chief of Staff. Cf. n. 47.

December 1973 reshuffle of the commanders of eight military regions, men who had up to then served as provincial party first secretaries but now gave up their civilian duties. But as so often with the Maoist state, the institutional and personal were intertwined, for on the occasion Mao called for the reshuffle he also indicated that Deng, the military hero, would be brought back into the PLA. While there was no possibility of the generals resisting Mao's demand, Deng's new role was reassuring as they gladly returned to the barracks.[121]

While back in the barracks, the PLA implicitly assumed a role quite unprecedented in its history, one which was neither the largely professional (albeit politicized) army of pre-Cultural Revolution days, nor the leading participant in civilian affairs after 1966. It now for the first time became the arbiter between competing civilian groups at the top. Previously, whenever the army became involved in Politburo-level disputes, it was fundamentally to endorse whatever position Mao adopted. Even now the role was not quite that of arbiter, first, because it was beyond imagination that the PLA would side with Jiang Qing's group, and, more immediately, because it would not act on this role while Mao lived. Indeed, the last year of Mao's life was essentially a waiting game, one where the traditional forces of the party-state held their hand even as their position was made more perilous by the death of Zhou Enlai, the ouster of Deng Xiaoping, the less noted sidelining of Ye Jianying[122] and others, disruption to Deng's institution-building program, and continuing social disorder – even if the most dramatic popular outburst, the April 1976 Tiananmen demonstrations, was an expression of popular support for the old guard.[123] Yet they waited, unwilling to use the overwhelmingly predominant resources at their disposal, for fear of precipitating a fatal downturn in Mao's fragile health – in Ye Jianying's words, "sparing the rat [Jiang Qing et al.] to save the porcelain [Mao]." While these leaders could secretly plot a course of action against the dying leader's wishes, he had to die first before they would take decisive measures to secure their own most vital interests.[124]

---

[121] See MacFarquhar, "The Succession," pp. 290–91.

[122] Following Deng's downfall, General Chen Xilian replaced Ye as the official responsible for the daily work of the MAC. Ye's status, however, allowed him to play a critical role in planning the arrest of Jiang Qing's group.

[123] On the Tiananmen events, see Richard Baum, *Burying Mao: Chinese Politics in the Age of Deng Xiaoping* (Princeton: Princeton University Press, 1994), pp. 32–37.

[124] See Keith Forster, "China's Coup of October 1976," *Modern China*, July 1992.

THE DYNAMICS OF THE MAOIST STATE: A SUMMARY

The twists and turns of the Maoist state can clearly be traced to the actions of Mao himself and the consequences of those actions. While initially playing the role of supreme arbiter but only sometimes initiator of policy, Mao presided over a regime with a well-defined (Soviet) economic model, a coherent set of Leninist party norms and stable institutional practices, and a practical approach where political realism served to balance revolutionary idealism. By 1958 this changed, however, as Mao personally launched and ran the Great Leap Forward which resulted in gross violations of party norms, major changes in institutional relationships, an unprecedented economic strategy built on wishful thinking rather than any sort of realism, and a demoralized society which suffered tens of millions of famine deaths. After an ambivalent period of recovery which Mao encouraged and allowed, yet also undercut, he initiated the Cultural Revolution which further undermined norms, institutions, realism, and social order, albeit in quite different ways. By the time of his death, the party-state had significantly weakened itself at the behest of its leader.

While Mao's capacity to alter drastically institutional patterns indicates the relative weakness of institutions in the Maoist state, it does not exhaust the question of organizational interests and behavior. The many organs of the state clearly had objectives flowing from their organizational missions, and vigorous bureaucratic politics of course existed, whether forthrightly, as in the mid-1950s, or behind ideological obfuscation as at other times. Yet in crucial ways such politics were always comparatively restricted, not to mention those periods when they were fundamentally compromised. Thus, even under the highly structured Soviet model, not only could political movements seriously disrupt organizational life, but more generally the individuals who took charge of China's bureaucracies were on the whole self-confident revolutionaries who saw themselves on a transformative mission and believed in a higher loyalty to the CCP as a whole. To paraphrase a party historian, although the heads of departments responded to organizational objectives, they themselves acted somewhat independently and took into account the overall party interest. The institutional influence, this scholar concluded, was relatively smaller. Similarly, given the importance of revolutionary status, even if Politburo-level economic officials were unhappy with Chen Yun's positions, it was very hard for them to express their discontent given Chen's superior standing.[125]

Organizational interests were more seriously compromised during the Great Leap, even as ministries and localities sought to capitalize on the new movement to obtain greater resources for their projects. For unrelenting political pressure mixed with revolutionary idealism placed both central bureaucracies and territorial committees in impossible positions: They were forced to make plans and set targets that not only could not be achieved, but caused great damage to their own interests and the greater national interest in the process. The situation was even more perilous during the Cultural Revolution, as the case of the presumptive institutional "winner" – the PLA – indicates. Not only was the army dragged away from its organizational mission, it was forced to suffer extensive internal purges and meddling from the likes of Jiang Qing. It was even faced with direct threats to its very institutional integrity, as in early 1967 when "rebel" groups attacked army bases, abused and tortured officers, and disrupted military training, leading key generals to beg Mao for permission to resist such assaults. Moreover, while PLA leaders would have been pleased with the significant increases in military spending during this period, it was due to a Mao-led drive for war preparations aimed at the Soviet Union rather than to institutional advocacy. Indeed, as the detailed work of John Lewis and Xue Litai has shown, while Mao's war fixation ironically created a situation where military specialists temporarily gained enhanced authority, it was a situation that quickly disintegrated, and one where, by the early 1970s, "few in the 'bowels' of the system any longer understood the authority structure, had any faith in it, or much cared."[126]

If bureaucratic politics were constrained or seriously compromised in the Maoist state, factional politics were both ever-present yet also contingent on overall party policy and especially Mao's initiatives. Such politics were endemic, given both the mixture of groups and different personal networks staffing official organizations from the top to bottom of the system, and given the control the powerholders in those organs had over material advantages and social status. The feuds which inevitably arose and became ingrained in view of the comparative immo

---

[125] See Teiwes with Sun, *China's Road to Disaster*, pp. 49, 189–90.

[126] See ibid., pp. 115–16, 172–76, 191ff; Teiwes and Sun, *The Tragedy of Lin Biao*, pp. 73–75, 118–20, 165; and Lewis and Xue, *China's Strategic Seapower*, pp. 40–42, 84–87, 239–40.

bility of careers often led to vicious infighting and cruel outcomes during political movements, the most extreme occurring during the Cultural Revolution when the breakdown of norms and structures led to the widespread activation of personal networks.[127] Yet, as one moved up to the higher reaches of the party-state, leaving aside the Cultural Revolution when "proletarian factionalism" was consciously engendered by Mao, the incidence of factionalism decreased as seen in the overall stability of both central and provincial leaderships before 1966. The cases of significant factional conflict which did exist were largely at the provincial level and fundamentally of the *shantou* variety – that is, between groups of distinctly different backgrounds, most notably the conflict between natives of an area who had been involved in local underground struggle and the representatives of the victorious outside forces that conquered the bulk of China in 1949. While different policy positions did come into play as in the most significant provincial purges in 1957–58, in substantial measure these were cases of the contending groups making use of changing policy from Beijing.[128]

The notion of continuous rampant factional conflict under Mao is even more difficult to credit at the very top. Here the critical factor in restraining such conflict was revolutionary status, the factor which Deng Xiaoping reportedly cited in eventually rejecting Gao Gang's approaches with the comment that "Comrade Liu [Shaoqi's] position in the party has been settled by history," and which led ranking leaders, including those with policy differences with Peng Dehuai, to try and defuse Mao's anger at the hapless marshal during the 1959 Lushan conference before Mao made denunciation of Peng mandatory. Even during the Cultural Revolution, for all the harsh attacks and even involvement in persecutions,[129] the leading figures of the establishment, as opposed to the

---

[127] See the heart-rending account of a sincere cadre repeatedly caught in factional currents he little understood from the late revolutionary period through the Anti-Rightist Campaign to the Cultural Revolution in Michael Schoenhals, ed., *China's Cultural Revolution, 1966–1969: Not a Dinner Party* (Armonk: M.E. Sharpe, 1996), pp. 315–26.

[128] See the excellent studies of the conflicts in Henan and Zhejiang respectively: Jean-Luc Domenach, *The Origins of the Great Leap Forward: The Case of One Chinese Province* (Boulder: Westview Press, 1995), pp. 29–35 and chaps. 4 and 5; and Keith Forster, "Localism, Central Policy, and the Provincial Purges of 1957–1958: The Case of Zhejiang," in Cheek and Saich, *New Perspectives*. On the overall pre-Cultural Revolution stability at the provincial level, see Teiwes, *Provincial Party Personnel*, pp. 34–39, 62–64.

[129] For example, the involvement of Zhou Enlai in the special case groups which detained and tortured disgraced leaders. See Michael Schoenhals, "The Central Case Examination Group, 1966–79," *CQ*, no. 145 (1996), pp. 88ff.

relative outsiders such as Jiang Qing, basically engaged in conflict with their peers only when required to do so by Mao, or in response to the forces unleashed by the movement, and their basic impulse seemed to be to protect vulnerable colleagues. The importance of revolutionary prestige can be further seen in the relations of Zhou Enlai and Lin Biao, heroes both before and during the Cultural Revolution. In both circumstances mutual respect existed as well as absolute acceptance of their relative status, even when Mao reversed it in 1966. During Mao's rule the only serious challenges to such status came from the Chairman himself, whether by, perhaps inadvertently, encouraging Gao Gang, launching an astonishing attack on Peng Dehuai, or creating an environment where past accomplishments were no protection against criticism from young people barely born when the revolution triumphed.[130] Elite restraint notwithstanding, such episodes contributed to the weakening of the regime.

Remarkably, given the various Mao-imposed factors that weakened the party-state, it remained exceptionally dominant over society throughout the Maoist era. The forms of domination varied, from the focused social engineering of the first eight years to wild attempts to introduce communism during the Great Leap to deliberately induced "rebellion" from below during the Cultural Revolution. As suggested, moreover, in key respects the capacity and reach of the state declined after the leap due to its self-inflicted wounds. But critiques of the totalitarian model as applied to the PRC which note that the state itself was not a monolith, that revolutionary values were not universally internalized by the population, that subcultures and self-interested behavior existed, and that grievances from below sometimes burst forth[131] rather miss the point. The failure to meet some idealized model cannot gainsay the state's totalistic pretensions and its extraordinary reach in fact. This reach was seen even during the Cultural Revolution, the party-state's weakest period, in the penetration of the most remote areas of the country; in the fact that much social conflict was along officially decreed lines, while other conflict, as among village lineages, still adopted the rhetoric of the movement; and in the inevitability that the resistence of any group in society could be overwhelmed when the authorities set their mind to it. Indeed,

---

[130] See Teiwes, *Politics at Mao's Court*, pp. 108–109; and Teiwes and Sun, *The Tragedy of Lin Biao*, pp. 24–42, 47–49.

[131] See Shue, *The Reach of the State*, chap. 1; and Perry and Li, *Proletarian Power*, introduction.

as Elizabeth Perry and Li Xun observe, "Maoist state initiatives ...
served to structure mass activism" – that is, however much the underlying sources of activism strayed from Mao's ideals, the very fact that it
developed in the virulent form it did against elements of the state, yet at
the same time in ways which were profoundly inimical to the interests of
social groups and society as a whole, was precisely Mao's doing. In addition, even in this chaotic period, the state had the capacity to carry out
truly monumental programs such as the transfer of industrial capacity to
the "third front" in the southwest, and to achieve significant if in key
respects illusionary economic growth when it moved to dampen excessive struggle.[132]

A more difficult, and uncomfortable, issue concerns why the party-
state was able to exert such dominance. Clearly, and unsurprisingly in
view of rapid social change, not to mention tense political campaigns,
there was significant social discontent and disobedience to authority from
the 1950s on.[133] Equally clearly, the strong coercive apparatus and use
sometimes of military force to put down disorder was a critical factor in
the party-state retaining control, yet in important respects CCP power
appears to have been legitimate. That is, the indications overall suggest
a population that either actively supported the state or passively
accepted its "right" to rule, grievance-led resistance to specific developments notwithstanding. A number of factors can be identified that would
have contributed to such legitimacy: the authority conferred on new
dynasties, a political culture of obedience to authority generally, the benefits gained as a result of ending decades of civil war and the process of
economic construction, the party's monopoly of the distribution of material rewards and symbolic status, nationalist pride that China had "stood
up," and, not least, the ever present indoctrination in an official ideology
which, especially for many intellectuals, was persuasive in many respects
and, in any case, was the only conceptual view of the world allowed.

---

[132] See A. Doak Barnett, *China's Far West: Four Decades of Change* (Boulder: Westview
Press, 1993), passim; Unger, "Cultural Revolution Conflict in the Villages"; Barry
Naughton, "The Third Front: Defence Industrialization in the Chinese Interior," *CQ*, no.
115 (1988); and Perry and Li, *Proletarian Power*, p. 5. Perry and Li's observation is made
in criticizing the totalitarian model.

   On economic growth, the problem, which was typical of Stalinist economies, was huge
waste and distorted priorities, but the state still achieved many of the objectives it set
for itself. See the post-Cultural Revolution official analysis of the period's economic performance in Schoenhals, *China's Cultural Revolution*, pp. 262–66.

[133] For an excellent survey of discontent in the mid-1950s, see Domenach, *Origins of the
Great Leap Forward*, chap. 2.

If one analyzes the segments of ethnic Han Chinese society that would have to grant legitimacy,[134] there are considerable indications that such grants were made. Absolutely crucial is the elite's own sense of regime legitimacy, something that when lost, as in the Soviet Union in the late 1980s, leads to the whole house of cards falling down. In the Chinese case, it is crystal clear that, personal deprivations and failed policies notwithstanding, the figures who made the revolution remained convinced of the party's cause, and that such attitudes extended deep into the official structures. It also appears that most ordinary cadres and intellectuals only gradually began to have doubts as the Cultural Revolution evolved. Prominent intellectuals, moreover, despite difficult circumstances and policy reservations since early in the PRC, saw their roles as assisting the state in adopting a proper course, rather than in opposing the party.[135] Student Red Guards, at least before disillusionment set in, often displayed religious fervor and genuine belief in the god-like Mao, and even those performing as rational actors overwhelmingly operated within the official ideology. Workers in state enterprises, notwithstanding workplace grievances, were advantaged in material and status terms. And peasants, who arguably received little in return for their support of the revolution, to a surprising degree retained faith in the party and Mao, participating in major anti-regime activities only in periods of great upheaval, and even then on a lesser scale than might have been anticipated.[136] In short, across a wide range of groups, there were significant degrees of belief in Mao and the system, and, with seemingly few exceptions,[137] an inability to

---

[134] This obviously leaves out the 5 to 6 percent of the population made up of ethnic minorities where, it would appear, CCP legitimacy has been in serious doubt.

[135] See the studies in Carol Lee Hamrin and Timothy Cheek, eds., *China's Establishment Intellectuals* (Armonk: M.E. Sharpe, 1986). The assessment of ordinary cadres and intellectuals is based on discussions with such people over a number of years.

[136] While there were disturbances in particularly hard-hit areas during the Great Leap famine, according to a provincial party first secretary at the time, the peasants generally were so accepting of their calamitous situation that there was little thought of robbing the obviously full granaries. Interview, July 1997. See also Becker, *Hungry Ghosts*, pp. 309ff and passim.

[137] The most important case from the 1970s was the dissident Li Yizhe group in Guangzhou that argued for socialist democracy and legal rights. Significantly, however, even this group treated Mao as sacrosanct, aimed its criticisms ostensibly at the officially denounced Lin Biao but in fact at the Jiang Qing group, had early connections with local party leaders, and advocated agitation methods characteristic of the Cultural Revolution. See Anita Chan, Stanley Rosen, and Jonathan Unger, eds., *On Socialist Democracy and the Chinese Legal System: The Li Yizhe Debates* (Armonk: M.E. Sharpe, 1985), introduction and passim. Cf. above, n. 107.

think in alternative conceptions. To be sure, there was an ebbing of the party's legitimacy through the sequence of disasters from the Great Leap to the Cultural Revolution, and disillusioning events like the "Lin Biao affair," but it is instructive that the last great expression of popular resistance in the Maoist era, the 1976 Tiananmen demonstrations, were in support of the experienced rulers of the state. Salvation was still to come through the CCP.

Mao Zedong left a difficult legacy for the post-Mao state: a fractured and grievance-riddled society, a party-state with reduced legitimacy and weakened dominance over society, faction-infested institutions, ambiguous official norms, and a divided top leadership. Once Jiang Qing's group was purged within a month of the Chairman's death, however, some resilient strengths were also in evidence. One was simply that there was no viable alternative to the CCP, or even much questioning of its overall conceptual framework, although the dissident voices that began to be heard over the "Cultural Revolution decade" would become more significant starting with the Democracy Wall movement in 1978–79. Other key assets involved the reassertion of elements so undermined by Mao over the 1966–76 period: Leninist discipline and respect for revolutionary status. The move to restore a disciplined party apparatus both internally and in its relations with society were an immediate priority, while the ostensibly more gradual reemergence of the dominant role of revolutionary heroes was also under way from an early date.[138]

While these developments indicated a very real desire to restore what the elite saw as the "golden age" of the 1950s, there could be no full-scale

It is, of course, impossible to measure the degree of acceptance or rejection of the regime by various groups. In some tension with the view advanced here, the prison memoirs of Yang Xiguang not only report understandable anti-communist attitudes among the most oppressed elements of the system but also claim similar sentiments on a fairly wide basis within the larger society, especially since the Great Leap famine. Of particular interest are Yang's reports of underground antiparty organizations formed since 1959. These undoubted sentiments and organizations notwithstanding, Yang's account is notable for the difficult journey it took many of those who suffered at the hands of the state, himself included, to reject communist assumptions, and how utterly novel or incomprehensible ideas of complete rejection seemed to inmates. See Yang Xiguang and Susan McFadden, *Captive Spirits: Prisoners of the Cultural Revolution* (Hong Kong: Oxford University Press, 1997), pp. 36, 71, 75, 104, 112, 115–16, 133, 138–39, 169, 210, 224–25, 280–81, and passim.

[138] A study is in progress by the present author, Warren Sun, and Chris Buckley which argues that the elite politics of the early post-Mao period, rather than a "succession struggle," is better viewed as an almost inevitable process of restoring proper statuses within the party.

turning back.[139] As Zhou Enlai's eventual successor as Premier, Zhao Ziyang, put it, "if it had not been for the Cultural Revolution during which everything had been driven to extremes, we would not have been able to see things so clearly. The emancipation of the mind we have achieved today would have taken a great deal more time." This "emancipation" came to involve measures to protect the elite itself from a future willful leader, a tacit understanding with society to replace totalism with a more limited strategic direction by the state, and the replacement of revolutionary idealism with a quest for economic modernization. It meant a sweeping rejection of "high Maoism," but by a system with crucial structural, normative, and political continuities with what preceded it, and by leaders who could no more detach themselves from the dead Chairman than they could deny their own lifelong revolutionary endeavors.

---

[139] See Frederick C. Teiwes, "Restoration and Innovation," *AJCA*, no. 5 (1981).

5

The Chinese State in the Post-Mao Era

DAVID SHAMBAUGH

If we do not institute a reform of our political structure, it will be difficult to carry out the reform of our economic structure.[1]

THE Chinese state evolved greatly during the post-Mao era. Deng Xiaoping left his successors a state (and society) very different from that which he inherited from Mao, while the post-Deng regime continues to restructure the state and reform its relationship with society. As Frederick Teiwes elucidates in the preceding chapter, Mao bequeathed to Deng a "totalistic" state characterized by highly personalized and concentrated power; an expansive and intrusive Leninist organizational apparatus that employed commandist, coercive, and mobilizational techniques of rule; with autarkic approaches to development and foreign affairs. The Chinese state under Mao was all-inclusive, playing multiple roles normally left to the private sector in many countries: employer, saver, investor, manager, economic planner, price setter, social provider, and redistributor of social and economic resources. All of these formerly totalistic functions performed by the Maoist state changed fundamentally under Deng, and are further devolving to subnational and nonstate actors in the post-Deng era.

The declining role of the state is best seen through the lens of the economy. Consider a few examples. When Mao died in 1976 the state was the monopolistic owner and employer of the means of production. By 1998 the state sector accounted for only 45 percent of Gross Domestic Product (GDP) and employed only 18 percent of the work force (those

The author is grateful to Bruce Dickson, Harry Harding, Lyman Miller, and Ren Xiao for comments on previous drafts of this chapter.
[1] Deng Xiaoping, "On Reform of the Political Structure," *Selected Works of Deng Xiaoping*, vol. III (Beijing: Foreign Languages Press, 1994), p. 179.

161

employed in the service sector have risen from less than 5 percent to nearly 30 percent today). As an investor in the economy, the share of central state appropriation has declined substantially, from 36 percent in 1982 to a mere 3 percent today.[2] This is largely a function of declining revenue extraction capacity by Beijing – the ratio of state revenue to GDP has plummeted from 31 percent in 1978 to just 11 percent in 1996. During the Maoist era the state expropriated and reinvested savings; today the state's fiscal agencies are dependent upon personal household savings deposits to keep the parasitical state industrial sector afloat (through redirected subsidies). Today those on state salaries earn far less than those in the cooperative or private sectors. Similarly, the state no longer provides all housing and welfare for citizens. Housing and property ownership rights are being privatized (fully 30 percent of Shanghai inhabitants own their own homes today), while nonstate pension and insurance schemes are being developed to cover the ever-increasing numbers who enjoy no welfare provision. In essence, the Maoist state sector became a huge drag on economies of scale and efficiency during the Deng and post-Deng eras.

During the Maoist era the state sector was the only option; today it is seen as the last option. While the Maoist system can be described as more monolithic than monocratic, the Dengist system was more authoritarian than autocratic. Deng inherited a stagnant economy, alienated society, and paralyzed polity, but he left his successors a robust economy, rejuvenated society, and less capricious political system. To be sure, these changes produced certain tensions and present the post-Deng leadership with unprecedented challenges of governance. Some China watchers even believe that the tensions and challenges will overwhelm the regime, bringing to an end the dynasty of Chinese communism.[3] Others believe that the system was on the verge of collapse before Deng rescued it, and that the state has generally "adapted" well to a changed environment and new challenges.[4] Still others argue that, despite significant normative

---

[2] China now additionally receives large amounts of foreign direct investment ($42 billion in 1998), earns large revenues from foreign trade (25 percent of GDP in 1998), and is the world's largest borrower from the World Bank.

[3] These prospects are explored later in this chapter and in Chapter 7. In particular, also see Arthur Waldron, "The End of Communism," in *Journal of Democracy*, vol. 9, no. 1 (January 1998), pp. 41–47; and David Shambaugh, ed., *Is China Unstable? Assessing the Factors* (Washington, D.C.: Sigur Center for Asian Studies, 1998).

[4] See Bruce Dickson, *Democratization in China and Taiwan* (Oxford: Clarendon Press, 1997).

and structural political changes, Chinese Communist leaders will always resist "democratic reforms" as they fear for their own positions, the continued sustenance of Communist Party rule, and social chaos.[5] In China, since Deng's death, there have also been stirrings and calls among intellectuals for renewed "political reform," although in late 1998 the regime opted to squash such sentiments by imprisoning advocates of democracy and giving stern warnings that dissent would not be tolerated. President Jiang Zemin told a session commemorating the twentieth anniversary of the famous Third Plenum (that kicked off reform), "From beginning to end, we must be vigilant against infiltration, subversive activities, and separatist activities of international and domestic forces. With a clear-cut stand, we must resolutely nip [such tendencies] in the bud. The Western mode of political systems must never be copied."[6] Outside China there is also a lively debate among China watchers over the Chinese Communist Party's ability to evolve in more pluralistic and democratic directions.[7]

Not in dispute is the fact that China, and the nature of the Chinese state, has changed markedly in the two decades since Deng Xiaoping returned to power. When Deng was rehabilitated in 1977, for the third time in his career, he set about implementing a comprehensive reform program. Deng's program changed the very nature of the state from being a proactive agent of social-political change to being a more passive facilitator of economic change and reactive arbiter of social-political tensions. The Chinese state "withdrew" from its former all-intrusive and hegemonic roles in the life of the nation.[8]

Deng's initiatives produced sweeping changes in the economic and social life of the nation, in foreign and military policy, and also in the political realm.[9] Had it not been for the 1989 popular protests in Beijing and thirty-three other cities across China, and the subsequent suppression in Beijing, it is quite likely that political reform under

[5] See Pei Minxin, "Is China Democratizing?," *Foreign Affairs* (January–February 1998), pp. 78–79.

[6] As quoted in John Pomfret, "China Reaffirms One-Party Control: In Name of Stability, Jiang Vows to Crush Democracy Movements," *International Herald Tribune*, December 19, 1998.

[7] See, in particular, the contributions to the symposium "Will China Democratize?" in the *Journal of Democracy*, vol. 9, no. 1 (January 1998).

[8] See Vivienne Shue, *The Reach of the State: Sketches of the Chinese Body Politic* (Stanford, Calif.: Stanford University Press, 1988).

[9] For assessments of Deng's impact in these policy realms, see David Shambaugh, ed., *Deng Xiaoping: Portrait of a Chinese Statesman* (Oxford: Clarendon Press, 1995).

Deng and his protégé Zhao Ziyang would likely have been as far-reaching as the Dengist reforms in other realms. During 1987–89 Zhao and his advisors had mapped out (with Deng's full endorsement) bold initiatives for reform of the political system – only for them to be shelved as they were arrested, purged, imprisoned, or escaped into exile abroad after June 4, 1989. Nonetheless, some of the political reforms enacted prior to 1989 endured into the post-Tiananmen period. Some of these were structural reforms, while others were normative. In both contexts all three institutional pillars of the Chinese state – the party, army, and government – were affected. Together they marked qualitative moves away from the Maoist state and polity. To be sure, there remain substantial continuities with the Maoist period, particularly organizationally, but the substantial changes Deng initiated were more notable.

When, in the mid-1980s, Deng began to address the issue of political reform, several issues were of primary concern: the overconcentration of power, the inefficient bureaucracy, and political strictures that inhibited economic growth. In a speech to the Central Committee Leading Group for Financial and Economic Affairs in September 1986, Deng outlined his strategy for dealing with these problems through streamlining, separating, and devolving political power:

> We have to discuss what the content of political reform should be and work out the details. In my opinion, its purposes are to bring the initiative of the masses into play, to increase efficiency and to overcome bureaucratism. Its content should be as follows. First, we should separate the Party and the government and decide how the Party can exercise leadership most effectively. This is the key and should be given top priority. Second, we should transfer some of the powers of the central authorities to local authorities in order to straighten out relations between the two. At the same time, local authorities should likewise transfer some of their powers to lower levels. Third, we should streamline the administrative structure, and this is related to the devolution of powers.[10]

As shown below, Deng largely succeeded in accomplishing his goals. In so doing, he initiated important processes, but with unforeseen consequences. Yet he knew that far-reaching reforms were needed, as China was falling further and further behind modern and newly industrialized countries. As a result of Deng's reforms, China has enjoyed an unprecedented period of economic development and social prosperity –

---

[10] Deng, "On Reform of the Political Structure."

but this has created tremendous strains on the Chinese state at all levels. To some extent, the state has evolved along with socioeconomic change, but in several key dimensions it has not. Whether it can survive in its present form (Communist Party authoritarian hegemony) is open to question – a subject explored in Harvey Nelsen's concluding chapter.

DEFINING THE POST-MAO STATE

Discussion of the "state" in contemporary China requires definition. There are indeed different ways to define its parameters and "measure" its capacities and effectiveness.

First, when discussing the "state" in the People's Republic of China, scholars almost always refer to the hybrid "party-state" because of the organizational penetration and political hegemony exercised by the Chinese Communist Party (CCP). As discussed below, I also believe that this organizational definition should include the coercive element of the state, that is, the People's Liberation Army (PLA) and People's Armed Police (PAP). Thus, in most political studies of contemporary China, and throughout this chapter, the "state" refers to the totality of party, government, and military – although each component is discussed individually.

Second, the "state" does not necessarily equate with "politics" or the "political system." Of course, the state affects the polity of any community or country via the political system and laws of that nation, but one must distinguish the "state" as an actor that affects more than the political realm. State actions obviously affect economies, societies, the environment, education, world affairs, and a variety of other realms. To address this, a voluminous literature on the "reach of the state" and "state capacity" has mushroomed in recent years. There is certainly no shortage of ways to evaluate the state in developed or developing countries. In the case of China, the potential measures are lengthy:[11]

- *The structure and organization of the state*: how is it organized?
- *The normative procedures of the state*: how legal, rational, regularized (or the opposite) is it?
- *The nature of elite politics*: how does the leadership interact and according to what norms and procedures?

---

[11] I am grateful to Harry Harding, Andrew Walder, and Wang Shaoguang for discussions on this subject.

- *The composition of elites and recruitment into the state*: how are the candidate pools defined, how representative and inclusive of society are they, and what are the mechanisms of selection?
- *The nature of policy making and implementation*: how bureaucratic, regularized, or ad hoc?
- *The functions of the state*: what are its principal purposes vis-à-vis society?
- *The degree of state penetration of society*: how pervasive and coercive? What are the buffers between state and society?
- *The extractive capacity of the state*: what is its ability to extract resources and taxes from society, how is this done, and is it seen as legitimate?
- *The regulatory capacity of the state*: how effective is it?
- *The coercive capacity of the state*: how well does it control the internal and external security forces?
- *The sources of legitimacy of the state*: on what is it based?
- *The historical and cultural origins of the state*: to what extent has it evolved indigenously and to what extent has it borrowed from foreign models?
- *The capacity to maintain social order*: how is this done and to what extent is coercion necessary?
- *The inclusiveness/exclusiveness of political participation*: how democratic are the forms and what is the extent of civil society?

A large literature has been published on most of these dimensions over the years. For the purposes of this chapter, though, I examine the state in post-Mao China along only three principal dimensions: *structural, normative,* and *spatial.* However, several of the aforementioned criteria are addressed under these rubrics.

THE STRUCTURAL DIMENSION

When discussing the structure of the contemporary Chinese state a basic distinction needs to be made between what may be described as the *organic* elements of the state, as distinct from *organizational* elements. Organizationally, the post-Mao Chinese state (like its predecessor) is comprised of three pillar institutions: the CCP, the State Council, the PLA, and the constituent elements of each – but these three institutions possess unique organic interrelationships and history that continue to have great affect on their functioning. That is, one must distinguish between the structural organization of the state and its component parts, and some underlying factors that give definition to the nature of the state – but do not show up in a table of organization.

For example, during the People's Republic of China there has long existed an integrated relationship between the PLA and the CCP over the years. Until the late 1990s, the Chinese military did not establish the separate professional and corporate identity commonplace in the West. Rather, the PLA has had a close symbiotic relationship with the CCP over time, in which there has been mutual structural interpenetration.[12] During the late Deng era this changed somewhat as the party exerted greater control over the army after 1989 – although after Deng's demise the armed forces exerted a greater autonomy from the party-state. Various mechanisms existed for the party to assert this control over the military: party committees, discipline inspection committees, and the General Political Department system. Similarly, the State Council (which is administratively responsible for governing many functional arenas of state power) has also historically had a symbiotic relationship with, and domination by, the party. As discussed below, the party-dominated *nomenklatura* personnel system was the key organizational device of dominance. Until the Deng period, this also took the form of systemic and systematic party controls over State Council organs, but as the result of administrative reforms undertaken during the 1980s and '90s, the State Council now enjoys substantial autonomy from the party. This reflected a fundamental change in the nature of state functions: The state no longer existed to administer mass campaigns, plan and run the economy, define and persecute class enemies, and so on. Instead, the scope of state power was intentionally downsized as it was deemed too intrusive to an economy and society increasingly regulated by the market, nongovernmental organizations, a variety of collective entities and individuals, as well as subcentral state actors. In both cases – State Council and PLA – the symbiotic relationship with the party has declined during the Deng and post-Deng eras.

Thus, when one speaks of the "state" in contemporary China, one must first consider the organic interrelationship that the government (i.e., State Council) and military sectors have with the Communist Party. This is true of the Maoist and post-Mao state. One of Deng's great reforms and lasting contributions was to distance the party from the "totalistic"

---

[12] On this complex subject, see David Shambaugh, "The Soldier and the State in China," *The China Quarterly* (September 1991), pp. 527–68; and Ellis Joffe, "Party-Army Relations in China: Retrospect and Prospect," *The China Quarterly* (June 1996), pp. 299–314.

(to borrow Tang Tsou's term) or "totalitarian" (to use Franz Michael's) control it knew under Mao, to devolve power to lower levels, to separate the party organizationally from other state and nonstate bodies (particularly in the economic sphere), and to permit conditions under which the military carved out an increasingly autonomous and professional identity. What this ultimately means for the sustenance of the CCP as a ruling party is difficult to predict, but there is no doubt that through these reforms Deng Xiaoping substantially altered the composition of the Chinese state.

These organic characteristics are not always evident when evaluating the post-Mao state organizationally. Examination of the table of organization of the party-army-state indicates uneven change; most organizational change has come in the State Council, with only minimal change in the Communist Party and PLA.

Disaggregating the State

The CCP and State Council must be disaggregated into four constituent levels: central, provincial/municipal, county, and local (see Fig. 5.1). The PLA has its own organizational structure, which is more distinct. Both the CCP and State Council hierarchies still stretch vertically from center to locality, creating separate parallel administrative systems (*xitong*), as they did in the Maoist period.

The central level of the post-Mao Chinese state is composed of:

- The Chinese Communist Party and its constituent units – the Politburo and Politburo Standing Committee; the Central Committee, its Secretariat, General Office, and departments and offices;[13] the Central Discipline Inspection Commission; the Central Military Commission; the Central Leading Groups; and Special Committees;[14]

---

[13] The Organization Department, Propaganda Department, United Front Work Department, International Liaison Department, Commission for Politics and Law, Commission for Comprehensive Management of Social Security, Commission for Protection of Party and State Secrets, Committee for Organizational Work, Guidance Committee on Ethical and Cultural Construction, Work Committee for Central Government Organs, Committee for Organs Under the Central Committee, Committee for Discipline Inspection in Central Government Organs, Policy Research Office, Central Party History Research Office, Central Documents Research Office, Central Party Archives, Central Party School, *People's Daily, Guangming Daily, Qiushi.*

[14] The Finance and Economics Leading Group (LG), Taiwan LG, Taiwan Economic and Trade LG, Foreign Affairs LG, Foreign Affairs Consultative Group, Rural Work LG, Party Building LG, Propaganda and Education LG, Foreign Propaganda LG, Communist Party History LG, Cryptography LG, Comprehensive Public Order LG.

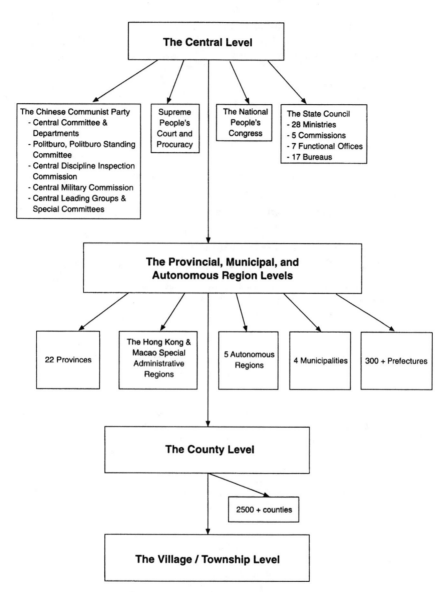

The Central Level

The Chinese Communist Party
- Central Committee & Departments
- Politburo, Politburo Standing Committee
- Central Discipline Inspection Commission
- Central Military Commission
- Central Leading Groups & Special Committees

Supreme People's Court and Procuracy

The National People's Congress

The State Council
- 28 Ministries
- 5 Commissions
- 7 Functional Offices
- 17 Bureaus

The Provincial, Municipal, and Autonomous Region Levels

22 Provinces

The Hong Kong & Macao Special Administrative Regions

5 Autonomous Regions

4 Municipalities

300 + Prefectures

The County Level

2500 + counties

The Village / Township Level

Figure 5.1 The Chinese State in 2000.

- The State Council and its twenty-two ministries,[15] five commissions,[16] thirty-three bureaus,[17] and four affiliated offices, three research institutions, and two general administrations[18] (following the 1998 reorganization);
- The National People's Congress, its Standing Committee, and constituent committees;
- The Supreme People's Court and Procuracy.

The second tier of the Chinese state consists of the twenty-two provinces, five "autonomous regions," and four large metropolitan cities that enjoy provincial-level administrative status (Beijing, Chongqing, Shanghai, and Tianjin). Also at this level, one must consider the 300-plus prefectures and 200-plus prefecture-level cities, although this is a designation falling into increasing disuse. The third tier of the Chinese state is the county (*xian*) level, traditionally the heart of Chinese government. In 1994 there were 2,541 counties and county-equivalent cities in China. Finally, there are the countless numbers of village- and township-level governments (*xiang-zhen zhengfu*) spread across rural China. The urban-level equivalent is the neighborhood committee,

---

[15] State Council Ministries (*Bu*) in 1998: Agriculture, Civil Affairs, Communications, Construction, Culture, Education, Finance, Foreign Affairs, Foreign Trade and Economic Cooperation, Information Industry, Judicial, Labor and Social Security, Land and Natural Resources, National Defense, Personnel, Public Health, Public Security, Railways, Science and Technology, State Security, Supervision, Water Resources. Source: Secretarial Bureau of the General Office of the State Council and Administrative Office of the Central Commission on Organizational Reform, eds., *Zhongyang Zhengfu Zuzhi Jigou* (The Central Government's Organizational Structure) (Beijing: Gaige chubanshe, 1998).

[16] State Council Commissions (*Weiyuanhui*) in 1998: National Defense, Science, Technology, and Industry; State Development Planning Commission; State Economic and Trade Commission; State Family Planning Commission; State Nationalities Affairs Commission. Source: ibid.

[17] State Council Bureaus (*Ju*) in 1998: Broadcast, Film, and Electronic Media; Building Materials; Chinese Medicine; Civil Aviation; Coal Industry; Commercial Administrative Management; Cultural Relics; Entry and Exit Border Formalities; Environmental Protection; Foreign Exchange Controls; Foreign Experts; Forestry; Government Offices Administration; Intellectual Property; Internal Trade; Light Industry; Machinery Industry; Maritime Affairs; Medicine and Chemical Agent Supervision and Management; Metallurgy Industry; Non-Ferrous Metals; Oil and Chemical Industry; Physical Culture and Sports; Postal; Press and Publishing Administration; Religious Affairs; Revenue Collection; Statistics; Technology Quality Supervision; Tobacco; Textile Industry; Topography; Travel. Source: ibid.

[18] State Council Offices (*Shi*) in 1998: Economic System Reform, Hong Kong and Macao Affairs, Legal Affairs, Policy Research. Research Institutions: Chinese Academy of Sciences; Chinese Academy of Social Sciences; Economic, Technological, and Social Development Research Center. Administrations: Audit; General Customs. Source: ibid.

although they often encompass a substantially smaller population base than their rural equivalents.

The armed forces have also undergone organizational change, streamlining, and downsizing in recent years. The most significant change to date came in the late 1980s, with the reduction of Military Region commands from eleven to seven and the creation of twenty-four Group Armies (*jituanjun*). The combining of two main pillars of the Maoist defense industrial establishment – the National Defense Industries Office and National Defense Science and Technology Commission – into one consolidated Commission on Science, Technology, and Industry for National Defense (COSTIND) was also a noteworthy change, as it also spun off the eight former defense industrial ministries (ministries of machine building) into corporations that produced for both civilian and military consumers. In 1998–99 the defense industrial complex was further reorganized, with a new PLA General Equipment Department (GED) created to oversee all defense research and production, and the ordered divestiture of all commercial assets by military units. All research institutes and factories that produce solely for the military will, in theory, fall under the purview of the new GED, while those that have successfully converted to civilian production will remain under COSTIND. In practice, though, this neat division of labor will be difficult to accomplish. During the 1980s, the PLA also created a Discipline Inspection Commission to parallel that on the party side (and to police party members in the armed forces), and has newly established party branches down to the company level.

Other than these reforms, the structure of the PLA today is no different than when Mao died – or, for that matter, as it has remained since the 1950s. This raises the question of whether the existing territorial and organizational command structure is suitable to its new doctrine of peripheral defense and "limited war under high technology conditions." It is known that the PLA is giving careful consideration to creating a joint-service staff system similar to the Joint Chiefs of Staff in the United States, in an effort to better coordinate and integrate the separate services in joint operations. Consideration is being given to abolishing or further truncating the military region commands, and eliminating the group army system in favor of a new configuration of regional "theaters" or "war zones" (*zhan qu*). The PLA High Command recognizes that both its force and command structures are outmoded and an impediment to creating a military capable of rapid deployment and engagement, joint operations, and high lethality in a peripheral environment. To meet these goals, in recent years the PLA has undertaken a program of downsizing forces, upgrading capabilities, and streamlining command and control.[19]

The organization of the Communist Party bureaucracy has changed little in the post-Mao period. Indeed, as John Burns notes, "it has remained fundamentally unchanged for more than fifty years."[20] The most important organizational changes that Deng stimulated were to resurrect the Secretariat of the Central Committee and create the Central Discipline Inspection Commission. Otherwise, the Politburo and its Standing Committee, the Central Committee Departments, and other central and regional party organs remain as before. However, Deng's goal was not to reorganize, but to make the existing structure *work better*. Deng Xiaoping was a quintessential organization man.[21] He believed in a strong Leninist party and worked hard to rebuild party organizations and discipline from their atrophied condition following the Cultural Revolution. Not only did he want to rebuild and strengthen the party; he particularly wanted to change the normative ways in which it functioned. It was not so much the *structure* of the party that concerned him, as it was the *process* of decision making and policy implementation. Organizationally Deng did not tamper much with the party structure he inherited from Mao.

This meant the continuity of several core elements of (Chinese-style) Leninism.[22] Yet, in each, we see qualitative changes initiated by Deng. As illustration, let us examine three core structural elements of Leninist party rule: (1) the *nomenklatura* personnel system; (2) the "interlocking directorate" relationship between the party on the one hand, and army and state on the other; and (3) party control over the media. These are three key instruments through which Leninist ruling parties exercise

---

[19] See my "The PLA and the PRC at 50: Reform at Last," *The China Quarterly* (September 1999), pp. 660–672; and my *Reforming China's Military* (Berkeley: University of California Press, forthcoming), chap. 3.

[20] John P. Burns, "The PRC at 50: National Political Reform," *The China Quarterly* (September 1999), pp. 580–594. For a thorough discussion of the CCP's formal organizations, see Kenneth Lieberthal, *Governing China: From Revolution Through Reform* (New York: W. W. Norton, 1995), pp. 155–182. Also see Zheng Shiping, *Party vs. State in Post-1949 China: The Institutional Dilemma* (Cambridge: Cambridge University Press, 1997).

[21] For further discussion of this aspect of Deng's leadership style, see my "Deng Xiaoping: The Politician," in Shambaugh (ed.), *Deng Xiaoping*.

[22] For further discussion, see Lucian W. Pye, *The Mandarin and the Cadre* (Ann Arbor: Center for Chinese Studies, 1988); and Burns, "The PRC at 50."

their political control: by controlling those who staff the state, by controlling the armed forces and other paramilitary and security elements of the coercive apparat, and by controlling and monopolizing information available to the populace. It must be said that in several other key areas of "totalitarian" Leninist control,[23] Deng did away with previous Maoist practices: the decline in the use of terror, bureaucratic hegemony, and intolerance of civil society. To be sure, with regard to the latter, Deng still practiced the Leninist/Maoist method of state cooptation of nongovernmental organizations (NGOs), but under Deng such organizations mushroomed and gained considerable "public space."[24]

The Nomenklatura

The *bianzhi*, or *nomenklatura* in Soviet terminology, is the method by which a Leninist ruling party staffs the party-state apparat. The armed forces maintain their own party *bianzhi* for leading positions as well as elaborate personnel procedures for appointments and promotions of high-ranking officers, but through the "interlocking directorate" the Communist Party similarly penetrates the military. The Leninist ruling party exercises organizational hegemony over these appointments and thereby dominates political life of the nation. The central *bianzhi* list today comprises the top 5,000 or so positions on the party-state personnel roster, all coordinated by the Organization Department (*Zuzhi Bu*) of the Communist Party. This includes not only all ministerial and vice-ministerial positions, all provincial governorships and First Party Secretary appointments, but also positions such as university chancellors and the presidents of the Academy of Sciences and Academy of Social Sciences. It also includes the top positions of the various "united front" organs established by the CCP to coopt and organize industrial workers, writers, women, and other civil actors (e.g., the All-China Federation of Trade Unions, the Chinese Writers Federation, and the Women's Feder-

[23] See, in particular, Carl J. Friedrich, *Totalitarianism* (Cambridge, Mass.: Harvard University Press, 1954); Friedrich and Zbigniew Brzezinski, *Totalitarian Dictatorship and Autocracy* (New York: Praeger, 1956, 1966); Brzezinski, *The Permanent Purge: Politics in Soviet Totalitarianism* (Cambridge, Mass.: Harvard University Press, 1956). For an excellent overview of the literature on totalitarianism, see Abbott Gleason, *Totalitarianism: The Inner History of the Cold War* (Oxford: Oxford University Press, 1995).
[24] See, for example, Timothy Brook and B. Michael Frolic, eds., *Civil Society in China* (Armonk, N.Y.: M.E. Sharpe, 1997).

ation). Cooptation of civil society is a key Leninist practice to control any potential challenges from below that may arise to challenge the Communist Party's hegemony (as occurred, for example, with the Solidarity Movement in Poland).

The mechanics of this system have varied over time.[25] The one constant has been that the Organization Department of the party controlled the *bianzhi* name list. Throughout the Maoist era and into the early Deng period, the *bianzhi* register reached two levels down into the bureaucracy. That is, the central CCP Organization Department and State Council Ministry of Personnel had the power to appoint party and state officials at the provincial and county levels, or down to the bureau level within a ministry. But during the 1980s the "two level down" system was truncated to one level down, thereby reducing, in one stroke, the main *nomenklatura* register essentially by half (approximately 10,000 to 5,000).[26] Following the political disturbances of 1989 and the party-army-state's subsequent crackdown, there is evidence that the process was further centralized.[27]

The major effect of these changes has been to delegate power to lower levels, allowing each level unit (whether a central ministry or territorial unit) greater control over its own bailiwick. This had the important net effect of lessening the central-level party's influence and control. Thus, with this key organizational alteration, the power of the central party-state to implement policy at lower levels has been substantially reduced, thus contributing to the "withdrawal" of the (central) state from the life of society. To be sure, lower-level units still feign compliance with certain central dictates, but the room for evasion of regulations and higher-level policy is considerable. Lax discipline and rife corruption further fuels noncompliance. The withdrawal of the state has only reinforced the "cellular" and protectionist nature of much of China's political economy, and has stimulated widespread variance in commercial, agricultural, and internal trade practices. Taken together, by reducing the scope of the

[25] John Burns has done the best work on China's *nomenklatura* system. See his *The Chinese Communist Party Nomenklatura System: A Documentary Study of Party Control of Leadership Selection* (Armonk, N.Y.: M.E. Sharpe, 1989); "China's *Nomenklatura* System," *Problems of Communism* (September/October 1987), pp. 739–70.

[26] See Melanie Manion, "The Cadre Management System Post-Mao: The Appointment, Promotion, Transfer, and Removal of Party and State Leaders," *The China Quarterly* (March 1985), pp. 203–33.

[27] John P. Burns, "Strengthening Central CCP Control of Leadership Selection: The 1990 *Nomenklatura*," *The China Quarterly*, no. 138 (June 1994), pp. 458–91.

nomenklatura, the party-state has effectively removed one of its traditional methods of Leninist control, thereby further isolating itself from the fabric of government and society.

The Interlocking Directorate

A second traditional characteristic of Leninist parties is the penetration of state and military organs by party personnel, and the reverse presence of state and military leaders in the Central Committee and Politburo – a system identified in the Soviet case as the "interlocking directorate." The CCP has certainly employed this practice, but here too substantial change has been witnessed in the post-Mao era. Actually, contradictory trends have been witnessed in the state and army. On the whole, the military has become more professional and less political, while the party has also been removed from many aspects of economic planning and decision-making. Party "core groups" (*dangzu*) throughout the state apparatus have also declined in number and importance,[28] but they have actually increased in the military. Following the Tiananmen massacre of 1989 and collapse of communist parties elsewhere, the CCP undertook a major effort to build party branches down to the regiment level. Despite this effort, the signs are that the armed forces are enjoying greater autonomy from interference by political commissars and party committees.

The party exercises its penetration of the PLA through three institutional mechanisms: party branches, the political commissar system under the General Political Department, and the Central Discipline Inspection Commission.[29] Unlike the Western tradition of apolitical professional militaries, the Chinese PLA has always been a politicized military and coercive tool of the CCP. As noted above, over time this has resulted in a symbiotic relationship between party and army. The PLA remains the ultimate guarantor of CCP rule, but it is also evident that in the post-Deng era the military is becoming more corporate and autonomous. After seventy years, the interlocking directorate and symbiotic relationship is being broken. The percentage of PLA officers on the Fifteenth Central Committee elected in 1997 was only 15 percent – the lowest since

---

[28] See the discussion in Lieberthal, *Governing China,* pp. 213–14.

[29] These mechanisms and the CCP-PLA interlocking directorate are detailed in my "The Soldier and the State in China: The Political Work System in the People's Liberation Army," *The China Quarterly* (September 1991), pp. 527–68.

the CCP came to power (the Thirteenth Central Committee of 1987 also registered 15 percent). There was no military member of the Politburo Standing Committee unveiled at the Fifteenth CCP Congress, and only two officers made it on to the Politburo. Moreover, the post-Deng High Command is distinctively comprised of commanders instead of commissars.[30] The new PLA leaders are combat-hardened veterans, drawn predominantly from the ground forces, who have spent the bulk of their careers commanding troops in China's interior. They are apolitical as a rule, and are real military professionals. They are focused on downsizing and upgrading the armed forces' fighting capabilities, and do not wish to be drawn into politics or the maintenance of internal security. This is a fundamental departure from the past. While virtually all officers in the PLA are party members, and the CCP has undertaken to rebuild party loyalty in the armed forces, the really noticeable trend is the markedly increased professionalization and decreased politicization of the military in the Deng, and particularly post-Deng, eras.

The other dimension of the interlocking directorate has been the party's traditional penetration of the State Council bureaucracy, subcentral government, and commercial enterprises. Until Mao turned on and attempted to destroy the party apparat during the Cultural Revolution, it directed and dominated these arenas. After regaining power in the wake of the Chairman's death in 1976, Deng Xiaoping set about rebuilding the party, but also redefining its role in these arenas. Deng was convinced that excessive party control had retarded the economy and constricted bureaucratic action at all levels of government.

One way in which he addressed this problem was through the *nomenklatura* system noted above. Another was by granting enterprise managers the power of economic decision-making. This was done under the policy of "separating party from government" (*dang-zheng fenkai*).

A third method was to grant increased autonomy to the National People's Congress and institute a system and legal culture in the country.[31] To be sure, the CCP still views law as an instrument to enforce its political hegemony and control society, rather than to grant society

---

[30] See my *China's Military Leadership: New Faces, New Trends?* (Stanford: Asia/Pacific Research Center, 1998); and my "China's Post-Deng Military Leadership," in James Lilley and David Shambaugh, eds., *China's Military Faces the Future* (Armonk, N.Y., and Washington, D.C.: M.E. Sharpe and AEI Press, 1999), pp. 11–38.

[31] From 1979 to 1997 the NPC enacted 311 laws and issued 700 sets of regulations and 4,000 administrative rules. Cited by Xinhua News Agency in Foreign Broadcast Information Service (FBIS), *China-Daily Report*, May 19, 1997.

and substate actors tools to challenge state power.[32] This is often described as "rule by law" rather than "rule of law." The primary institutional vehicle for the promulgation of a legal system has been the National People's Congress (NPC). Since its inception in 1954 the NPC had long been treated by the CCP as another united-front organ to be controlled, but to provide a facade of citizen representation.[33] But over time the NPC has gained more and more autonomy and now functions as a substantial check on government (but not party) policies. While it has no formal watchdog duties vis-à-vis the Communist Party, the party's influence in NPC lawmaking processes has declined.[34] But, at the end of the day, the party's control over the NPC system at the national and provincial levels is exercised through the *nomenklatura*. Only CCP authorities can convene people's congresses, and delegates must be screened by the party.[35]

A fourth method was to streamline the central bureaucracy. This has come in four rounds of restructuring – in 1982, 1988, 1993, 1998 – resulting in a substantial reduction of ministries and commissions, ministers and vice-ministers. The 1982 reorganization of the State Council, for example, resulted in the reduction of ministries and commissions from 98 to 52 and, concomitantly, reducing ministers and vice-ministers from 505 to 167. The overall number of administrative cadres and staff of central government organs was reduced by more than a third, from 49,000 to 32,000.[36] To be sure, some of these changes were cosmetic – such as the merging of the Ministries of Water Conservancy and Electric Power into one – but Deng's administrative reforms (Zhao Ziyang and Zhu Rongji's, to be more precise) did have the net effect of streamlining government organs, reducing overlapping functions, and substantially lessening party control over a wide range of economic and technical policy arenas. The 1988 and 1993 restructurings were more form than substance, but the 1998 reforms represent a more serious attempt to rationalize and downsize the administrative structure. The total number of

---

[32] See Pitman B. Potter, "The Chinese Legal System: Continuing Commitment to the Primacy of State Power," *The China Quarterly* (September 1999), pp. 673–683.

[33] See Kevin O'Brien, *Reform Without Liberalization: The National People's Congress and the Politics of Institutional Change* (New York: Cambridge University Press, 1990).

[34] See Murray Scot Tanner, "The Erosion of Communist Party Control over Lawmaking in China," *The China Quarterly*, no. 138 (June 1994), pp. 381–403.

[35] Burns, "The PRC at 50."

[36] Richard Baum, *Burying Mao: Chinese Politics in the Age of Deng Xiaoping* (Princeton: Princeton University Press, 1994), p. 139.

ministries and commissions in the State Council was reduced from 40 to
27. As in past downsizing, however, there has been more of a merger of
ministries (thus creating the impression of a net decline) than their elimination. The Ministry of Geology and Mineral Resources was merged into
the new Ministry of Land and Natural Resources; the Ministry of Information Industry was created out of the old Ministry of Post and Telecommunications, the Ministry of Electronics, and the Ministry of Radio, Film,
and Television; and so on. Some energy ministries, such as the Ministries
of Coal, Chemicals, Petroleum, and Gas, were abolished and regrouped
as bureaus under the new State Economic and Trade Commission. The
former State Education Commission and State Science and Technology
Commission have been reduced in rank to ministries, while a number
of former ministries were reduced in rank to bureaus or lesser-level
administrative institutions.[37] Nonetheless, the 1998 restructuring resulted in a reduction of State Council bureaucrats from 47,000 to 31,000,
with additional redundancies of 80,000 personnel at provincial and
municipal levels.[38] By any measure, this initiative represents serious
reform.

Party Control of the Media

Another key indicator of loosened state control can be found in the publishing and broadcast industries. During the Maoist era the party totally
and tightly controlled information available to the public via the media.
Today it is neither total nor tight.[39] While the CCP Propaganda Department (*Xuanchuan Bu*), the Central Leading Group on Propaganda and
Education (*Xuan-Jiao Lingdao Xiaozu*), the Central Leading Group on
Foreign Propaganda (*Duiwai Xuanchuan Lingdao Xiaozu*), and New
China News Agency (*Xinhuashe*) still exercise considerable control over
what appears in the print and broadcast media, it is no longer monopolistic or monolithic. The party's watchdog agency, the State Press and

---

[37] For a useful overview of these changes, see Julie Reinganum and Thomas Pixley,
"Bureaucratic Mergers and Acquisitions," *The China Business Review*, vol. 25, no. 3
(May–June 1998), pp. 36–41. A useful Chinese Source is Ren Xiao, *Zhongguo Xingzheng
Gaige* (Reforming China's Administration) (Hangzhou: Zhejiang renmin chubanshe,
1999).

[38] The biggest cuts have come out of the former industrial sector ministries (up to 70
percent), while the Ministry of Finance lost 50 percent of its employees and the Ministry
of Foreign Affairs 15 to 20 percent.

[39] For excellent analyses of the media in China today, see Orville Schell, *Mandate of Heaven*
(New York: W.W. Norton, 1996); and Anne Stevenson Yang, "Word Games," *The China
Business Review*, vol. 25, no. 3 (May–June 1998), pp. 42–48.

Publications Administration, is but a shadow of its former Orwellian self. In the environment of slackened control, a plethora of newspapers and magazines (devoted to all number of subjects) have mushroomed. By 1998 more than 2,000 daily and weekly newspapers and more than 8,000 periodicals were published in China, 565 publishing houses operated, while over 1,000 television stations and over 3,000 radio stations were on the air.[40] The content of television programs is no longer dull and propagandistic, with Chinese mainland television now quite similar to that broadcast in Hong Kong and Taiwan. Talk radio has also swept China, with callers openly expressing dissatisfaction with state policies and local conditions. Indeed, in some municipalities, local mayors subject themselves to caller criticism. With the opening of the country to the outside world, Chinese citizens now also have direct access to satellite television, a wide range of foreign radio transmissions (although some like VOA, the BBC, and Radio Free Asia are still jammed on certain frequencies), and foreign publications. Access to the internet is another critical source of independent information, and a dent in the party's armor. By the end of 1998, there were 2.1 million registered internet accounts in China, with an estimated three times that number online, as many people share accounts. Computer and internet use is ballooning in Chinese society, with the CCP and Xinhua trying desperately to fight rearguard action by trying to control servers and block websites.

Despite its continued grip over the Xinhua media system, the party has lost control of the key Leninist device of controlling what people read, see, hear, and learn. Without control over the media, the party can no longer control people's minds.

NORMATIVE CHANGES

There have also been important normative changes in the post-Mao party-state. The most notable changes have to do with the ways that decisions are taken and implemented. During the Maoist era the Chinese party-state functioned largely as a creature of the Chairman's dictates, as detailed by Frederick Teiwes in the previous chapter. Of course, this was not always the case (as during the early 1960s), but decision-making by personal fiat was often the norm. But beneath the Chairman factionalism reigned. Under Deng, decision-making became more *consensual*,

---

[40] As cited in Burns, "The PRC at 50," citing *Ta Kung Pao* (Hong Kong), April 17, 1998, in FBIS, *China-Daily Report*, April 20, 1998.

consultative, and *collective*, and factionalism was substantially reduced.[41] Under Mao, when the Chairman sought advice from colleagues or subordinates, it was often a trap to test their political loyalties.[42] Deng's more consensual style had important implications for "inner-party life" and, more generally, for freedom of speech in society at large. Deng believed that Mao, as Stalin before him, had severely undermined "inner-party democracy" through the creation of a cult of personality and his dictatorial decision-making style. While Deng himself often made decisions by fiat and assumed the role of paramount leader, he nonetheless placed a priority on building bureaucratic coalitions, seeking expert advice, and involving other leaders in policy deliberations.[43] Deng was authoritarian but not autocratic. Yet late in his life, like Mao, Deng grew distrustful of his successors and the bureaucracy. He twice dumped his anointed successors (Hu Yaobang and Zhao Ziyang), and in 1992 he became frustrated with Li Peng and Jiang Zemin over their failure to push ahead with rapid economic reform. Like Mao under similar circumstances, an ailing Deng "leapfrogged" his successors and the bureaucracy and took his case straight to society with a whirlwind inspection tour of the special economic zones in the south. His end run worked; Deng succeeded in shifting the political and economic agenda. But his more lasting legacy was to reconstitute the state bureaucracy and institute a more rational (in the Weberian sense) system of policy-making and implementation.

Under Zhao Ziyang, Jiang Zemin, and Zhu Rongji, policy-making has also become more consultative. All three leaders set up think tanks and research institutes and drew upon advice from them.[44] This has been an important feature of rationalizing the decision-making process, as various advice is sought, pilot studies are undertaken, and feasibility projects are used.

---

[41] See Harry Harding, *China's Second Revolution: Reform After Mao* (Washington, D.C.: Brookings, 1987), pp. 211–14.

[42] This was a characteristic first noted by Lucian Pye in his *The Dynamics of Chinese Politics* (Cambridge, Mass.: Oelgeschlager, Gunn & Hain, 1981).

[43] See my "Deng Xiaoping: The Politician."

[44] See Harding, *China's Second Revolution*; Carol Lee Hamrin, *China and the Challenge of the Future: Changing Political Patterns* (Boulder: Westview Press, 1990); Nina Halpern, "Social Scientists as Policy Makers in Post-Mao China: Explaining the Patterns of Advice," *The Australian Journal of Chinese Affairs*, no. 19–20 (1988); A. Doak Barnett, *The Making of Foreign Policy in China* (Boulder: Westview Press, 1984); "Characteristics of Zhu Rongji's Think Tanks," *Xin Bao* (Hong Kong), January 15, 1999, in FBIS, *China-Daily Report,* January 20, 1999.

Another normative feature of elite politics – factionalism – has persisted in the post-Mao era, but its manifest forms and intensity have changed. With the exception of the remnant orthodox "leftists" and neo-Maoists, the parameters of elite factionalism have narrowed and a more centrist consensus across a range of policy issues is evident. Where factional differences have existed, they tend to be more a matter of degree in policy debates than of wholesale substance. When factionalism did emerge under Deng rule, such as when Zhao Ziyang split from the top leadership in 1989 or the Yang brothers connived to control the armed forces in 1991–93, they were effectively purged. The post-1989 leadership has been remarkably centrist and coherent. Those who veer too far from the center of the political spectrum risk removal from the leadership.

The relative absence of factions does not signify that patron-client networks did not continue to penetrate and crisscross the party, army, and state during the Deng period. In the upper echelons of the party there is clear evidence of clientalistic networks tied to both Jiang Zemin and Hu Yaobang. Li Peng built a strong following in the state apparatus, while General Zhang Zhen did the same in the military. Two of General Zhang's key clients, Zhang Wannian and Fu Quanyou, have themselves promoted networks of those aligned with them. Patron-client ties remain the *sine qua non* of Chinese politics, although it must also be recognized that rule and law-based procedures increasingly govern recruitment and retirement processes. Indeed, one of the most noteworthy normative changes of the Deng period was to establish more meritocratic criteria for selection and promotion of cadres. Clientalistic loyalties or factional affiliations are no longer the predominant criteria for professional advancement. Whether in the party, government, or military, specialized training and competence now matters. The technocrat reigns in post-Mao China.[45] Similarly, Deng instituted a system of regularized retirement for cadres, military officers, and enterprise managers.[46]

Thus, normatively, Deng Xiaoping set in motion several reforms that

---

[45] See Hong Yung Lee, *From Revolutionary Cadres to Party Technocrats in Socialist China* (Berkeley and Los Angeles: University of California Press, 1991); Li Cheng and Lynn White, "The Fifteenth Central Committee of the Chinese Communist Party: Full-Fledged Technocratic Leadership with Partial Control by Jiang Zemin," *Asian Survey*, vol. 38, no. 3 (March 1998); and my "The Fifteenth Party Congress: Technocrats in Command," *Issues & Studies* (January 1998).

[46] See Melanie Manion, *Retirement of Revolutionaries in China* (Princeton: Princeton University Press, 1993).

changed the ways in which the party-state functioned. These normative changes profoundly affected procedural aspects of state behavior. They have made the post-Mao state more efficient, responsive, and capable. These reforms may not be easily observable or measurable, but in the long run they have left a defining impact on the Chinese party-state and society.

In addition to these three aspects of the contemporary Chinese state, as Chapter 1 highlights, one must also consider several normative traditions and elements of rule that the communists inherited from their Confucian ancestors:

- There is an imperative of moral or virtuous (*de*) rule.
- Such rule was to be benevolent (*wangdao*) instead of coercive (*badao*), and hierarchical instead of diffuse.
- The state was to be unified and the society it governed stable.
- The elites that staffed the state apparat were to be carefully screened and selected.
- The state and its administrators were to adhere to a single guiding ideology, which they would be indoctrinated with through education and a variety of intermediary institutions.

Thus when one examines the Maoist and post-Maoist state one sees essential continuity with these Confucian precepts. In these important respects the Chinese state has changed little over the millennia.

These definitions must be borne in mind when considering both the continuities and the changes in the post-Mao party-state. When one examines the structural or spatial dimensions, more continuity is evident. But when the normative dimensions of state behavior are judged, change is more evident.

While the organizational changes have served to reduce the scope and power of the Chinese Communist party-state, the normative changes introduced under Deng have even further undermined it. On the one hand, the normative changes introduced have rescued the party-state from its previous moribund state, and have made it a party more responsive to its members and society. On the other hand, however, the normative changes have further eroded the party's capacity to rule society.

THE SPATIAL DIMENSION: STATE AND SOCIETY

Deng's reforms of the party-state were probably felt the most by the citizens of China. During the Maoist era, the reach and tyranny of the state grew to proportions unknown in Chinese history. No sectors or locales were immune to state intervention. The state attempted to regulate most aspects of the social, political, and economic life of the nation, and succeeded in doing so to remarkable degrees. Citizens were impacted on a daily and personal basis. Social engineering was carried out through an elaborate organizational network established by the Maoist state, as well as periodic mass campaigns. Both urban and rural China were caught up in the Great Maoist Experiments. Millions suffered, died, or were killed as a result. Nary a class went untouched – peasants, workers, intellectuals, cadres, soldiers, and minorities were all subjected to the Maoist state's machinations and repression. Even Mao's fellow leaders were attacked and purged during a unrelenting series of inner-party witchhunts – not the least of which was the Great Proletarian Cultural Revolution (1966–76), Communist China's equivalent to the Great Purges in the Soviet Union during the 1930s.

If one of the hallmarks of the Maoist state was the penetration of society, then the Dengist state was noticeable for its withdrawal. The organizational mechanisms of state penetration and manipulation were substantially reduced or dismantled altogether:[47] the "work unit" (*danwei*) in urban areas, the production brigade/team/commune in rural areas, party cells and branches in government and military units, neighborhood "residence" committees, and so on. Even the system designed to restrict and regulate the movement of population around the country – the *hukou* (residence permit) system – atrophied, resulting in large-scale migration of over 100 million rural residents into urban centers in search of work.

The withdrawal of the party-state from society can be seen in many ways. Many of these are obvious and visual. One no longer sees the uniformity of dress and conformity of behavior among citizens. The reduction in state control of the media and expansion of commerce has opened burgeoning entertainment and advertising industries. Discotheques, karaoke clubs, and concerts are now commonplace. Satellite television penetrates into many Chinese homes and the government has stopped jamming many foreign radio broadcasts as well, thus giving citizens an unprecedented "window on the world." Restrictions on foreign travel have been relaxed and several million Chinese have gone abroad (to be sure, still a miniscule percentage of the population). Opportunities to

---

[47] See Andrew G. Walder, "Social Structure and Political Authority," in Ramon Myers and Thomas Metzger, eds., *Two Societies in Opposition* (Stanford: Hoover Institution Press, 1991).

practice religion – both traditional Buddhism and Daoism as well as Christianity – are being grasped by many.

Commerce is the common denominator to much new social activity in China. Countless Chinese have taken the plunge into the commercial sea (*xiahai*), and have thereby taken up pursuits previously unimaginable – and now uncontrollable by the state. To be certain, not all such activity has been positive. Crime and corruption have flourished. Both an underworld and underclass have appeared. Hedonism and commercialism have replaced Maoist egalitarianism. A moral vacuum and ideological void exists in society. While hundreds of millions have had their lives improved, the benefits of growth have not been evenly distributed and many have not benefited from the boom. Of those who now live on the edge, many have slipped into lives of crime or destitution. Social stratification has increased markedly and, along with it, class jealousy. After decades of social leveling under Mao, class divisions reappeared under Deng.

As a result of declining state control over society, public discourse accompanied growing private freedoms. Citizens enjoy considerably more latitude to speak their minds in private and public – as long as they do not criticize the "Four Cardinal Principles" laid down by Deng: Marxism-Leninism-Mao Zedong Thought, the socialist road, the people's democratic dictatorship, and the supremacy of the CCP. As long as citizens do not directly criticize the party-state or its leadership, much is permissible. Invigorated public discourse has been noticeable in several spheres. The variety of coverage has increased markedly in newspapers, magazines, and books. As noted above, the publishing industry has flourished. Professional discourse has also improved and colleagues in many professions now share their ideas and findings through associations, meetings, and publications. The state no longer even attempts to control such discourse.

While a "public sphere" developed in Deng's China, the same cannot be said for civil society. If the test of civil society is the tolerance and sanctioning by the state of autonomous and enfranchised groups – including those with political agendas – this is where the post-Mao state drew the line. Certainly NGOs have proliferated in post-Mao China, but the Deng and Jiang government's approach was to coopt them and suppress any that had even a marginally political agenda. In some cases the government would create such organizations (GONGOs, or government-organized NGOs), and in all cases NGOs must register with the government and be sponsored by a state organ. Particularly in the wake of the collapse of communist party-states in Eastern Europe and the former Soviet Union, the Chinese Communist regime became convinced that the approval and allowance of any citizen-organized organizations outside of state cooptation or control would lead inexorably to the formation of organized political groups that would ultimately challenge Communist Party control. The example of Solidarity in Poland, and the effect it had on the ultimate demise of Communist Party control in that country, served only to reinforce this predisposition among the Chinese leadership. The arrests, imprisonment, and crackdown in 1998 on attempts of some activists to form a China Democracy Party is a clear indication that, after fifty years in power, the CCP is no closer to tolerating opposition.

In terms of human rights, the post-Mao state was simply more selective in its repression than its predecessor. That is, political rights were restricted for all under Mao. Under Deng and Jiang, the vast majority of citizens have enjoyed improved political participation (especially those in rural areas who benefited from village-level elections), but anyone who openly and directly challenges the state will quickly attract the attention of the state's coercive apparatus (although some promising signs of relaxation took place in 1997–98). Economic and social rights also markedly improved after Mao.

In sum, the "space" created between state and society in post-Mao China is a good measure of the profound changes in the nature of the state itself. Its writ is not large. By giving society such space, Deng succeeded in his goal of enlivening society and thereby unfettering cultural and commercial impulses. The direct beneficiaries have been the citizens of China, but the state has benefited indirectly as it has provided China with a new basis of legitimacy.

CONCLUSION

This chapter has outlined a number of ways in which the post-Mao state differed from its predecessor. We have noted that Deng, his colleagues, and successors undertook a number of structural, procedural, and normative reforms that resulted in the relative "withdrawal" of the party-state from its former dominant position. In other ways – particularly the organization of the party-army-state and its continued political hegemony – we have shown that the post-Mao and Maoist states share many commonalties and continuity. But few dispute that Deng changed more than he retained.

Where these changes leave the Chinese party-state is uncertain.

Harvey Nelsen explores some of the complexities in his contribution to this volume, but it seems to this observer that the shrinkage and withdrawal of the state, and the concomitant diversification of society, will make it extremely difficult for the single CCP party-state to survive. Its previous hegemony and control have eroded extensively and substantially. The continued refusal of the Chinese leadership to undertake any really meaningful political reforms (village-level elections notwithstanding) and to improve the transparency and accountability of the state does not bode well for its longevity.

There would appear to be two lessons here. The first is the example of many other developing and former socialist polities, whereby the political pressures for interest articulation grow and, along with them, the pressures for enfranchised civil society. If the state does not create such institutionalized channels for political articulation, frustrations build inexorably and politically explosive potential wells up from below, not unlike a steam generator without a pressure valve. Sooner or later the pressure erupts. The second lesson for the state is to try and preempt or co-opt such an explosion through the gradual sanctioning of civic groups and other institutionalized channels for political participation. These channels need not challenge the state, but rather permit demands for increased public goods to be expressed. As economies grow and wealth accumulates, the citizenry increasingly demands better quality of life – better health care, education, environment, public infrastructure, and so on. If the channels to articulate such demands are cut off by the state, opposition grows and the state and ruling party themselves become its object. Yet, if the state moves to create such channels, it could just as easily trigger a slippery slide to its overthrow, as the state is unable or uninterested in meeting such social demands.

Such is the dilemma confronting the post-Deng Chinese state: politically reform or fall from power *or* politically reform and still fall from power. The choice for the Chinese state today may not yet be so stark, but there is no mistake that pressure is building. If and when the CCP's hegemonic grip on state power ends in China, qualitative change should certainly be expected – and most likely in a more liberal direction – but no doubt many aspects of the post-communist Chinese state elucidated in this volume will endure. Certainly the challenges of governance that have confronted and bedeviled the Chinese state (indeed all states) over time – demographic pressures; poverty reduction; welfare provision; full employment; revenue collection; provision of public goods, social order, infrastructure, and other investment; national security; and other responsibilities – will remain. Other new challenges, such as environmental protection, have arisen. In the twenty-first century the Chinese state will be confronted with unprecedented challenges of governance. To meet these challenges the Chinese state must recognize a fundamental fact: many of these responsibilities and challenges are better managed by the market, by NGOs, by subcentral state actors, and by Chinese citizens themselves. The central state may be more of an obstacle than a solution to these challenges.

6

The Chinese Communist
Economic State
in Comparative Perspective

JAN PRYBYLA

THE aim of the communism that was implemented over vast areas of the world in this century (the real thing, not intellectual or *salon* communism) was to bring about a seamless unity of the state's official belief system, state monopoly of political and military power, state-prescribed social norms and relations, state-defined culture, and, importantly, state ownership, control, and management of the economy – in short, to bring into being a monolithic totalitarian state: all-embracing and omnipotent, a oneness of state and society. Allowing for temporal, regional, and national variations, the institutions of the state itself (party, government, police, the judiciary, the military, mass organizations, economic planning apparatus) were highly hierarchical, commandist, centralized, pervasive, and pathogenically bureaucratized.

The totalitarian ideal was never fully attained – in China especially, localism continued to exert its traditional influence – but most variants of real socialism came very close to it at one time or another, in some instances over extended periods. To gain total control of the economy, which is what concerns us here, the communist state in almost every case had to tackle a double task: physical rebuilding of an economy ravaged by war and/or civil conflict and a restructuring (reform) from first principles of key economic institutions, primarily of the mechanism of allocation and coordination, and the system of property rights. In almost every case the first task proved to have been the easier of the two. Thus in China, by 1952 the physical infrastructure of agriculture, industry, and trade had been for the most part repaired and in some instances improved compared with the pre-World War II peak years. Institutional reform not only took longer, but its modalities and path were more complex and tortuous, ending in the 1980s with abandonment of the original communist objective of total state ownership and control and management of the economy by the monoparty state, thus illustrating, some say, with appropriate adjustments, the Chinese circular conception of history. In China, too, the heritage of regionalism, localism, familism, factionalism, and networking has exerted a persistent influence on current policies. It has been instrumental in preserving age-old cellular and centrifugal forces and propensities within society despite the totalitarian character of the state organization and the mind-shackling quality of the party's creed, now badly, perhaps irretrievably tattered.[1]

The path and modalities of the Chinese communist state's seizure of and eventual partial retreat from the economy were also affected by the party's early history of armed opposition in remote border areas (e.g., agrarian and military communism), the chastening lessons learned during the tenure of economic power (e.g., the destructive effect on the economy of "politics in command," the fatal error of logic inherent in the notion of central physical planning), and the idiosyncracies of the leading personalities in charge of the movement in its early and later stages (Mao, Deng). In communist China, as in the former Soviet Union, conclusions from the bitter lessons of experience with the system could not be fully drawn and implemented until the chief architects (Mao, Stalin) had been embalmed. In the ex-Soviet Union such conclusions were theoretically defective because they did not address the root cause of the systemic problem, which was the paralyzing effect on the economy of total state dominance. So nothing was done beyond rhetoric of the *glasnost* and *perestroika* variety, plus some formulaic Kosyginistic patching-up and tinkering with the parts, until the whole edifice collapsed in 1991 from dry rot in the foundations, thirty-seven years after Stalin's death. By contrast, China's initial disenchantment with the Soviet model (1956), subsequent deterioration of Sino-Soviet relations, and the shocks administered to the economy and the bureaucracy individually and severally by the Great Leap Forward and the Cultural Revolution concentrated Chinese apparatchiks' minds on the real issue of structural defects, resulting in market-oriented systemic reform a little more than two years after Mao's passing, and in the world's most dynamic, market-tending, developing economy not long thereafter.

---

[1] Yu-ming Shaw (ed.), *Tendencies of Regionalism in Contemporary China* (Taipei: Institute of International Relations, National Chengchi University, 1997).

SOCIALIST CONSTRUCTION

Laying the Foundations (1949–1952)

Communist China's leftward journey from what the regime called a semi-feudal, semicolonial, embryonically capitalist economy to neo-Stalinism (1953–57), then on to an extreme left variant of Stalinism (the Great Leap Forward, 1958–60), and later to Mao's *chef d'oeuvre*, the organized chaos of the Cultural Revolution (1966–(69)–76), was preceded by a spell of destructive construction (1949–52) which laid the groundwork and cleared the way for a Soviet-type economic polity. It was a period of ruthless mass movements that covered land reform (stopping short of advanced collectivization), confiscation of the Nationalist regime's "Chinese bureaucrat" and foreign industrial and commercial capital, the initial socialization of domestic industry, trade, and handicrafts (e.g., elementary and advanced state capitalism, supply and marketing cooperatives, handicraft producers' cooperatives), and their liquidation and full nationalization following the "Three-Anti" (*san fan*) and "Five-Anti" (*wu fan*) terror campaigns of 1951–52, takeover of the banking system, restoration of fiscal order through reorganization of the tax system, and centralization of fiscal powers. Each mass campaign resulted in the taming, cooptation, socioeconomic demonization, and neutering or outright killing of the regime's actual, real, imagined, suspected, or potential enemies, miscreants, and infiltrators beyond redemption, paranoically classified into several hostile classes ("people outside the people" who "deserved to die"). This groundbreaking for Soviet-style "socialism with Chinese characteristics" went by the political name of "new democracy." It was envisaged as an antechamber enabling economically under developed China to skip the fullness of the capitalist stage with its parliamentary ("bourgeois") democracy, and proceed directly to socialism by 1953. In an ideological aside, it was conceded thirty and some years later that this conceptual leap forward represented an idealistic and subjectivist misreading of Marx's historical *Stufenlehre*. It was, therefore, necessary to correct the mistake, backtrack, and pass through a bit of capitalist unpleasantness, the politically correct name for which would be "socialist market economy." But by then hardly anybody was listening. Something like a new democratic entranceway to socialism, but at the upper end of capitalism, known as "people's democracy," equipped with elementary cooperatives, phony political parties, and other united front appurtenances, was present in 1945–49 in the Central and East European countries taken over by the Soviet armies.

Although today all this reads like touring an old ideological curiosity shop, it was taken very seriously in its time by leaders, people, and scholars alike, for excellent reasons. One of them was that the impulse, repeatedly indulged in during Mao's lifetime, to pit the mobilized collective will against the evidence of facts, to disdain and dismiss evolutionary change and leap into the future, compounded what Hayek had diagnosed as the fundamental error of logic of the socialist system concerning the nature of economic information and the key role of (private) property, and that this compound affected the everyday lives of millions of people with dire personal and social consequences. Unfortunately, for decades, even as evidence to the contrary was piling up, many politicians and even more academics in the West supported not only the Marxist fatal conceit but the leaping twist given to it by the Maoist "misreading" (Franz Michael was an outstanding and lonely exception to this rule). By the end of 1952, industry, handicrafts, and trade (both foreign and domestic), but not agriculture, were in state hands either directly or through the agency of state-subservient cooperatives. After China's entry into the Korean war (October 1950) foreign trade was redirected toward the Soviet Union and Eastern Europe (almost 70 percent of the total in 1952) as part of an emerging policy of "leaning to one side." By 1955 practically all foreign equity participation in Chinese industry had been ended and the situation did not change until 1979, when the restriction was considerably eased.

It was during 1949–52 and for a few years thereafter that the basic agencies of nationwide political governance and state control of the economy were fashioned and honed. Three influences were at work: the organizational structures inherited from the republican and imperial past (continuity), administrative experience gained in the "old liberated [mostly rural] areas" since 1931 (innovation), and the example of the Soviet Union, particularly with respect to the public security apparatus, the central planning commission, and the functional, "branch" ministerial principle of industrial organization (imitation). The last was arguably adopted because at the time the Soviet Stalinist strategy of rapid industrialization was thought to have been effective, especially in its concentration on capital goods industries with military applications, and because it was seen as doctrinally correct and politically expedient – Stalin's definition of socialism was dogma (except in Yugoslavia), and realistically, in the political climate of the time, the USSR was China's only potential supplier of financial and technical assistance. The three influences on the choice of governmental institutions reappear in the future, albeit with different relative emphases put on continuity, innovation, and imitation, depending on the period.

Initially, out of necessity, and again after 1968 (also from necessity) the task of day-to-day government in China devolved, by and large, to the People's Liberation Army. The principal instruments used at the local level were the military control commissions, provisional bodies charged with establishing social order, screening former Nationalist officials, punishing political undesirables, and organizing more permanent "local people's governments" at the village (*xiang*), market town/township (*zhen*), and county (*xian*) levels. At first the commissions were staffed with military personnel trained in civil administration, later replaced by civilian party members. Concurrently, the top leadership set up some eighty central state (national) ministries and organized the higher reaches of regional government at the level of provinces (*sheng*), autonomous national minorities regions (*zi zhi qu,* August 1952), larger cities (special municipalities), municipalities (*shi*), special districts, and districts (*qu*). Property rights of territorial government units below the central state ministries were very limited until 1957 when important operational rights, including some decisions on the acquisition, use, and disposal of assets, were transferred from the top to lower-level governmental units with the intention of reducing the rigidity of the system and removing from the shoulders of central planners and their immediate subordinates the national ministries, burdens they were not well equipped to carry. Until June 1954, use was also made of six Great Regional Administrations/Councils (paralleled by six regional bureaus of the party organization, abolished in 1954, revived in 1961–62, and removed again in 1967) whose task was to supervise, on behalf of the central leadership, the work of provincial people's governments in their respective regions.

The whole system was given the chop of approval in September 1949 by the Chinese People's Political Consultative Conference (CPPCC), predecessor of the National People's Congress that came into being five years later. The CPPCC consisted of 662 delegates drawn from the Communist Party and its satellite formations, the regions, army, and mass organizations. Included also were seventy-five "specially invited personalities," among them Mme. Sun Yat-sen and members of the Guomindang peace delegation who had gone over to the communist side. Thus, in conformity with the theory of new democracy, the CPPCC and the

Central People's Government Council (the predecessor of the State Council) contained some domesticated noncommunist formations which made the system into what the theory said it was: a united front of all those who could be united under communist leadership and control. The semblance of popular participation reached down to the provincial and local (municipal and county) levels through the establishment of "All-Circle People's Representative Conferences," members of which were elected, that is, selected by the Communist Party leadership from among mass organizations and "democratic parties" composed of remolded or semiremolded intellectuals, compliant businessmen, technical experts, and so on. After the emergence of the National People's Congress in 1954, the CPPCC became an assisted living home for the democratic parties, a consultative body with little power, advisory or otherwise.

On the available evidence, the governmental institutions erected during the years of reconstruction and institutional reform (1949–52) and carried over to the First Five-Year Plan (1953 57), when some of them underwent modifications and rounding-off (e.g., the establishment of rural production brigades and teams as units of advanced collective farms roughly corresponding to the township and village levels of government), performed as expected by its architects. Despite the diversion of resources to the Korean conflict (1950–53), rehabilitation of the economy from the ravages of warlordism, Japanese despoliation, and civil conflict was accomplished under the regime of governmental institutions created during the early years of the People's Republic. Their ruthless thoroughness combined with the weariness of a people subjected for decades to the dislocations and horrors of war was instrumental in the establishment of a degree of order and social stability indispensable to the work of physical reconstruction and systemic reform.

Soviet-Type Socialism (1953–57)

The period of the First Five-Year Plan (1953–57) was devoted to the construction in China of a Sinified adaptation of the Soviet Stalinist (1929–53) economic edifice, which by the time it was completed in 1956 was judged by Stalin's successors as being in need of thorough inspection, if not structural overhaul. The basic characteristics of the Soviet Stalinist economic model are well known.[2] The four supporting and

[2] Eugene Zaleski, *Stalinist Planning for Economic Growth, 1933–1952* (Chapel Hill: University of North Carolina Press, 1980); Naum Jasny, *Soviet Industrialization, 1928–1952* (Chicago: University of Chicago Press, 1961).

mutually reinforcing pillars are: (1) quasi-total nationalization of the means of production and distribution (either directly or through surrogate collectives), and abolition of the market and its prices as the economy's allocative and coordinating mechanism; (2) pursuit of rapid, forced, extensive, and selective, that is, highly imbalanced, growth emphasizing producer goods industries and slighting services and agriculture, the latter to the point of peonage; (3) austerity resulting from a deliberate neglect of consumption imposed by the plan's strategy of heavy industrialization carried out almost exclusively from domestic forced savings (extracted primarily, but not exclusively, from the collectivized peasantry) and fueled by very high rates of investment: "Steel was a final good to Stalin, and bread an intermediate one," as Abram Bergson aptly put it; and (4) national autarky, which when combined with the emphasis on extensive growth, that is, growth resulting from additions of technically unimproved factors rather than from technologically and organizationally based improvements in factor productivity, eventually produced an atrophy of innovation and loss of competitiveness on world markets.

Although each pillar contributed through its structural defects to the collapse of the much patched-up communist economic edifice, the weakest of them was the first: the substitution of bureaucratic resource allocation/coordination and state property for market rationing/coordination and private property, which as von Mises and Hayek had argued long before, made economic calculation impossible in the planned system. Lacking this compass the decision makers hadn't a clue where they were going, and without a reliable measuring rod of costs and benefits the system toward its end became value-subtracting, that is, irrational without being aware of it. The cost of inputs in market terms exceeded the price of outputs, the difference being made up by state subsidies. That's no way to run a business. But it was the way, with Soviet expert assistance and a few loans, that the Chinese chose to follow in 1953, in part from a lack of acceptable alternatives ready to hand.

Both unfortunately, if judged by what followed in 1958 and 1966, and fortunately for China when looked at in a longer-term perspective stretching beyond 1978, at the very time China set out on the Stalinist path to industrialization, Stalin died. Once they were sure he would not rise from the dead (ca. 1954–55), his successors in the Soviet Union and Eastern Europe began to discuss more openly, albeit superficially, the shortcomings of the Stalinist way. In East Berlin, Poznan, Warsaw, and Budapest (1953, 1956) the reconsideration was prompted in large measure by popular uprisings. Actually, the Chinese neo-Stalinist First Five-Year Plan was not ready to be put into effect until 1955, and by then everybody had second thoughts about Stalinist economics.

If the first propagandistic statistical compendium, the *Ten Great Years,* is to be believed (after the publication of which in 1960 China fell numerically silent for more than twenty years), the results of the First Five-Year Plan were gratifying compared with the initial output levels and the Stalinist institutional agenda.[3] But there were problems due to the dawning realization (1) that the Soviet model was inherently flawed in its reliance on physical/engineering-type criteria expressed in weights and measures on both the input and output sides, an error which, among others, produced perverse incentives to workers and managers and encouraged cheating on a systemic scale; (2) that the model could not be transplanted to China in its entirety because of China's different factor endowments and level of development compared with the Soviet Union at a comparable period; (3) that there was the already mentioned loss of confidence in Stalinism in general and Stalinist economics in particular, and the increasingly strained interstate and interparty relations between China and the USSR; and (4) that there existed a related Chinese desire to find a nativist solution to the problem of development, combined with Mao's determination to force the rate of socialist transformation beyond even Stalin's febrile teleology.

The later acerbic debates between the Chinese and Soviet leaderships were foreshadowed by factional strife among China's elites, referred to during the doctrinal reexaminations of the 1980s as the "two-line struggle." The growing disagreements, many of which revolved around issues of economic philosophy, were hidden from public view until 1957, officially the terminal year of China's First Five-Year Plan. It is interesting to note with reference to point (2) above, that collectivization of agriculture, an indispensable component of the Stalinist model of industrialization, because it was the mechanism which extruded agricultural surpluses from an impoverished peasantry for investment in heavy industry ("squeezing blood from a turnip," as Stalin phrased it), was not carried out in China until 1956. When it occurred, the process took just one year (1955–56: the "Little Great Leap"). In the Soviet Union herding the peasants into *kolkhozy* took the better part of a decade. Soviet collectivization had been bloodier and attended by a manmade famine of horrific

---

[3] Jan S. Prybyla, *The Political Economy of Communist China* (Scranton, Pa.: International Textbook Company, 1970), pp. 116–223.

proportions, not matched in China until the aftermath of the Great Leap Forward (1958–60). The main class enemies, the landlords and "rich peasants," had been either physically wiped out or socioeconomically neutralized in China during the land reform movement of the early 1950s, before the advanced collectivization of 1955–56, whereas the slaughter of the Ukrainian and Russian *kulaks* was carried out concurrently with the Soviet collectivization drive. Almost as soon as all the building blocks of the Chinese Stalinist model were in place, the model was abandoned.

The rejection began during the "liberal interlude," a brief and far from torrid affair with markets, modest private property (household plots in the countryside), somewhat enlarged autonomy for local governments and enterprise managements, material incentives, less class struggle, greater openness to the outside world, and marginally more freedom of thought and expression for the intellectuals (the Hundred Flowers campaign). The interlude lasted from September 1956 to early June 1957. It was dominated by the party's economic moderates, many of whom were later branded as "capitalist roaders." The tone was one of relative moderation and pragmatism based on the belief that the disproportions, rigidities, inconsistencies, and shortages of the Stalinist Juggernaut that had just been rolled out could be fixed by rectifying the party's and government organs' "style of work," that "you could make a totalitarian regime acceptable simply by rectifying the conduct of those who held power," and by pushing the economy a little to the right.[4]

Beneath the calm surface of the liberal interlude there was much leadership controversy, which toward the end of 1956 unfolded in the shadow of the Polish and Hungarian challenges to communist dictatorship. In a regime whose mindset rejects the give-and-take of opinions, the probability is strong that disagreements on policy will at some point be personalized, criminalized, and that the losers will pay a stiff price for their deviance. One subject of contention concerned the very substance and role of government organizations in the new socialist order under construction. The well-defined and rigid hierarchical lines of authority among government administrations and between the party and government, and the less visible, but real and important informal networks of interpersonal power relations, indeed, the very necessity of bureaucratic structures, began to be questioned by the more radical elements in the leadership who had the ear of a Mao become more than ever suspicious

---

[4] Roderick MacFarquhar, ed., *The Hundred Flowers Campaign and the Chinese Intellectuals* (New York: Praeger, 1960), p. 13.

and intolerant of largely imaginary plots, cabals, and "revisionist" stray-ings from the socialist road. The 1957 administrative refurbishings men-tioned earlier reduced the number of central ministries by roughly two-thirds, and with few exceptions (e.g., defense-related industry) removed from the survivors the bulk of responsibility for detailed plan-ning and supervision within their areas of competence.

Maoism I: The Great Leap Forward (1958–1960)

The relatively moderate tone and, within the accepted ideological para-meters, comparative reasonableness of the *Proposals for the Second Five-Year Plan (1958–62)*, which emerged from the party's Eighth National Congress (September 1956, one month before the Polish uprising and the Hungarian revolution) were thrown out with the launching on June 8, 1957, of the Anti-Rightist Campaign, a cataclysmic mind-cleansing recti-fication movement, and the four mass campaigns that comprised the Great Leap Forward: the mobilization of peasants for water conserva-tion and flood control work, a nationwide drive for tool improvement by poor and lower-middle peasants, construction of millions of local small-scale labor-intensive workshops (the "five small industries," better known as the backyard furnaces campaign), and the creation in the summer and fall of 1958 of 26,000 giant rural people's communes (farms, basic units of state power in the countryside, and "schools of communism" rolled into one) out of the 740,000 collective farms set up less than two years earlier. These were the four elements of Mao's Great Leap alternative to the economic moderates' *Proposals* and to what he considered to have been a too structured and bureaucratized Soviet model, the pace of which he found too slow and the scope too restricted for China to reach full communism in his lifetime. Besides, segments of the bureaucracy, looming larger in his mind than they were in reality, were seen by Mao as presenting a threat to the absolutism of his rule. They had to be continually shaken up by intraparty permanent revolutions that involved refined personal cruelties and humiliations.[5] Shortly after it began, the Leap ended in a disaster the magnitude of which was missed in the West.

The Great Leap was Maoist thought applied to the economy. Parts of it, its autarky and egalitarianism for one (excluding Mao's personal

---

[5] Li Zhisui, *The Private Life of Chairman Mao: The Memoirs of Mao's Personal Physician* (New York: Random House, 1994).

entourage at one end, and nonpeople at the other), reach back to the guerrilla days of the border regions and Yanan. Its extraordinary primitivism mirrors Mao's ignorance of economics – exceeded only by Pol Pot – part and parcel of the autodidact's larger lack of erudition and his anti-intellectualism. But in other respects (although even in its crudity and economic illiteracy) the Leap was the left side of Stalinism. The leaping itself finds precedents in Stalin's repeated "stormings" (*shturmovshchiny*). The accent put on steel ("taking steel production as the core and achieving a comprehensive leap forward"), if not the minimalist way of producing it in homemade furnaces, was vintage Stalinism. Not least, the "awful mess" (Liu Shaoqi's phrase), made by the leaping was a Stalinist norm. Despite talk about grain being the "key link," the peasants' main preoccupation during the period was with making what turned out to be unusable "native" steel, inventing deep plows that worked only under specific topographical and soil conditions, and digging ditches from nowhere to nowhere. Little time was left for planting and harvesting. The whole operation was carried out at breakneck speed in a theoretical, institutional, and statistical near-vacuum. Instead of the output of 300 million metric tons of grain projected for 1962 (Mao aimed for 475 million tons), actual grain production in 1962 came to 155 million tons (143 million tons and 147.5 million tons in 1960 and 1961, respectively, compared with 195 million tons in 1957). Steel production for 1962 was planned at 12 million metric tons (5.6 million tons of actual output in 1957). Production in 1962 was 6 million tons. Much of the 19 million tons of steel turned out in the peak year 1960 was "native" and unusable. The following year steel output fell to 8.7 million tons, and a large portion of that was useless.[6]

The attempt to "telescope" the transition to full communism had a paralyzing effect on state institutions because of the upheaval it created among governmental organizations and the disarray it caused in the ranks of their routine-bound occupants now abruptly detached from their desks and sent to do earthwork in the countryside. At the height of

---

[6] Yuan-Li Wu, *Tiananmen to Tiananmen: China Under Communism 1947–1996. After Disillusionment a Nation at a Crossroads* (Baltimore: University of Maryland School of Law, Occasional Papers/Reprint Series in Contemporary Asian Studies, No. 1, 1997), p. 130. Figures based on data provided by Bo Yibo, former head of the National Economic Commission, in *Ruogan Zhongda Juece yu Shijian de Huigu* [*Certain Major Decisions and Events in Retrospect*], 2 vols. (Beijing: CCP Central Party School Press, 1991, 1993). On the Great Leap-caused famine, see Jasper Becker, *Hungry Ghosts: China's Secret Famine* (London: John Murray, 1996).

the Leap the staff of the State Statistical Bureau was reduced to half a dozen active professionals in what was a centrally planned economy where statistics on all manner of physical and financial phenomena were supposed to take the place of the guiding and coordinating job done by spontaneously generated prices in a market economy. Monumental resource misallocations and ecological damage resulted. In addition, Stalinesque gigantism of the newly created rural people's communes, the disrepute in which material incentives were officially held ("economism"), and excessive egalitarianism in the distribution of mostly psychic rewards posed managerial problems of gargantuan dimensions. The partial administrative decentralization crafted during the liberal interlude turned into a disorderly runaway happening, an administrative fractioning by default. Whereas in 1957 (1952 price basis) 46 percent of the gross value of industrial output was attributable to enterprises under central control and 56 percent to locally controlled firms, in 1959 centrally run enterprises produced only 26 percent of total industrial output and half of heavy industrial production (1952 price basis). The figures, even if assumed to reflect very roughly the actual orders of magnitude (a heroic assumption given the statistical situation of the time), probably understate the effective central control over industrial output in 1959 due to the breakdown of communications between the center and the production front. As for local administrations in charge of the other half of heavy industry and of 74 percent of the output value of all industry, the situation was later captured by the author of "Evening Chats" (*Beijing Evening News*, June 22, 1961) in a historical simile overtly referring to the reign of Empress Dowager Ming Su: "The local officials lower down did exactly as they pleased."

Readjustment to the Right (1961–(1962)–1965)

The "awful mess" created by pushing Maoist Stalinism to its left extreme had to be cleaned up. This began to be done, albeit gingerly, by the bureaucratic machine after the July 1959 Lushan meeting of the Central Committee and continued, not without constant challenges and interference from Mao and the party's left-wing zealots, after the Central Committee Plenum in September 1962 at which Mao resurrected the topics of class struggle, income inequality, and revisionism. "The policy of readjustment, consolidation, filling-out, and raising standards," as this second relatively liberal interlude was called, followed five general guidelines: restoration of farm production and institutional order in agriculture

("agriculture as the foundation"), a more balanced development of industry ("industry as the leading factor"), reassertion of central planning and control, attenuation of class struggle, and retreat from domestic autarky (though not from calls for self-reliance).

The rural people's communes were dissolved in fact, if not in name; private plots of commune members were reintroduced together with family production quotas and assignments of land to individual families – precursors of the household production responsibility system of the late 1970s. Primary markets in rural areas were revived in the fall of 1960, the grain tax was reduced, and the "three levels of ownership" (production team, brigade, commune) were consolidated, the smallest of them, the production team, becoming the basic planning, production, and accounting unit. The abortive attempt to introduce a "free supply"-type (i.e., gratis) system of income distribution was dumped, and piecework wages based on assessment of "work points" for given tasks (differential material incentives) were reintroduced. Most of the backyard furnaces were axed out of existence, and numerous small coal mines, fertilizer plants, homemade power generating stations, and other political "baby plants" met the same fate.

First place was given to light industry and handicrafts, which supplied the countryside with articles of daily use, small farm tools, and building materials, and earned foreign exchange into the bargain. Investment in heavy industry, especially steel, was to be trimmed. Material incentives, intersectoral balance, internal consistency, and feasibility became the order of the day. The exodus from the land during the First Five-Year Plan and the Great Leap was to be reversed by not recruiting workers from the countryside for three years and by sending back home those young people who had left the farms (the Educated Youth to the Countryside movement). The back-to-the-land population transfer smacked of Maoism. It was, however, engineered by the bureaucratic "moderates" for practical economic reasons: to raise the educational and technical level of the countryside (no more inventions by class-correct but illiterate peasants) and to lessen the danger of urban unemployment and overcrowding. At the same time it found approval with the leadership leftists who liked mass movements in principle and saw this one, as all the past and future ones, almost exclusively in ideological terms. For them, the transfer would remove impressionable young people from the "bourgeois" allurements of the cities and distance them from the ideologically unremolded urban school teachers. This seemed all the more urgent because at the time ascendant bureaucratic revisionists were removing from some intellectuals rightist labels stuck on them during the Anti-Rightist Campaign of 1957. At the same time, sending educated young people to the countryside would raise the youngsters' revolutionary consciousness and temper them by daily association with the laboring peasant masses. Instead of using their heads, they would learn through their calloused hands ("learning by doing").

That the economic shift to the right, that is, toward markets and private property, was in the nature of an emergency measure, a band-aid, not a systemic reform – it began to lose momentum and then to retreat under a renewed onslaught from the left as early as 1963 – is .perhaps best brought out by the reemergence of central planning and reassertion of central control over agriculture and industry. Although not intended to be a return to the bureaucratic centralization of the neo-Stalinist First Five-Year Plan period, but rather to the decentralization principles of 1957 combining central government supervision through economic accounting (the Soviet *khozrsaschet*) with wider operational decision-making discretion at the enterprise level and reduction in local party control over economic activities, the 1961–65 readjustment remained, nevertheless, well within the right of center, red technocrat – almost Brezhnevian – understanding of real socialism's economic orthodoxy. It was certainly not, as was later alleged by the triumphant leftists, a symptom of deep-seated "capitalist-roading" tendencies among leaders of the Liu Shaoqi and Deng Xiaoping ilk. To inject some sanity into the chaotic farm situation created by the communes, the Agricultural Bank of China was revived in 1963, placed directly under the State Council, and instructed to take charge of the communes and production teams in addition to its normal functions of extending interest-bearing loans and advancing funds for compulsory procurements of farm produce. Simultaneously reflecting perhaps pressures from the party's left, bank officials were to go down to the farms, immerse themselves in poor peasant culture, and develop political organs at the *xian* level and above.

To indulge for a second in the "what if?" school of historical thinking: what if Mao had been mummified at that point? It is conceivable, but not very likely, that in that event the intrasystemic adjustment might have evolved into real intersystemic reform, as it did in Mao's absence after 1978, with the same leading personnel in charge, minus those murdered in the meantime. However, for the seeds of capitalist thinking to mature in the minds of Mao's coterie, the big bang and personal shock of the Cultural Revolution were probably necessary. Even then, habits of the Leninist mind, Stalinist temper, and Maoist heart remained in evidence in both Deng's and his successor's attitude not only with respect to the privatization of property rights (reluctant) but, and especially so, toward the authoritarian governance of the political environment of the economy (enthusiastic).

What economic rationality had been introduced during this period began to unravel after 1963. Until then, but particularly during the immediate post-Leap famine emergency (1961–62), the economic policy makers took the stance of class reconciliation and attenuation of the Leap's autarky. The last took the form of a tentative trade opening to the nonsocialist world, which was in large measure a function of the rapidly deteriorating Chinese state and party relations with the Soviet Union. Leaning to one side was terminated and replaced by a new policy of leaning to all sides, Third World included.

The moderately revisionist shift to the right in the wake of the backward consequences of the Great Leap Forward began to come to an end with the leftist Socialist Education Campaign designed during the September 1962 Tenth Plenary Session of the Eighth Central Committee at which Mao urged his colleagues not to forget class struggle. The campaign was launched in the spring of the following year. It was the opening salvo and dress rehearsal for the apocalyptic Great Proletarian Cultural Revolution. It consisted of several smaller but extremely venomous campaigns directed at party intellectuals (e.g., the "one divides into two, and two combine into one" denunciation of the idea – two combine into one – of class reconciliation as a permanent feature of socialist society); the campaign for the whole nation to learn from the People's Liberation Army radicalized since 1959 under the command of Lin Biao; the village Socialist Education Campaign, which included the printing in 1965 alone of more than 12 million village compendia of Mao's thoughts; the politicization of experimental plots and farms; cultural reform of the Peking opera and literature ("Replace Old Things with New"); campaign for part-work, part-study schools and for spare-time education and research; and several production campaigns based on the principle that economics is the handmaid of politics and politics is summed up in the thought of Mao (e.g., the Agriculture Learns from Dazhai and Industry Learns from Daqing campaigns). Included also was a decision to construct new defense-related factories in the more inaccessible regions of the country's interior and to move there, from coastal and central China, feeder plants as well as important factories of which only one of a kind existed in the country. Known as the strategy of the Third Front, the relocation (which ended only in 1972) was in some ways a Stalinist phenomenon in its massive transplantations, feverish pace, wasteful overinvestment in capital-intensive industries, and negative side-effects on consumption. In 1962 the per capita output index (1957 = 100) was 81 for grain, 45 for edible vegetable oil, 43 for pork, and 54 for cotton cloth.[7] By September 1965 the stage was set for the official opening of the apocalyptic drama of the Cultural Revolution.

Maoism II: The Cultural Revolution (1966–(1969)–1976)

To borrow a phrase, the Cultural Revolution was the "mother" of all mass campaigns. As its name suggests, it was aimed primarily at the super-structure of ideas, specifically at incorrect thinking by intellectuals and revisionists, that is, anti-Mao thinking by bureaucrats, but it had impor-tant repercussions on the economy, most of them disruptive. There is no doubt that personal vendetta verging on paranoia, acute mean-spiritedness, and lack of human decency were the cause, as they had been in Stalin's terrors of the 1930s, '40s, and early '50s, and as it is with any dictator, however great or dictatorial, who wields unlimited power. But, as is *de rigueur* in such circumstances, more elevated reasons were adduced for the benefit of the Chinese masses, the young especially, and friends abroad, many of whom waxed lyrical about the ingenious novelty and virtues of this atrocity. Socialism, went the Maoist argument, was being corroded from within by top party and government persons in authority "taking the capitalist road." They and their followers, however mighty or humble, were to be dragged out, publicly debased, and cast into the outer darkness. The slate had to be wiped clean of all ideologi-cal deviants, indeed, of all accretions of the past, so that a new society could be built on foundations made from Mao's thought. The Great Leap Forward failed, went the argument, not because its economics was wrong, but because people's minds, especially those of the leaders, Liu Shaoqi, "China's Khrushchev," in the lead, were not ready to receive it. With due respect to Marx, the dialectical motor of history was to be found not in the economic base of society – the material productive forces and rela-tions of production – but in revolutionary ideas expounded by Chairman Mao. Hegel, whom Marx had turned on his head, was put by Mao back on his feet again. Dialectical idealism was in command.

The Cultural Revolution peaked in 1969, but its aftershocks continued until after the death of Mao and the arrest and trial of the Gang of Four

---

[7] Wu, *Tiananmen to Tiananmen*, p. 145, citing Bo Yibo.

in 1976. Its negative economic consequences were due not only to the institutional chaos it had caused but to the new institutions it built on the rubble. During its most intensive years (1966–69), ending with the Ninth National Congress in April 1969, the planning and statistical apparats rebuilt during the previous interlude of economic readjustment hit the dust again. Indeed, the state bureaucracy as a whole – the surrogate in centrally planned socialism for the signaling, rationing, and macro-coordinating functions of opportunity-cost prices in a market system – was thrown into utter confusion, and the institutional structure of the party-state – of both the party and the state – was for all practical purposes reduced to ashes. The remnants of old government cadres accused of "economism" were soon at loggerheads with parallel leftist Cultural Revolution groups run by Mao's people who preached endemic stoicism. A disorganized decentralization of economic organization by default followed once more.

The economic philosophy of the Cultural Revolution was synthesized in the "Anshan Constitution," a document reportedly drawn up by Mao himself in 1968, and its rural equivalent, the Dazhai Work Point System. The Anshan edict required politics to be "in command" of all work; worker participation in management and management participation in physical labor; worker innovation; and abolition of "reactionary rules and regulations." These instructions went in tandem with the slogan "Better Troops, Simpler Administration" launched by Mao in the spring of 1968. The idea was to downsize overstaffed departments, eradicate bureaucratic habits of mind through public struggle and criticism (abuse), and eliminate the expert-above-the-masses mentality and other poisonous weeds of new class elitism. The way to achieve this was to dispatch large numbers of cadres, managers, technicians, experts, bureaucrats, officials, and uppity educated youngsters to the countryside where they would have to learn new habits, manners, and ethics from poor and lower-middle peasants. The movement was soon transformed into a massive outflow from the cities, joining and adding millions of former Red Guards (who, as Mao informed them in July 1968, had disappointed him) to the flow of young people already in progress. The Anshan and Better Troops initiatives were antibureaucratic but also anti-intellectual and anti-expert in spirit, Maoist in their emphasis on the inventive capacity of the masses and in their scorn for material incentives lumped together with other reactionary rules, regulations, and admittedly bloated bureaucratic structures.

Under the Dazhai system, commune members' performance was to be evaluated not only, or even mainly, in terms of the amount (never mind quality) of work done, but by the degree of the workers' revolutionary spirit. But how was this to be computed? Through connections (*guanxi*)? One suggested way was to make periodic awards based on scales established by revolutionary pacesetters, which still left the question unanswered. Hidden class enemies who despite twenty years of proletarian vigilance had managed to conceal their family backgrounds and forge family records were to be dragged out and banished. Private plots of commune members were to be reduced in size and then eliminated, the objective being the total socialization of the country's productive property structure ("Two privately owned chickens = capitalism; one privately owned chicken = socialism"). The slogan of commune self-reliance was revived and peasants were ordered to pay for their own medical insurance, schools, and agricultural machinery stations, on top of absorbing millions of reluctant and resentful town dwellers sent down to the countryside for revolutionary tempering.

With due regard to differences in the specific circumstances of place and time, the Chinese Cultural Revolution resembled Soviet War Communism. It was based on the conviction that Marxist historical stages could be telescoped by mobilizing revolutionary will and resort to terror. In practice, it meant turmoil on a scale approaching civil war, great hardship, and intimations of foreign (this time Soviet) armed intervention, particularly after the Soviet invasion of Czechoslovakia in 1968 and the March 1969 Damansky Island (Zhen Bao) incidents on the Ussuri River.

There has been a good deal of speculation about the economic costs of the more than decade-long upheaval. The short-run price measured in disrupted agricultural and industrial output and the consequent low levels and stagnation of rural and urban real incomes is generally acknowledged, despite the paucity of statistics on the matter. It was revealed in 1988 that in 1978, two years after Mao's death, for the country as a whole, annual per capita farm income averaged 134 yuan ($78 at the then applicable exchange rate of 1 yuan = US$0.582) and that annual urban wages per worker averaged 614 yuan ($357). This means that living standards were at or below the spartan levels of the 1950s. More controversial are the longer-term consequences of the cultural folly, especially if Maoism I and II are added up and the initial date of the second outburst is pushed back, as it probably should be, to 1964, and extended through Hua Guofeng's ambivalent reign to 1978.

These long-run effects concern more elusive questions of what had been lost by directing the energies of the nation into idle work, like the many rivers and streams redirected to nowhere, and the ditches with no water in them dug by the frenzied masses during the Leap. A literature of the "wounded" blossomed briefly after the death of Mao. It reflected on the senselessness of the treadmill and wondered at the futility and cruelty of it, without ever directly taking to task its inventor.

During the post-1978 period of socialist deconstruction and hesitant capitalist construction, many formerly rusticated, educationally impaired youths became entrepreneurs. They built up extensive business and arbitrage networks from connections made during their stints in the countryside, eagerly took risks, and generally navigated with ease and profit through the uncharted waters of the newborn neomercantilistic capitalism with Chinese characteristics. The loss of economic expertise by mature cadres and still ambulatory scholars shell-shocked by the Cultural Revolution was primarily in areas of central administrative command planning and Marxist economic theory, hence no loss for the new economic order instituted after 1978. By the mid-1980s, knowledge and experience in the ways of the market was supplied by the monied Chinese diaspora of Hong Kong and Taiwan, once it was established that the people in charge in Beijing and, even more important, those lower down in the increasingly more assertive provincial, municipal, special economic zone, county, and other local receptacles of political power would not strangle capitalist strivings but, on the contrary, were not averse to having their extended palms greased as tradition dictated.

The Ambivalent Interlude (1976–1978)

Hua Guofeng was Mao's rearguard acolyte in charge of things from the time of Mao's death in September 1976, and formally until his ouster in mid-1981. However, his grip on political power and grasp of economics, never very firm, were considerably weakened and befuddled after the Third Plenum of the Eleventh Central Committee (December 1978) dominated by Deng Xiaoping, who had been rehabilitated (for the second time) and reinstated to various key party posts in July of the previous year. Economic policy under Hua was, to stretch the metaphor, goulash communism. It had in it a pinch of Stalinism: in 1976–78 nearly 58 percent of all industrial investment went to capital-intensive heavy industry; the rate of fixed capital investment was nearly as high as during the Great Leap; consumption and agriculture were neglected; input-output relations in production continued to be disrupted; and a grandiose ten-year Stalinomaoist vision ("plan") for national economic development (1976–85) based on imported rather than nativist technology was presented to the Fifth National People's Congress in February 1978. Added to this was a dash of Maoist helmsmanship, like the leap into the huge Baoshan steel project without any feasibility studies, and resort to radical left sloganeering techniques of the "two whatevers" genre.

SOCIALIST DECONSTRUCTION

While the jockeying for political power was in progress (1976–(78)–81), disturbing – for Marxist-Leninists – thoughts of profound economic transformation must have begun to germinate in the minds of influential leaders such as Deng Xiaoping, Hu Yaobang, and Zhao Ziyang. The fact was that not Stalinism, Maoism, nor the mixture of the two (1976–78), nor the relatively pragmatic intrasystemic revisionism of 1961–65 were workable long-term vehicles for the economic modernization of China. Thus ideologically legitimate economic system options were exhausted. The more daring government advisors looked to Hungarian reforms on the one hand, and Yugoslav innovations on the other. There was nowhere to go but to the right, cross the Chinese Rubicon, groping for the other (capitalist) side, the land of the East Asian tigers. Ideologically, of course, it was a dreadful, apostate, almost unthinkable prospect – yet thinking about it was, in Marxist terms, historically inevitable. No wonder, therefore, that unlike the warmed-over communists of Central and Eastern Europe, Chinese communist leaders from Deng to Jiang Zemin rejected allegations that their intent was to build in China a full-blown modern capitalist economy. At a minimum, they said, they had put up Chinese "screens" to keep the worst of Western bourgeois cultural pollutants out. They were probably quite sincere in these denials, as witnessed to by their reluctance to divest the state of its majority ownership in the economy's "strategic" industrial heights, although they feared massive unemployment in the sprawling state sector and the threat of social instability resulting from de facto privatization.

Partial Systemic Transformation in China (1978–1997)

Cognizant of the critical situation in the countryside and of the fact that, like Polish peasants in 1956, Chinese rural people in many localities in the late 1970s were busy dismantling the people's collectives on their own initiative and with positive production results, Mao's successors decided to follow suit in the early '80s by introducing the so-called "production responsibility system to households." This was an arrangement under which households became tenants and the state, at the local level, was the landlord. Specifically, the households were vested with extensive property rights of use to the land plots allotted to them by the authorities, that is, with the right to make decisions on what to produce and how to produce it. They were at the same time obligated to remit to the state an agricultural tax assessed in kind at official state-fixed prices attached to the quota produce, which were normally below prices for the same items on the reopened free farm produce markets. The tax in kind was used by the government to supply basic foods (grain, vegetable oils) to the cities at lower subsidized prices, as well as to consumers in agriculturally depressed areas. Any surplus left over after payment of the tax could be disposed of by the households at will (unlike what happened under Stalin in the USSR, there was such a surplus in Dengist China because the tax was not extortionistically confiscatory). In property terms, the households gained residual rights to income. In this way family income became positively related to the productivity of the household plot, thus improving significantly incentives to farmers compared with the production team-based collective work point system compensation of the past. In time, a restricted right to transfer the family farm strips was given to households. The mini-farms could be enlarged (up to a designated size), sold, or leased with permission of the local authority. This right, however, stopped short of the extensive legal rights of land transfer that characterize a full-fledged market system.

The partial property reform in the countryside had a one-shot positive incentive effect on output and productivity, which began to dissipate by the mid-1980s. Since then, for a variety of reasons not exclusively ideological, to this day there has been no decision to fully privatize land ownership. To some extent – but it is not the whole explanation – the failure to do so, to give farm families legal security of ownership, may have contributed to the less vigorous output and productivity performance of Chinese agriculture and farm income stagnation after 1984. In terms of the coordination mechanism, the former detailed commands to farm managements were replaced by a three-track price system: prices paid to households for deliveries under the agricultural tax obligations (quota deliveries), prices the households could obtain for the remaining produce on the rural and urban free markets, and (subsidized) prices charged for grain and other products by the state to urban consumers and peasants in food deficiency areas. In sum, the decision had been made not to leap into a private property-cum-market price agricultural system, but to move gradually in that direction through (1) prolonged, perhaps indefinite, phases of partial private ownership rights loosely defined, and (2) resort to tiered farm prices (some free, some fixed with a trend toward the free). In 1990, 30 percent of agricultural prices were state-fixed, 17 percent subject to state guidance, and 53 percent determined by market forces. By 1994, 7 percent were set by the state, 3 percent were state guided, and 90 percent set in the market.[8] One gets the impression that in both cases ideological considerations did play a role, but not the determining one.

Decollectivization also gave impetus to dispersion and decentralization of decision-making. Dispersion means the sharing of allocative decisions between the state and nonstate actors, in this case millions of peasant households, which means, in turn, that the state's reach is no longer near-total as it had been at certain times in the not-so-distant past. The authority of the state remains considerable but not totalitarian. Decentralization means that some decision-making power has shifted from central state authorities to the localities. This state sprawl does not automatically translate into more civilized bureaucratic attitudes (reports of tyrannical and "treats"-extorting village chieftains abound), but it does as a rule strengthen the drift toward more locally informed pragmatism, away from centralist fantasy. It points to continuity of the formal state organization, despite the many changes during the half-century of the state's existence that sometimes (1958–60, 1966–69) assumed catatonic proportions. It also hints at imitation of the special economic zones and technological parks earlier successfully used by, among others, Taiwan and South Korea. What is not shown is the shift since the early 1980s toward state regulation of the economy through indirect monetary interventions on the Japanese model in line with the remonetization of the increasingly market-oriented system, after a long spell of demonetized, administrative governance.

Structural reform in industry was, until 1984, experimental and confined, by and large, to Sichuan Province.[9] The process proceeds, and today roughly 80 percent of "production materials" (presumably producer goods) are traded at market prices, though the markets range from imperfect to oligopolistic. More than 90 percent of industrial consumer

---

[8] Thomas G. Rawski, "Reflections on Three Decades of 'China-Watching,'" *Issues & Studies*, September 1996, p. 22.

[9] David Shambaugh, *The Making of a Premier: Zhao Ziyang's Provincial Career* (Boulder: Westview Press, 1984), chap. 6.

goods are sold at prices formed by market forces. Despite official protes-
tations to the contrary, the instrumental or technocratic (very un-
Marxist) premise is that what matters is not who owns the means of
production – the state or nonstate (i.e., private or freely associated cooperative parties) – but to what regime of coordination – market or administrative plan – property rights are subjected. In other words, the
ownership question is secondary.[10]

In this view, industrial property structure in China is comprised of two
groups of enterprises: (1) those governed primarily by dynamic markets,
and (2) those governed by bureaucratic rules (remnants of the commandist plan) no matter at what level of government these rules are formulated and/or applied.[11] The first group consists of private firms, both
domestic and foreign, including township and village enterprises (TVEs);
"collective" enterprises, including TVEs owned by township and village
governments; joint ventures of various kinds, mainly between foreign corporations and domestic firms owned by the state, often at the echelon of
the province, municipality, special economic zone, or city; and market-
oriented state enterprises, the state here being any government above
that of the township. The degree of market exposure varies, depending
in part on the quality and reach of the connections networks and the
number and consistency of the bureaucratic protective strata that a firm
has built up. Group 1 output has grown by at least 20 percent a year in
the last half-dozen years or so. Group 2 firms are nominally governed by
the plan, or what there is left of it, and operate on the old *danwei* (work
unit) principle: they benefit from guaranteed flows of resources at below
market equilibrium prices; their output is purchased by the state at prices
fixed by the state; they get loans from the state banking system without
going into debt, and subsidies that strain the state's budget. They also

---

[10] This view is embraced by some Western social democratic politicians (e.g., Tony Blair)
and a number of economists (e.g., Joseph Stiglitz, Thomas Rawski, and, more hesitantly,
William A. Byrd), one of whom (Rawski) advises China-oriented economists to "ignore
politics, understand economics," advice which if carried out would leave us in darkness
during China's prolonged spells of "politics in command." William A. Byrd's, *The Market
Mechanism and Economic Reform in China* (Armonk, N.Y.: M. E. Sharpe, 1991) is an
important study. As I read her, Jean Oi shares the "reinventing government" view that
"a minimalist state is not necessarily the answer [to efficient resource allocation]. The
goal should be more effective government," and that "privatization is not the only way
to stimulate economic growth." Jean C. Oi, "The Role of the Local State in China's
Transition Economy," *The China Quarterly*, no. 144, December 1995, pp. 1146, 1148.

[11] The following account of the instrumental view of industrial reform is drawn from my
"China's Economic Reforms: A Synoptic View," *Journal of Northeast Asian Studies*,
Spring 1996, pp. 75–77.

carry heavy responsibilities for the welfare of their employees and the employees' dependents; their workers cannot be fired; and retirees get pensions from the general wages pool. Despite bankruptcy laws, the *danwei* rarely die – so far, at least. But change in that respect is in the offing because of the drag on growth and distortionist effects on the economy produced by their shoddy products, unpaid bills, interenterprise debt chains, and the strains they put on the state budget as tax consumers and on the banking system as bad debtors. Group 2 does not include all of the roughly 100,000 mostly large, capital-intensive (two-thirds of the country's fixed capital investment) enterprises designated as being "state-owned" (SOEs) employing 100 million people (300 million with dependents), and producing two-thirds of industrial output. It includes only those SOEs of which the material inputs, outputs, exchanges, finances, tax regime, employment, and management are administratively commanded, usually from central or provincial/municipal heights, and which for much the greater part get their financing from the state banking system, and more generally are exempt from the discipline of market competition. Because of the ambiguity and opaqueness of China's transitional economic arrangements, it is almost impossible to say where exactly the borderline between them and the more market- and profit-oriented (but not fully marketized) SOEs runs. Rather than a well-defined boundary between the two, there is an imperceptible transition through a zone of winks and nods, treats, old boys' networks, nepotistic preferences, and shadowy (often shady) linkages between the functions of business entrepreneurship, management, and officialdom. The system is in flux and its foundations are shaky, but so far it has worked remarkably well.

Compared with the reformist strivings of Russia and the ex-communist countries of Central and Eastern Europe, some of which exhibited (e.g., Poland) initial tendencies toward a quick, radical, all-embracing dismantling of socialism, the Chinese prescription has been gradual, less concerned with precise property ingredients, and exceedingly sensitive to social upsets, the arrest of which the leadership did not shirk from resorting to armed Tiananmen-like remedies. Caution and gradualness, however, come with a price tag: the postponement of the hardest choices and the tackling of the most vexing problems to the last, presumably based on the logic that such difficulties can be addressed with less friction and unwanted sociopolitical fallout when the gross domestic product is bigger. The Poles, Czechs, and Hungarians and some other East Europeans, even the Russians and others in what used to be the USSR, attach more importance to unambiguous and fundamental changes in property structures (privatization) than do the Chinese. That is so, in part, because privatization of property is related to individual liberty and civil society. Economic reforms in the ex-communist countries outside China have been accompanied, in some instances preceded, by profound political deconstructions of real socialism and a movement to, or at least toward, representative constitutional democracy, whereas the Chinese political transformation has been so far of more modest qualitative dimensions.

Compared with the pre-1978 situation, the number of business laws enacted in China in the past two decades has been impressive. Less admirable has been the persistence of ambiguity and arbitrariness, and of inconsistency in the interpretation and application of the laws by organs of the authoritarian state. The incomplete nature of the economic reforms, the continued powerful position of the unelected state in the mercantilistic neomarket economy, and the ubiquity of personal-exchange and patron-client relationships have spawned monumental top-to-bottom corruption that threatens to spiral out of control. As a complement to *guanxi*, corruption can be useful in getting around bureaucratic impediments to market reform, on condition, however, that it does not become the behavioral norm, in which case it destroys the market, which ultimately must be based on trust verified by transparency of transactions.[12] Although the pace has slowed of late, so far neither foreign nor diaspora investors, while complaining a lot, have been discouraged from putting their money into China – as has been the case in Russia – by the corrupt practices of China's merchant-officials. They regard these as an extra cost of doing business in a place that in their estimation has the potential of becoming in a not-too-distant future the largest market in the world.

Although the merits of autarkic development lost their shine in the early 1970s, it was not until the mid-1980s that an outward orientation (controlled openness) became part of reformist policy. In large measure because of the *huaqiao* – the monied "overseas" Chinese in Hong Kong, Taiwan, and other places farther afield – the policy of the half-open door (open wide on the side of exports, but only a crack on the import side)

---

[12] On the purely economic cost of corruption: Paul Mauro, *Why Worry About Corruption?* (Washington, D.C.: International Monetary Fund, 1997). For an interesting socioeconomic defense of the culture of gift and favor exchanges through *guanxi* in the context of a highly bureaucratized and decentralized neomarket economy with Chinese characteristics: You-tien Hsing, *Making Capitalism in China: The Taiwan Connection* (New York and Oxford: Oxford University Press, 1998), chap. 6, "Reform Coalitions and Blood Connections."

has been a huge developmental success, particularly in the coastal provinces. Integrating China more closely in the world trading and financial system and seeing that it plays by the rules of international commerce is probably one of the better ways of helping to sustain the reformist impulse.

CONCLUSION

Using a gradualist and relatively pragmatic approach to institutional reform, China since 1978 has removed most of the spoiled remains of the central planning system, and has marketized the greater part of the economy's allocative and coordinating mechanism. To be sure, many of the markets are quite imperfect, as they are linked by networks of interpersonal connections. They mingle, do not blend, but so far have worked well all the same. The already noted tendency to combine institutional tradition, native innovation, and imitation is alive and well, with Japan, South Korea, Taiwan, and Singapore having replaced the former Soviet Union as sources of inspiration and objects of selective emulation. A large industrial nonmarket state sector continues to exist. Property structures have been diversified and quasiprivatized in the sense that bureaucrat-capitalists in charge of assets operate within a generally competitive market environment. Property laws remain far from adequate. There are many laws, but no independent judiciary and commonplace arbitrary enforcement. Trade is half free (exports), half not (imports), resembling early Japanese, South Korean, and Taiwan semiprotectionism with a cheerful disregard for intellectual property rights. There has been phenomenally rapid growth from low initial levels. The growth has been useful, that is, beneficial to the living standards of very large numbers of people.

Some serious and potentially disruptive problems remain. Of these, the existence of a largely unreformed, inefficient, heavily indebted sector of industrial behemoths (Group 1 SOEs) not subject to competitive market pressures is one infection that has now spread to a fair number of TVEs (which together account for about two-fifths of China's total industrial output, provide some local governments with up to 80 percent of their revenues, and employ nearly a quarter of China's labor force).[13] Despite desultory attempts to rationalize some of them through various schemes

[13] Craig S. Smith, "Municipal-Run Firms Helped Build China; Now They're Faltering," *The Wall Street Journal*, October 8, 1997, pp. A1, A13.

of "corporatization," the Group 1 enterprises have, in fact, grown in number by about a half since the reforms began, and now hold about 50 percent of China's industrial assets. Of Group 1 firms surveyed in 1995, the average debt-to-assets ratio was 80 percent, and 95 percent of all their working capital came from state bank loans borrowed in conformity with the old socialist principle that a loan from state banks to state enterprises is not a debt. Another big, potentially crippling, snag is the precariousness of the financial system generally and the banking sector specifically. This sector, owned by the state, has an estimated $200 billion in accumulated nonperforming "policy" loans, that is, loans made by the banks by order of the government (five times the equity capital of all Chinese banks). Four-fifths of these bad debts are owed by Group 1 SOEs. Absent structural reforms, China's banking system is unfit for an emerging commercial power, and its present condition represents an open invitation to financial collapse.

There is also the massive overinvestment in manufacturing and real estate, which China shares with a number of other East and Southeast Asian economies that over the past several decades experienced rapid government policy-driven growth, where governments in their attempt to trump the market have on occasion impressively miscalculated. Contributing also to the investment glut has been "euphoria investment" from outside, especially from Hong Kong, concentrated before the territory's July 1, 1997, retrocession on politically well-connected, mainland-controlled companies listed on the Hong Kong stock exchange – a case, perhaps, of private miscalculation. Areas of overinvestment on the east and southeast Pacific rim include real estate, automobiles, steel, some petrochemicals, wood pulp, copper, glass cement, and frozen chicken. In the context of shrinking regional demand in 1997–98 recurrent real estate bubbles and industrial overcapacity have resulted in the accumulation of large inventories (estimated for China at 3 trillion yuan ($361 billion) at the end of 1996). In Shanghai's government-sponsored Pudong Development Zone, the vacancy rate is reportedly around 70 percent while construction of new office towers continues apace, in part because, as one Shanghai real estate executive put it, "no one has to pay the money back."[14] The effect of all this has been the piling-up of massive inter-enterprise debt chains and excessive inventories.

The Chinese economic state thus exists as an eclectic mixture of

---

[14] Craig S. Smith, "China Appears to Ignore Region's Tough Lessons," *The Wall Street Journal*, November 4, 1997, p. A17.

market and nonmarket institutions, prices, processes, and mechanisms. This odd assemblage is proving increasingly unworkable, and the government will have to make some tough decisions – enfranchising property rights, freeing prices, creating labor markets, and complying with World Trade Organization standards – if it is to continue its impressive reform record. Given its past record, one cannot be too optimistic that the Chinese Communist Party is capable of such tough decisions.

7

The Future of the Chinese State

HARVEY NELSEN

THINKING about the future is an exercise in humility. Thinking about China's future, if its modern history is any guide, is an exercise in frustration. No major country has gone through as many radical policy shifts as has the People's Republic of China (PRC) since its founding in 1949. But a number of factors point to greater continuity in the future. Thus, this chapter hazards a presentation of a "most likely" scenario of state development over the mid-term future.

CHANGE IN COMMUNIST AND ONE-PARTY STATES

Writing some thirty years ago, during the heyday of communism, Richard Lowenthal identified a fundamental contradiction in Marxist-Leninist states. On the one hand, they are utopian, seeking the creation of a new socialist man and the elimination of class differences. On the other hand, they mobilize their populations for rapid economic development and modernization. As development occurs, however, it gives rise to a new elite of bureaucrats, scientists, engineers, military officers, and skilled blue-collar workers. This new elite, in turn, undermines the egalitarian goals of the revolution.[1]

As history has demonstrated in recent decades, the new elites eventually triumph over the communist ideologues. On the surface, there is little left to separate communist from nationalist revolutions in developing nations. Both undertake fundamental social change in pursuit of national

---

The author is particularly grateful to David Shambaugh for comments and suggestions on earlier drafts of this chapter.

[1] Richard Lowenthal, "Development versus Utopia in Communist Policy," in Chalmers Johnson (ed.), *Change in Communist Systems* (Stanford, Calif.: Stanford University Press, 1970), pp. 33–116.

power and economic growth. In theory, the most important remaining differences between communist and nationalist revolutionary models are that the former are characterized by state ownership of the means of production and central planning substitutes for market forces. Yet the Chinese state still declares itself to be Marxist-Leninist even though the market economy now is dominant, and the state is divesting itself of most dependent enterprises. Probably the most important differences between communist and nationalist revolutions are the historical legacies left by the communist revolutions. Expropriation, class struggle, totalitarian governmental methods, and mass mobilization techniques create pathological political cultures. The growth of healthy sociopolitical institutions is slow and painful, even after utopian communists have been removed from power. The nongovernmental organizations so integral to civil society are not allowed to take root under communism. So their growth is slow even after communist governments are deposed. When communists remain in power, as in the case of the PRC, a "civil society" seems a distant goal indeed.

Modern history has also demonstrated that the communist systems eventually fail due to bureaucratic inefficiencies, increasing corruption, and the availability of the more successful liberal-democratic model. So why has the Chinese Communist Party (CCP) survived while so many of its communist brethren are no longer with us? There are a number of reasons; here we concentrate on those related to the conceptual framework provided by Lowenthal. In the conclusion of this chapter, we revisit the issue in terms of future prospects.

Deng Xiaoping's economic reforms of the 1980s shifted the Chinese revolution from a communist toward a state-authoritarian model. He moved away from state planning and allowed the rise of market forces. He privatized agriculture, opened China to foreign investment, and pursued an export-oriented economic development policy. More recently his successors, Jiang Zemin and Zhu Rongji, have begun sharply reducing the burden of state-owned industry. These post-Mao policies have produced a rapidly developing economy. Yet the political structure remains thoroughly Leninist.

Leninist regimes are ruthless in defense of their authoritarianism.[2] As Lowenthal observed:

---

[2] One Leninist regime which gradually lost its ruthless character and became open to democratic reforms is the Guomindang (GMD) Party on Taiwan. But it did not carry out class struggle, and was cooptive in its politics, bringing into the regime many who opposed

the ruling bureaucracy will be rational and legal in its methods so long as it does not feel threatened in its privileged position by pressures from below. But once such pressures make themselves felt, it will be quick to proclaim that the fatherland is in danger and to tamper with legal guarantees in the name of a national emergency.[3]

The bloodshed in Tiananmen Square on June 4, 1989, fit Lowenthal's analysis all too well.

China's blend of supply and demand economics and rigid political controls led Nicholas Kristof of the *New York Times* to coin the salubrious term "market Leninism" to describe the PRC.[4] The critical question arises: how long can such a seeming oxymoron survive? Will the market forces and increasing opening to foreign influences destroy the Leninist political system? A number of factors need to be considered.

Lucian Pye provides a useful conceptual framework for prediction to answer these vexing questions. He argues that transnational forces have tended to undermine authoritarian systems. Trade, finance, communications, science, and technology have all worked on a global scale to weaken despotic governments. The main challenge for most authoritarian regimes has been economic growth. In Pye's words: "The forces of modernization have made it harder for political willpower to mobilize and dominate a society."[5] He argues that there is a fundamental clash between the culture of modernization and the various national political cultures. This results in a confrontation between universal standards and parochial values. The former are essential for economic performance and effectiveness, the latter are critical for creating national loyalties and distinctive national political styles. National identity is necessary for a spirit of community.[6] Successfully developing countries have been able to both open their doors to the outside world and sustain their internal identity. Underdeveloped countries have not been able to accomplish this. One important factor in being able to open the doors is "the shock of failure."[7]

its policies. The different operational modes of the CCP and GMD cause Bruce Dickson to conclude that the successful Taiwanese model of democratization cannot be replicated in the PRC. See Bruce Dickson, *Democratization in China and Taiwan: The Adaptability of Leninist Parties* (Oxford: Clarendon Press, 1997).

[3] Lowenthal, "Development versus Utopia," p. 116.

[4] Nicholas Kristof and Sheryl WuDunn authored a fine overview of the contemporary scene: *China Wakes: The Struggle for the Soul of a Rising Power* (New York: Times Books, 1994).

[5] Lucian W. Pye, "Political Science and the Crisis of Authoritarianism," *American Political Science Review*, vol. 84, no. 1, March 1990, p. 9.

[6] Lowenthal, "Development versus Utopia," p. 11.   [7] Ibid., p. 15.

Pye's analysis bodes ill for the Chinese Communist Party. The shock of failure doomed Maoism in China. As Chapter 6, by Jan Prybyla, graphically illustrates, the combined catastrophes of the Great Leap Forward and the Great Proletarian Cultural Revolution provided ample evidence that Maoist politics and economics should be relegated to the rubbish heap of history. But David Shambaugh's chapter shows that the pragmatic policies of Deng Xiaoping provided a new lease on life for the communist leadership. Market Leninism has worked, at least for a time. But Shambaugh's chapter also illustrates the decayed nature of the Chinese communist state.

Harry Harding's consideration of Chinese bureaucracy supports the pessimistic perspective on fundamental political change. Writing in 1981, Harding found that the PRC leadership relied primarily on incremental "internal remedialism" when responding to problems in the state system (the Great Proletarian Cultural Revolution was an obvious exception to this generalization). This approach is rooted in Chinese political culture. The imperial system used a "Censorate" to discover and report malfunctions and malfeasance in the bureaucracy. Corrections were made and punishments meted out to miscreant officials, but system change was glacial in its pace.

Shortly after Harding published his work, Deng Xiaoping created a Central Discipline Inspection Commission within the CCP which paralleled the functions of the Censorate. The autocrats in Beijing dismiss external balance of power systems as untrustworthy since the CCP would not be able to control them.[8] The CCP itself was initially intended to serve as a balance wheel correcting the problems of a centralized bureaucratic system. But in the 1950s, the party became the state.[9] The political reform agenda of Deng Xiaoping in the 1980s again tried to separate party and governing functions. He was much more successful in separating party and economic functions, especially at grass-roots levels. But that was a natural consequence of allowing the market economy to develop.

In the post-Deng era, the "paramount leaders" have less personal

---

[8] The author interviewed the senior editor of an internationally famous Chinese journal. When asked about the likelihood of a free press leading the way to systemic reforms in China, he responded that a press freedom would most likely be the *last* freedom to be achieved in the PRC.

[9] Harry Harding, *Organizing China: The Problem of Bureaucracy, 1949–76* (Stanford, Calif.: Stanford University Press, 1981), chap. 11. See, too, Shiping Zheng, *Party vs. State in Post-1949 China* (Cambridge: Cambridge University Press, 1997).

authority and must rely more on consensual decision-making. Mao had immense ideological and charismatic authority. Deng had little of either, but he had a great deal of power derived from *guanxi*, or sponsor-protégé, relations which he had built up through many years of service in party, military, and government leadership positions. President Jiang Zemin and Prime Minister Zhu Rongji represent the next phase of Chinese leaders who are recruited from the technocratic elite. Such men will have to rely on political and economic tradeoffs to get things accomplished. Interest groups will play a role much more important than in the past history of the PRC. Since no leader will have sufficient authority and power to undertake fundamental change, "internal remediation" would seem the most likely form of state evolution. Systemic change will then be gradual and piecemeal. The PRC will probably still be an authoritarian state a decade from now. Putting Harding's work in Pye's conceptual framework, Chinese parochial values can be expected to prevail over universalistic global standards.

A contrary and more optimistic view of China's future comes in the form of a democratic system emerging from a neoauthoritarian government. One theorist – Wu Jiaxiang – bases his ideas on Samuel Huntington's *Political Order in Changing Societies*. Huntington sees the need for a transitional stage between autocracy and democracy. Wu hypothesizes that the market economy – economic democracy – will lay the groundwork for a political transition to follow. Wu believes the growth of market forces in an autocratic system will lead to social crises. At that point a strongman model becomes desirable, and he will create sustained changes leading to further democratization. Turkey's experience with the reform dictatorship of Kemal Attaturk serves as an historical example. Democracy will not become a given. It will have to be pressed for during and after the strongman rule. Wu calls for the revitalization and downsizing of the National People's Congress (NPC) and Chinese People's Political Consultative Conference (CPPCC) to provide the organizational backing for a future national-level democratic government.[10]

The neoauthoritarian Wu Jiaxiang comes full circle to meet Wei Jingsheng, China's most famous prodemocracy dissident. Wei argues that modernization cannot succeed without democratization. Wu believes that economic forces will lead to a log-jam between autocratic

---

[10] Willem van Kemenade, *China, Hong Kong, Taiwan, Inc.: The Dynamics of a New Empire* (New York: Knopf, 1997), pp. 235–36.

political forces and a liberalizing society. Both see democracy as the outcome of economic forces already unleashed in the PRC. Both Wu and Wei believe that "the shock of failure" awaits China in the not-too-distant future.

The optimism of Wu and Wei fails to convince. There are examples of market-based economies which have coexisted comfortably with corrupt autocracies. See, for example, Indonesia from 1965 to 1998 and South Korea from 1960 to 1990.

However, Samuel Huntington's theory on how single-party systems evolve is relevant to the future of the PRC. Such systems operate effectively in the early phases of modernization when centralization of political power also helps economically. But the modernization process eventually leads to a dispersion of power. This poses the problem of how to reconcile the continued primacy of the single party with the representation of functional socioeconomic groupings.[11] The CCP's answer is that the party is necessary to counterbalance the fissiparous tendencies of a heterogeneous society. The CCP defends against the possibility of anarchy.

One-party systems emerge from what Huntington calls "bifurcated societies." A nation in the throes of a political revolution is obviously bifurcated. However, historical evolution and the course of the revolution eventually remedy most bifurcations. The ideology of a one-party system requires a strong "us-them" division; the party must be virulently "anti-something." As the original enemy disappears, the party has a problem justifying its dominance. Monopoly party control is further endangered when new bifurcations develop which are engendered by party policies.

Membership in a strong one-party system is difficult to obtain, and the party experiences frequent internal purges.[12] Huntington's findings imply that if party membership is no longer a highly desirable commodity, the party is in decline. That would seem to be the case in the PRC today. Young people are less prone to compete for CCP membership, and service in the armed forces is avoided as a career option. The People's Liberation Army (PLA) used to be an important vehicle for upward mobility and one of the easiest ways to gain CCP membership. Now it is seen as "hard time" at starvation wages.

---

[11] Samuel Huntington, "Social and Institutional Dynamics of One-Party Systems," in S. Huntington and Clement Moore (eds.), *Authoritarian Politics in Modern Society* (New York: Basic Books, 1970), p. 8.   [12] Ibid., p. 13.

How does Huntington's model apply to the evolution of the CCP? Huntington finds that single-party systems go through a three-stage evolution. First is "transformation," which in the case of China was the Maoist phase. This period often sees the emergence of a charismatic leader to lead the drive for revolutionary change. Ideology provides a strong guide for remaking society. The second phase, "consolidation," sees the emergence of a more consensual society. Ideology becomes less important; indeed, efforts to revive ideology would indicate a political crisis. As the party becomes institutionalized, political power tends to be either shared among several leaders or concentrated in one man for a limited tenure of office. This is happening in the post-Deng period. Prime Minister Li Peng was one of the first top-level national leaders to leave his position due to the fact that his two terms of office expired (the constitution does not allow for a third term.)[13]

Huntington's third phase for the evolution of one-party systems is "adaptation." In this phase the party deals with the emergence of a new innovative, technical-managerial class, and the development of complex group structures typical of a more industrialized state. The party must also contend with the reemergence of a critical intelligentsia and demands by local and popular groups for participation in and influence over the political system. The political dynamics pit the newly emerged forces against the mid-level party bureaucrats who tend to be the most status quo-oriented. The top levels of the party serve as the arbiters and mediators of change.[14]

Bruce Dickson applies Huntington's model to the contemporary CCP. He finds that the Chinese communists are failing the "adaptation" phase. They are not coopting new socioeconomic elements into the political leadership. The CCP deals with political opposition through exclusion and suppression. The only reforms tolerated are those needed for efficiency rather than responsiveness to pluralistic needs. The longer this leadership mindset continues, the more difficult and less likely real reforms become. As grievances accumulate, they increase the danger of sociopolitical explosions. Incremental reforms are apt to set off a chain

---

[13] Li Peng is the first Premier to leave office under tenure and reappointment restrictions. There have been at least two Presidents who also retired because their term of office had expired, but that position used to be largely honorific. It has become more powerful during Jiang Zemin's tenure.

[14] Huntington and Moore (eds.), *Authoritarian Politics*, pp. 24–25.

reaction such as occurred through Gorbachev's policies of *perestroika* and *glasnost*. This reality strengthens the hand of the hard-liners at the top levels of leadership and weakens the leverage of the would-be reformers. Leninist parties seek to determine their environments rather than adapt to them. During the "adaptation phase" this becomes increasingly difficult, but so far the CCP has remained in its Leninist controlling mode, at least in terms of politics.[15]

Huntington argues that policy formulations can be quite heterogeneous so long as the arguments take place within the party. Thanks to Deng Xiaoping, "efficiency reforms" have grown quite strong within the CCP. He set retirement ages for all party, government, and military positions and limited terms of office. This resulted in the emergence of a new leadership generation comprised of better educated and more cosmopolitan officials. While certainly not democratic in their outlook, this new elite is much more open to pragmatic change and consideration of policy alternatives. "Responsive reforms" – political changes attempting to accommodate the new socioeconomic conditions – are harder to find. A modest degree of political pluralism has developed with the NPC exercising increasing authority outside the purview of the CCP. But the NPC is by no means a competitor for ultimate power or policy-making authority.[16]

Village-level elections were authorized in 1987 and are currently conducted in about 60 percent of the rural communities. But these may not qualify as "responsive reforms." In many cases, candidates are selected by higher-level administrators. County and township governments still operate through appointment powers with far greater authority than the democratically elected village governments.[17] Thus the likelihood of democracy growing from the grass-roots level to a national political model would be a very slow process at best. Meanwhile, Beijing has shown little tolerance for democratization as a top-down movement. Since Mao's death, three national level leaders have tried to liberalize the politics of the CCP and move it toward the center. All three were dismissed from their posts.[18]

---

[15] Dickson, *Democratization in China and Taiwan*, chap. 1.

[16] Minxin Pei, "Is China Democratizing?," *Foreign Affairs*, vol. 77, no. 1, January–February 1998, pp. 68–82.

[17] Jiang Wendi, "Fostering Political Democracy from the Bottom Up," *Beijing Review*, vol. 41, no. 11, March 16–20, 1998, pp. 11–14.

[18] Harry Harding, "The Halting Advance of Pluralism," *Journal of Democracy*, January 1998, p. 11.

ALTERNATIVE VIEWS OF THE FUTURE OF THE PRC

In 1998, the *Journal of Democracy* published a symposium on the future of democracy in China. Ten well-known China scholars were asked to address a number of questions which can be summarized as: (1) Will the CCP still be in charge of the PRC ten years from now? (2) What are the prospects for democratization? and (3) What is the likelihood of chaos and possible territorial disintegration of the state?[19] There was a surprising amount of agreement among the contributors. All but one believed that the PRC would still be intact in ten years and most believed that some form of CCP would still be in charge.[20]

The symposium generally agreed on the eventual democratization of the PRC, but no one could predict how long the process might take. The authors seemed to predicate the eventual attainment of democracy on "neoliberal institutionalism." This increasingly popular model predicts the gradual political-economic homogenization of the international system. The efficiencies of market economics and the political stability and flexibility provided by democratic governments will eventually prevail over all other contenders. The process includes the rise of a "civil society," the growth of a middle class, high levels of education, and the homogenizing effects of global trade and investment.

In his concluding article, Andrew Nathan reviewed the analyses of his colleagues. He found that the contributors were unable to discover actors in the Chinese political-economic system who both repre-sent democratic values and have real power to accomplish their goals.[21] Neoliberal institutionalism looks to the rise of a bourgeoisie as an important factor in eroding authoritarianism. But the Chinese bour-geoisie is quite different from its Western namesake. The emerging Chinese middle class is not apt to challenge the state since it takes the form of a bureaucratic-business elite network.[22] Wealth is generated

---

[19] "Will China Democratize?," *Journal of Democracy*, January 1998, pp. 1–64. The scholars who contributed their views were Robert Scalapino, Zbigniew Brzezinski, Suisheng Zhao, Juntao Wang, Andrew Nathan, Yizi Chen, Harry Harding, Arthur Waldron, Thomas Metzger, and Michel Oksenberg.

[20] Yizi Chen was the exception. He believes that contradictions inherent within "market Leninism" will cause national economic collapse prior to the ten-year time horizon stip-ulated in the symposium.

[21] Andrew Nathan, "Even Our Caution Must Be Hedged," *Journal of Democracy*, January 1998, p. 64.

[22] Ibid., p. 61.

through special prerogatives, quasimonopolies, and, in general, the use of political power to achieve economic benefits. Politicians from the local level to the nation's capital work hand-in-glove (and hand-in-pocket) with entrepreneurs. They have a symbiotic relationship with one another.

This writer finds himself in agreement with the contributors to the *Journal of Democracy* symposium. Regime change in the PRC does not seem imminent. But it would be worthwhile to assess the merits of some alternate viewpoints.

Dankwart Rustow offers an attractive model for the Chinese case. He studied twenty-three cases of nations which transitioned to democracy as a result of endogamous forces. He excluded Japan which had its constitution imposed upon it during American military occupation at the end of World War II. Rustow expected to find economic indicators – relative wealth, emergence of the middle class, and levels of industrialization – to be a fundamental factor in democratization. This was not the case. Instead, the most important variable was unity. If a sense of national identity was absent or weak, or if regional conflicts were strong, democracy was killed before it was born. But if unity prevails, authoritarian governments struggle with the issues which Huntington identified as salient in the "adaptation phase" of single-party rule. New economic forces and elites emerge, and the old political oligarchy must find ways of dealing with their demands. When the struggle between the new emerging forces and the old guard goes on for some time without decisive resolution in favor of one side or the other, democratic means are adopted to accommodate the differences. Over time, these means become institutionalized and democracy becomes "habituated," in Rustow's term.

This applies well to China, if one begins by excluding Tibet and Xinjiang. These two regions clearly do not feel a sense of unity with Han China. But the ethnic Han regions which constitute most of China and all of the densely populated territories have a remarkably strong tradition of unity. This is due in large part to the ideographic nature of the language. Despite the existence of a number of mutually unintelligible dialects, all Chinese read a common written language. This has provided a profound cultural identity over the centuries, and in the view of this writer, renders very unlikely the scenario of a geographic breakup of China.

The second part of Rustow's scenario also seems appropriate to the PRC. It is unlikely that the CCP will be willing or able to squelch the demands of new socioeconomic forces over time. Neither is it likely that the new elites will undertake successful revolutionary action against the CCP. Thus, democratic compromise looks possible or even likely. But there is a fly in the ointment. Rustow points out that the time required for this process of democratic evolution varies immensely from case to case.[23] This brings us back to the consensus view of the China scholars polled in the *Journal of Democracy*. They generally believed that democracy would eventually develop. Rustow provides a model to predict how this might happen, but no one can tell us when.

A few years ago, there was a popular expectation that the end of the Cold War would see the collapse of all communist governments around the world. Those that collapsed did so for one or more reasons. First, their governments had been imposed upon them by the USSR. Second, they experienced "the shock of failure" brought on by the communications revolution which enabled the citizenry to compare their economic situation with their capitalist counterparts. The liberal democratic model provided an obvious alternative to their regimes. Third, the governments proved unwilling or unable to use military force to defend communist governments – even their own. The former Soviet Union and German Democratic Republic were prime examples of governments unwilling to use military force to defend their regimes.

None of those three factors have much relevance to China. Its revolution is indigenous, like that of Cuba. Both Havana and Beijing have survived economic catastrophies – largely of their own making – which would have brought down most governments. Second, the PRC has not experienced the shock of failure since the political chaos of the Great Proletarian Cultural Revolution. Economically, the citizens of the PRC were able to compare themselves unfavorably to Taiwan, but by that time, Deng's market reforms were under way and marked advances in living standards had begun. So there was no widespread sense of hopelessness. Finally, the PRC has shown willingness to use military force to suppress dissent in the form of public demonstrations – see June 1989 in Tiananmen Square. The regime also continues to use its legal system to suppress individual dissidents.

A different argument predicts the collapse of the PRC based on the "ideological bankruptcy" of communism today. That assertion is misleading. Ideology means two different things. First, ideology refers to a

---

[23] Dankwart A. Rustow, "Transitions to Democracy: Towards a Dynamic Mode," *Comparative Politics*, vol. 2, no. 3, April 1970, pp. 337–63.

core set of ideas and political values on which a society is generally agreed. As Chapter 2 illustrates, China has sought consensus on political values ever since the collapse of the Qing dynasty in 1911–12. During the first decade of the PRC, there was a euphoric sense that the model had finally been achieved. But, as Chapter 6 argues, the 30 million dead in the Great Leap Forward and the political chaos of the Cultural Revolution wrote finis to the Maoist model. The fact that Beijing does not now have a coherent ideology cannot be solely blamed on the CCP. The ideological vacuum has lasted almost a century. Confucianism, for example, was mortally wounded during the May Fourth Movement at the end of World War I. It was effectively attacked as a cause of China's weakness in the face of foreign exploitation. As a hierarchical political code which calls for obedience and discipline, Confucianism is favored by the supporters of "neoauthoritarianism" in the PRC. But does the populace agree, know about, or even care whether Confucianism is utilized in this new defense of the CCP? With the exception of certain family values, Confucianism has lost its ability to organize shared values for the Chinese.

Second, ideology serves as a rationalization for a particular political and economic order. It is primarily in this second sense of the word that China is ideologically troubled. And yet even here – ideology as a guide for a political-economic system – the PRC still has assets. "Socialism with Chinese characteristics," as Beijing calls it, has become a euphemism for pragmatic policies. Since neither "socialism" nor "Chinese" are clearly defined by Beijing, few restrictions apply to policy formulation. An ancient metaphor describes the policy process: "Crossing the stream by feeling for stones." Pragmatism works so long as the basic institutions function reasonably well. Gradual and incremental improvements, experimenting with new policies, and tackling problems as they arise makes a great deal of sense when the political system itself is viable. It is only when system collapse has been suffered that people turn to true ideologues like Mao Zedong.

Some analysts see the growth of economic decentralization leading to a political devolution of the PRC.[24] However, the center still holds carrots and sticks in terms of economic policy over the provinces, and the center still has the power of appointment. The provinces compete for economic concessions which are granted by Beijing, but they can also later be with-

---

[24] See, for example, James Miles, *The Legacy of Tiananmen: China in Disarray* (Ann Arbor: University of Michigan Press, 1996), chap. 10.

drawn by the same central government.[25] Thus the institutional strength is just not there to mount a challenge to national authority, even if the political will were found.

One possible route toward a more humane, pluralist, responsive, and democratic political system in China is federalism. This could enable the Chinese citizenry to exercise greater control over their political lives by restricting the arbitrary power of Beijing. A trend toward federalism has been under way for some years. The market reforms required greater powers and autonomy for the provinces. This nascent federalism, however, has occurred within the framework of a unitary state. But the central characteristic of federalism is a constitutionally guaranteed division of powers.[26] China's political tradition has been one of centralization. Decentralization is associated with breakdown and chaos. Political cultures do change, but two big obstacles must be overcome prior to moving toward a federalist system. First, the Beijing leadership will have to be convinced that power-sharing is in their interest. With a zero-sum view of political power, this will prove difficult. Second, the poorer provinces must receive assurances that their economic development will not be forgotten. One important role of the central government in the PRC has been to redistribute wealth from the richer to the poorer regions. Beijing has been less effective in playing that role under market Leninism than it was under Maoism, but the demands for social justice remain.

Other analysts foresee the collapse of the government based on an inability to deliver basic economic services to the population. Exiled political thinker Chen Yizi looks at the failing state enterprises and rapidly growing unemployment and asks: "How can a communist regime, long accustomed to buying obedience with jobs and welfare, maintain its legitimacy even while it takes jobs and benefits away from its subjects?"[27] Unemployment may pose the greatest single threat to political stability in the PRC.

Chen's case is strengthened by the recent announcement by Prime Minister Zhu Rongji that he intends to both rectify the money-losing

---

[23] Dorothy Solinger, "Despite Decentralization: Disadvantages, Dependence and Ongoing Central Power in the Inland – The Case of Wuhan," *The China Quarterly*, no. 145, March 1996, pp. 1–34. See also Zhao Suisheng, "China's Central-Local Relationship: A Historical Perspective," in Jia Hao and Lin Zhimin (eds.), *Changing Central-Local Relations in China: Reform and State Capacity* (Boulder: Westview Press, 1994), pp. 19–34.

[26] Ibid., p. 31.

[27] Yizi Chen, "The Road from Socialism," *Journal of Democracy*, January 1998, p. 9.

state-owned enterprises and reduce the bureaucratic payrolls in the 1998–2000 time frame. This is an ambitious and potentially dangerous program to accomplish in such a short time period. Unemployment is already running at the highest levels since the communists consolidated their power in the early 1950s.[28] Whether private-sector growth and new jobs stemming from international investment can absorb millions of additional layoffs remains to be seen. Of course, the ultimate safety net is the Chinese family, which cushions unemployment through sharing and help by other family members. In the long-term, the PRC plans to establish something akin to a "social security" system for the aged, unemployed, and ill. But for now, there is little the government can offer.

It can, however, attempt to keep the lid on tight. In April 1998, a high-level CCP "Leading Group on Comprehensive Public Order" was revealed in the Hong Kong press. Its purpose is to defuse various threats from laid-off workers, disgruntled farmers, underground political organizations, and ethnic unrest in Tibet and Xinjiang. The office will coordinate the efforts of public security forces and various ministries and departments dealing with trade unions, propaganda, and ethnic minorities.[29] This office reminds one of the "Drug Czar" position created in the U.S. federal government after top-level officials in the executive and legislative branches came to believe that something had to be done, and that a central coordination effort was needed. Clearly the threat of major social unrest has caught the attention of Beijing. Returning to Professor Chen's pessimistic prediction of regime collapse, if it is to come true, it will probably happen within the next three to five years when the unemployment pressures are at their worst. Jobless workers have less to lose from state suppression. Their families are already suffering.[30] The CCP has good reason to fear high levels of unemployment as a serious threat to social stability and a possible threat to the party's hold on power.

Mass opposition to the CCP has always required intra-elite conflict. Without paralysis or division in the instruments of coercion, extensive mass movements never get off the ground. But in David Bachman's analysis, the policies being undertaken by Premier Zhu Rongji are poten-

---

[28] In an "off the record" statement in March 1998, a well-known Chinese economist from Shanghai estimated that the real unemployment rate in China was approaching 25 percent.

[29] *China News Digest*, April 24, 1998, citing reports in the *South China Morning Post*.

[30] David Bachman, "Emerging Patterns of Political Conflict in Post-Deng China," presented at the conference on "The PRC After the Fifteenth Party Congress: Reassessing the Post-Deng Political and Economic Prospects," Taipei, February 19–20, 1998, p. 22.

tially divisive to the CCP elite. State enterprise reform, bureaucratic cutbacks, and banking reforms all are fundamentally redistributive in their political and economic effects.[31] So Bachman is leaving the door open for a new "democratic spring" such as China experienced in 1989. Like Chen Yizi, Bachman's evidence and argument would imply the greatest likelihood for mass unrest in the next few years.

The last alternate viewpoint to be considered emphasizes the problem of corruption. It was a major cause of the 1989 "Democracy Spring" demonstrations in cities throughout China. Corruption leads to alienation, cynicism, and loss of legitimacy for the government. But contrary to the views of some, it is not apt to result in the collapse of the CCP. There are two kinds of corruption: productive and unproductive. Examples of unproductive corruption are graft and theft of the public coffers. Productive corruption consists of illegal wealth accumulated in return for actions taken; see bribes as an example. Most corruption in the PRC is of the less dangerous "productive" type. It is often little more than a fee for services rendered. Underpaid bureaucrats, physicians, and school teachers will take money in return for granting the services desired. Andrew Nathan sees corruption as a means to get things accomplished when the rules are not clear. He further asserts that corruption serves as a substitute for democracy rather than as a prod toward it.[32] While it is true that bribes enable the ordinary citizen to get things done, the outrage at high-level official corruption expressed in the mass demonstrations of 1989 would tend to undercut Nathan's "democracy substitute" argument. But he may be right in the sense of corruption slowing the growth of democracy. The powers that be, enriched as they are off the current system, will resist with all their might political reforms which would threaten their purses. Thus the government-led anticorruption campaigns have had little effect. Without checks and balances in the political system and a free press, the opportunities to use positions of authority for ill-gotten gains will continue to be irresistable.

SEVEN REASONS WHY THE CCP WILL ENDURE IN THE NEAR TO MEDIUM TERM

First, authoritarian governments can and do prolong their hold on power by invoking threats to justify their rule. The threats may be foreign or

---

[31] Ibid.
[32] Nathan, "Even Our Caution Must Be Hedged," p. 63.

domestic, and they may be legitimate or chimerical. The August 1991 military coup d'etat against Gorbachev warned that unless emergency measures were undertaken, the Soviet Union would fall apart. The coup failed, and the USSR did indeed collapse. China's foreign policy will be largely determined by Beijing's domestic political needs. The "myth of national humiliation" will be invoked to inspire Chinese nationalism against perceived slights by foreign nations.[33] The CCP argues that only its rule can provide the stability and integrity required to keep its economic reforms working. Is the CCP wrong? If you were a Chinese citizen would you be willing to take a chance on sweeping change?

Second, there is an absence of likely alternatives to the present regime. The reasons why democracy still seems distant were described in the previous section of this chapter. But what about the collapse of communism into a military dictatorship?

There is little likelihood of China devolving into a military dictatorship due to CCP failures. Huntington found that military authoritarianism usually results when one-party regimes fail to institutionalize themselves.[34] The PRC has gone beyond that stage. Also, the traumatic experiences of the PLA during the Great Proletarian Cultural Revolution and in the streets of Beijing in June 1989 would mitigate against the use of overt military power in the political process.

The CCP enjoys a number of effective controls over the PLA. First the Chairman of the Central Military Commission is the civilian President Jiang Zemin. This powerful organization allows Jiang to exercise the power of appointment in the top levels of the armed forces. Second, in the scramble for resource allocations for military modernization, the CCP can play one service off another. Jet fighters take funds away from a modern submarine fleet. Finally, Chinese military modernization requires the active support of numerous civilian hierarchies. Scientific manpower and funding, personnel recruitment, and a supportive industrial policy are all required. But the PLA is in no position to redefine national priorities.[35] So it will just have to go along in order to get along.

---

[33] Myth is used here in the anthropological sense: a powerful underlying belief conditioning the thinking of a society. There is no more powerful myth in contemporary China than that of its national humiliation suffered at the hands of foreign powers over the past 160 years. It serves as an important source of Chinese nationalism and strengthens the hand of the central government.

[34] Huntington and Moore (eds.), *Authoritarian Politics*, "Conclusion," p. 513.

[35] Bachman, "Emerging Patterns," pp. 17–19.

The power of the civilian leadership over the interests of the PLA was reflected in the decision to sign the comprehensive nuclear test-ban treaty. The PRC nuclear arsenal is not very sophisticated. It lacks multiple independently targeted reentry vehicles for its ICBMs. Its tactical nuclear capability is questionable at best. Without any opportunity to continue nuclear testing, these serious weaknesses will be indefinitely perpetuated.[36] Yet the PRC not only agreed to sign but actually ceased testing in 1997. It is clear that foreign policy and international relations criteria prevailed over the interests of the armed forces in this case.

Third, lessons have been learned from Tiananmen, 1989. The CCP has shown a willingness to use large-scale lethal force against its own population. But the costs of doing so – political and economic – were high indeed. The liberals and dissidents – those who are not in jail – also remember Tiananmen and do not attempt to arouse demonstrations or mass movements. The sole exception to that generalization might be the daring few who are committed to developing organized labor in the PRC. Labor activists are among the first to be arrested. Beijing wants no replication of the Polish experience with the Solidarity trade union.

Many conservative intellectuals offer support for the regime through the vehicle of "neo-authoritarianism." China's future is compared to present-day Singapore: a democracy in name, but an authoritarian government in reality. There are many nuanced differences among the neoauthoritarians and significant differences between them and the CCP apparatchiks. But the end result is support for the status quo.[37] In 1997–98, liberal intellectuals began to find their voice once again. University lecture series occasionally featured critics of communism. The works of a few anticommunist Western philosophers were translated into Chinese. Proposals were allowed to circulate for the expansion of grass-roots elections and the reform of the NPC electoral system.[38] But a modus vivendi seems to have been reached. The liberals won't directly attack CCP rule, and the CCP will allow criticism around the edges. Such criticism serves as a relief valve and possibly as a source for new and effective "efficiency reforms" which would have the effect of perpetuating CCP control. Meanwhile, student interest is not focused on political activism. The release of the famous Wei Jingsheng caused hardly a ripple

---

[36] Ibid.

[37] Feng Chen, "Order and Stability in Social Transition: Neo-Conservative Political Thought in Post 1989 China," *The China Quarterly*, no. 151, Sept. 1997, pp. 593–613.

[38] Steven Mufson, "It Looks Like Spring Again in China," *Washington Post*, National Weekly Edition, vol. 15, no. 26, April 27, 1998, p. 12.

on China's campuses. But students are interested in long-term change such as how to implement the rule of law in China.[39]

Fourth, the CCP will continue to manipulate nationalism for its own ends. China will continue its imperial control over restive minority peoples, and that control will also serve the interests of authoritarianism. The Han Chinese will increasingly see the Xinjiang Moslems and the Tibetans as threatening the Chinese state, especially as the number of terrorist incidents increase. Reunification with Taiwan is more problematic. In reality the continuance of CCP rule is the major obstacle preventing some form of reunification. Taiwan would be far more interested in negotiating with a democratic regime in Beijing. But the CCP claims that only its strength – political, military, and economic – can rein in the trend toward "independence" on the part of the Taiwanese electorate. Beijing ultimately relies on sticks rather than carrots to protect the status quo. It is, however, very unlikely that threats will result in a political settlement.

Fifth, economic growth will slow but not stop. It is not likely that "market Leninism" will prove to be an oxymoron. Indeed, the late economic guru Chen Yun may be laughing in his grave. He had argued against rapid expansion of market forces in the 1980s, proferring his "birdcage" theory of economic development for China. If the cage is too small – read as insufficient market forces – the bird is apt to grow sick and die. If the cage is left open – read as unlimited market forces – the bird will fly away. So the best compromise is a large cage. He won his argument in 1988 when the reforms were severely retrenched. But he lost it again in 1992 when the current economic policies were adopted. If he is able to look down from his Marxian heaven and watch the Asian capitalist countries go through their torments of the late 1990s, he could say, "I told you so." China's remnant socialism has thus far saved it from the worst effects of the Asian economic shocks. Its currency is not fully convertible, so it was able to resist the pressure on it to devalue. Its banking system is rife with bad debt, but the government controls the financial system so the threat of bankruptcy is ameliorated.[40] Foreign investment slowed, but has not dried up since investor confidence in China did not evaporate as it did in Indonesia. As discussed above, unem-

---

[39] Frederick Teiwes, "Succession, Institutionalization, Governability and Legitimacy in the Post-Deng Era," presented at the conference on "The PRC After the 15th Party Congress," Taipei, February 19–20, 1998, p. 11.

[40] In late 1998 and early 1999, China closed a few of its weakest banks.

ployment is a grave problem. Social unrest is already occurring. But it is difficult to construct a scenario in which such unrest would be apt to destroy the regime. Beijing always has the option of retreating on its retrenchment policies.

Sixth, the political system functions from the top down. Bruce Dickson points out that "feedback" mechanisms are essential for successful adaptation. Leaders of Leninist parties are ambivalent about feedback. While recognizing a need to develop links with the society in order to achieve goals, they believe they know the interests of society better than does society itself.[41] Elections to village committees provide accountability for village officials, but they are not designed to provide feedback on the behavior and policies of the CCP.[42] So the indicators are that the Leninist system will simply muddle through rather than undertake the hazardous course of systemic reforms.

Seventh, the legal system serves as a relief valve. While China is far from a nation which operates by the rule of law, the courts increasingly provide opportunities to settle grievances. The process began with revised marriage laws in the Maoist era. The leadership attempted to strengthen women's position in society, and that required the power to sue for divorce. The opening of the PRC to foreign investment and the marketization of the economy caused a rush to create a commercial law code. Most recently, citizens are being provided some recourse against government malfeasance. An "Administrative Litigation Law" went into effect in 1990. Citizens can sue government offices for abuse of powers. The law is most often invoked against arbitrary police actions, and the settlements of claims are frequently in favor of the plaintiffs.[43] The ability to bring suits to settle grievances – personal, commercial, and administrative – should keep many social problems from reaching explosive levels.

Human and civil rights may prove to be a wild card in China's future. China has signed the United Nations conventions on social and economic rights and the pact on individual and political rights. As yet they have not been ratified by the NPC, so they have no force in domestic Chinese law. Ratification could reinvigorate the civil rights advocates in the PRC who would have a stronger legal base upon which to press their demands. The development of Czechoslovakia from a communist government to a pluralist nation was accomplished in

---

[41] Dickson, *Democratization in China and Taiwan*, p. 23.   [42] Ibid., p. 25.
[43] *New York Times*, April 27, 1998, p. 1.

part through demands that the regime honor the human rights agreements it had signed. Andrew Nathan believes human rights issues may lead to further mass movements and eruptive rather than gradual change.[44]

In the long run, the rising importance of the legal system may well condemn the CCP to extinction. As Richard Lowenthal argues, "transition to a rule of law in the full meaning of the term seems incompatible with any type of single-party rule."[45] But the full ramifications of this contradiction will require many years to develop – especially in a political culture that has for 2000 years emphasized "the rule of men" over "the rule of law."

CONCLUSION

The best hope for a politically vibrant and pluralistic China rests in generational change, yet even this is problematic. Mikhail Gorbachev came to power as a younger-generation transition figure in the 1980s. His experiences in attempting to reform the former Soviet Union serve as a negative example to Chinese within and without the CCP. Most citizens have no desire to follow in the footsteps of the failed USSR. So systemic change will be approached cautiously and incrementally. As Westerners, we chafe at the repressive nature of CCP authoritarianism, but the Chinese generally would prefer this to the alternative of *luan*, or turmoil. Thus the CCP is likely to be with us for some time. Hopefully the face of its authoritarianism will soften, but fundamental change is apt to be slow in coming. Eventually, the growth of civil society, the effects of globalization, and increasing levels of wealth and education will lead to a liberal democratic outcome. But that appears to be a distant goal.[46]

The United States and its allies must be prepared to live with a "market Leninist" China for years to come. The relationship will be especially problematic in the next few years. Beijing can be expected to keep

---

[44] Nathan, "Even Our Caution Must Be Hedged," p. 64.

[45] Richard Lowenthal, "The Ruling Party in a Mature Society," in Mark G. Field (ed.), *Social Consequences of Modernization in Communist Societies* (Baltimore: Johns Hopkins University Press, 1976), p. 94.

[46] Baogang He argues that liberal democracy – as opposed to radical-populist or paternalistic models – is the most likely form of democratic governance for China's future. But he is not optimistic that the preconditions for such an emergence can be realized in the near future. Baogang He, *The Democratization of China* (New York: Routledge, 1996), esp. pp. 226–31.

a tight lid on political dissidents while it undertakes economic reforms. The reforms will likely be accompanied by unemployment and unrest. Under such circumstances, the leadership will be paranoid about the maintenance of political stability.

It will be very difficult for Western democracies to stand by and watch these violations of political rights. But if American policy-makers press hard for policies designed to mitigate communist control over China, the most likely result would be to slow the reform process. External pressures heighten Chinese chauvinism, which works to the advantage of the autocrats. It was the quiet diplomacy of "constructive engagement," as the Clinton administration called it, that resulted in the release of China's most famous dissidents, Wei Jingsheng and Wang Dan. Many American politicians will be tempted to strengthen their vote-getting ability at home by attacking the Beijing autocracy. That is an unfortunate political truth. A better approach for dealing with an authoritarian and increasingly powerful China came long ago from Theodore Roosevelt: "Walk softly but carry a big stick."

Index

Administrative Litigation Law, 234
Agricultural Bank of China, 201
agriculture, 62. *See also* communes
Aid Korea, Resist America campaign, 131
All-Circle People's Representative Conferences, 193
Anshan Constitution, 204
Anti-Rightist Campaign (1957), 126, 136, 197

Bachman, David, 229–30
Bamboo Gang, 91
Bank of China, 62
banking, 214
banner system, 19, 22–3, 28, 29
baojia system, 21, 52
Bartlett, Beatrice, 24–5, 29
Beiyang regime, 45–54
Blue Shirts Society, 58
Boards: Civil Appointment, 20; Public Works, 20; Punishment, 20; Rites, 18, 20, 22; War, 20, 22

cadres, 131–2, 181
Cao Kun, 47, 52
Censorate, imperial, 20
Central Asia, 25
Central Executive Committee, 55, 57, 58
Central Leading Group on Foreign Propaganda, 178

Central Leading Group on Propaganda and Education, 178
Central Military Commission, 231
Central People's Government Council, 193
Central Political Council, 55, 58
Central Standing Committee, 88
Chen Cheng, 69
Chen Li-fu, 69
Chen Yi, 122n47
Chen Yizi, 227
Chen Yun, 134, 137, 139, 153–4, 233
Cheng Hsiao-shih, 100n44
Chiang Ching-kuo, 9, 77, 81, 87, 88, 92
Chiang Hsiao-wu, 91
Chiang Kai-shek, 7, 54, 71; and constitution, 63; errors of, 69–70; establishes control, 57–8; power of, 64, 66, 68; vision for China, 59–60
China, imperial: banner system in, 19; center-region relations in, 37–9; civil administration in, 19–22; demographic growth in, 36–7; economy of, 5, 23, 35–6; evolution of state in, 1–3; and frontier areas, 34–5; imperial authority in, 26–30; local government in, 5–6, 31–4; Manchu-Chinese relations in, 24–6; military forces in, 19, 22–3; political order in, 17–23; reach of state in, 30–7; response to West, 39; social stratification in, 5, 31–2; state legitimization in, 4–6

China, People's Republic of:
bureaucracies in, 106; consolidates
power, 129–33; decision making in,
109, 179–80; during Cultural
Revolution, 10, 114, 120n43, 123,
124–5, 143–8, 154, 155, 200–206,
219; decline of Maoist state, 148–52,
161–2; economy of, 12–13, 190–3;
factionalism in, 181; follows Soviet
model, 108–9, 133–6, 193–7; future
of, 13–14, 185–7, 216–35; during
Great Leap Forward, 113n20,
120n43, 123, 136–9, 154, 197–9, 203,
219; interlocking directorate in,
175–8; and legacy of Revolution,
107–11; local government in,
117n35; media in, 178–9;
nomenklatura in, 10–11, 12, 115–16,
167, 173–5, 176, 177; post-Leap
recovery, 139–43, 199–203; post-
Mao state in, 11–12, 166–70; state-
society relations in, 182–5; systemic
transformation in, 207–13; as
totalistic state, 106, 112–29, 153–60.
See also Chinese Communist Party;
Deng Xiaoping; Mao Zedong;
People's Liberation Army
China, Republic of, 6–8; Beiyang
regime, 45–54; and civil war, 68–70;
democratization in, 98–104;
economy of, 8, 53n33, 61–4, 82–6;
and one-party state, 78–81; reasons
for failure, 59–65; state
organizational structure, 55–7, 75–8;
state political behavior in, 57–64;
on Taiwan, 8–9, 74–5, 87–98; visions
of state in, 43–5; wartime state in,
65–70. *See also* Chiang Kai-shek;
Guomindang; Taiwan
Chinese Communist Party, 113–17,
165; Central Committee, 113,
151n118; Central Discipline
Inspection Commission, 172, 175,
219; in civil war, 68–70; core groups
(*dangzu*), 175; decentralized model
of rule, 10; and Deng Xiaoping,
11–12; Eighth National Congress,

197; Eleventh Central Committee,
206; future of, 14; gains power,
107–11; General Political
Department, 167, 175; levels of
bureaucracy, 172–3; Party Center,
114, 118n39; party secretaries, 124,
130, 137; Mao's importance in,
10–12, 105, 110–11, 113–14;
membership in, 221; Organization
Department, 173–4; and PLA, 110,
151–2, 175–6, 231; Politburo, 114,
123, 145; pragmatism of, 107–8;
Propaganda Department, 178;
reasons for dominance of, 157–8;
Secretariat, 114, 138, 145, 172;
Standing Committee, 114; Third
Plenum, 113n20, 163
Chinese People's Political
Consultative Conference (CPPCC),
127–8, 192–3, 220
Ch'u T'ung-tsu, 31–2
civil service, 21–2, 51
civil war, 68–70
class divisions, 184
coercion, 11
collectivization, 134–5, 195–6
communes, 197, 198–9, 200, 207
communication, internal, 22, 127
Communist Youth League, 151n118
Confucianism, 4, 182, 227
Constitutional Council, 47
constitutions: of early Republican
period, 45, 46n11, 47, 49–50; of
Nanjing period, 55, 58, 63, 69, 70–1;
post-1949, 76, 93, 94
Control Yuan, 55, 75, 93, 97n30
corruption, 68, 69, 212, 230
Court of Sacrificial Worship, 18
Crossley, Pamela, 24–5, 27n20
Cultural Revolution, 10, 114, 120n43,
143–8, 155, 200–206, 219; and PLA,
123, 124–5, 154
Cultural Revolution Group, 114, 145,
148, 150

dangwai, 78, 80, 89, 90–1
dangzu, 115n27

danwei, 183, 210–11
Dazhai Work Point System, 204–5
decentralization, 11, 120, 137, 209, 227
decision making, 109, 134, 179–80, 209
Deliberative Council of Princes and
    Ministers, 28
democracy, 220, 223, 224, 226; on
    Taiwan, 81, 91–6, 98–104
Democracy Spring, 230
Democratic Progressive Party (DPP),
    87, 90, 93–4, 95, 96, 100, 101, 102
demonstrations, 89–90, 163
Deng Xiaoping, 114; becomes
    distrustful, 180; consensual
    decision-making of, 179–80; and
    Cultural Revolution, 149, 151;
    desire to rebuild party, 11–12,
    172–3; and Gao Gang, 132, 155; and
    Great Leap Forward, 138; impact
    of, 161, 162, 163–4; loses power,
    152; and PLA, 121, 122; reforms of,
    168, 207, 217, 219, 223; reinstated,
    206; sources of power, 220; and
    Zhou Enlai, 139
Deng Zihui, 117n36, 141n95
directorate, interlocking, 175
Duan Qirui, 47–8
Duara, Prasenjit, 34
dynastic cycle, 39

economy, 157n132, 161–2, 184; during
    Cultural Revolution, 203–6; in early
    People's Republic, 12–13, 189,
    190–3; during First Five-Year Plan,
    193–7; during Great Leap Forward,
    197–9; after 1978, 207–13; in post-
    Cultural Revolution period, 206–7;
    in post-Leap period, 199–203; of
    Taiwan, 82–6
Educated Youth to the Countryside
    campaign, 200–201
education, 4, 89
elections, 69, 77–8, 80, 89, 90, 93, 95,
    97, 100; in PRC, 127, 223, 234
Electronic Research and Service
    Organization, 85
emperors, 17–18, 25–6, 27, 29–30

ethnic minorities, 158n134, 233
Examination Yuan, 57, 75
examinations, civil service, 22, 51, 75
Executive Yuan, 55, 75, 100, 101n45

factionalism, 72; in Beiyang
    government, 49, 53; in
    Guomindang, 79–80; in imperial
    China, 28, 29; in Nationalist
    government, 58, 64, 66, 68; in PRC,
    110, 132, 139, 142, 148, 150, 154–6,
    180, 181, 195
Fairbank, John King, 27n20
fanmaojin, 134, 136
February, 28, 1947, incident, 74–5
federalism, 14, 227
Feng Guozhang, 47
First Five-Year Plan (FFYP), 133,
    134n80, 193–7
Five-Antis campaign, 131, 190
Four Cardinal Principles, 184
Fu Quanyou, 181
Fulin, 18

Gao Gang, 132–3, 155
gentry, 31
Grand Council, 19–20, 21, 25, 29
Grand Secretariat, 19, 21, 22
Great Leap Forward, 113n20, 120n43,
    123, 136–9, 154, 197–9, 203, 219
Great Proletarian Cultural
    Revolution. *See* Cultural
    Revolution
Guomindang, 8, 217n2; and business,
    100; and democratization, 100–103;
    and Nanjing government, 54–5;
    receptiveness to change, 73–4; on
    Taiwan, 78–81, 87–98; Taiwanization
    of, 94, 98, 103; during wartime, 65,
    68. *See also* China, Republic of

Harding, Harry, 219
Hau Pei-tsun, 95, 100
He, Baogung, 235n46
He Long, 117n36, 122n47
He Yingqin, 69
Hevia, James, 16

Ho Ping-ti, 31–2
Hongli, 30
Hongtaiji, 18, 19
Hu Hanmin, 57
Hu Yaobang, 139n91, 180, 181, 207
Hua Guofeng, 149, 206
hukou system, 183
human rights, 185, 234–5
Hundred Flowers movement, 135–6, 137, 196
Huntington, Samuel, 220–3, 231

ideology, 4, 116, 226–7
Imperial Board of Astronomy, 18
Imperial Clan Court, 19
industrialization, 133, 134n80, 191
industry, reform of, 209–11
Industry Learns from Daqing campaign, 203
inflation, 79
intellectuals, 158, 232
interest articulation, 127, 128, 186
internet, 179

Japan, 74, 84, 85, 88
Jiang Qing, 114, 142, 145, 147–8, 149
Jiang Zemin, 163, 180, 207, 217, 220, 231
Johnson, Chalmers, 83
Journal of Democracy, 224–5, 226
judicial reform, 50
judicial system, 125–6
Judicial Yuan, 55, 75

Kang Ning-hsiang, 90
Kang Sheng, 142
Kangxi Emperor, 18–19, 22, 23, 28, 30
Kao, Henry (Kao Yu-shu), 80
Kaohsiung, Taiwan, 80n10
Ke Qingshi, 139
Korean war, 131
Kristof, Nicholas, 218
Kuhn, Philip, 30, 32, 33
Kuomintang. *See* Guomindang

land reform, 61, 80, 131
landownership, 208

leadership, collective, 111, 134, 144
Leading Group on Maintaining Social Stability, 229
Learn from Dazhai campaign, 203
Lee Teng-hui, 9, 76, 77, 81, 93, 98, 101, 103
legal system, 177, 234
Legislative Yuan, 47, 55, 60, 75, 77–8, 79n9, 93–4, 95, 97, 99
legitimacy, 158–9, 227
Leninist party/regime, 109, 138, 172–3, 175, 217–18
Li Fuchun, 115n27, 140
Li Hongzhang, 37, 38
Li Peng, 180, 181, 222
Li Xiannian, 115n27
Li Yizhe group, 158n137
Li Yuanhong, 47, 52
Liang Qichao, 7, 45
Lien Chan, 94
lijia system, 21, 52
lijin, 23
Lin Biao, 117, 122, 130n71; and Cultural Revolution, 147–8; death of, 144, 148; and Gao Gang, 132; uninterested in power, 142; and Zhou Enlai, 156
Lin Liguo, 149n111
Lin Yang-kang, 95
literature of the wounded, 206
Liu, Henry, 91, 92
Liu Kwang-ch'ing, 38
Liu Shaoqi, 109, 114n24, 117, 203; and Cultural Revolution, 144; and Gao Gang, 132; and Mao, 133n76, 140; and PLA, 121; promotes "trusts," 141
local government, 60–1
Lowenthal, Richard, 216, 235
Lushan conference, 113n20, 123, 137, 139, 155

Machiavelli problem, 43n2, 72
magazines, 179, 184
magistrates, 6, 21, 60–1
Manchuria, 68
Manchus, 24–6

Mann, Susan, 33
Mao Zedong: and collective decision making, 109; and Cultural Revolution, 143–4, 156; and Great Leap Forward, 136–9; importance of, 153–4; legacy of, 159–60; and mass activism, 135, 157; and PLA, 121; rejects Soviet economic model, 137; role in CCP, 105, 110–11, 113–14, 132; and totalist state, 10–11; war fixation of, 154
market Leninism, 218, 219
Marshall, George C., 70
martial law, 76, 77, 92, 93
Marxist-Leninist state, 216–17
mass movements, 27, 119–20, 131, 135, 137, 157, 190, 202
mass organizations, 128–9, 151n118
McCord, Edward, 38
media, 178–9, 219n8
Meilidao (*Formosa*), 90
Metzger, Thomas A., 45
Michael, Franz, xix–xx, 16–17, 24, 27n20, 31, 37–9, 41, 191
Military Administrative Committees, 130
Military Affairs Commission, 54
Military Affairs Committee (MAC), 121–2, 151
military control commissions, 192
military, 19, 100. *See also* banner system; People's Liberation Army
ministries, 20, 21–2, 42, 77n5, 119, 178
Ministry of Defense, 121
Ministry of Interior, 57
Ministry of Justice, 50
Modern Chinese History Project, 27n20
modernization, 49–52
monopolies, state, 23
Mote, Fritz, 37n39

Nanjing Decade, 8
Nanning conference (1958), 136–7
Nathan, Andrew, 224, 230, 235
National Assembly, 46, 47, 48–9, 69, 75, 77–8, 93, 94, 95, 97

National Defense Industries Office, 171
National Defense Science and Technology Commission, 171
National Development Conference, 97n37
national identity, 91, 101–3
National People's Congress (NPC), 126–7, 176–7, 220
National Resources Commission, 60
National Security Council (NSC), 76–7, 100
nationalism, 71, 231, 233
Nationalist party. *See* Guomindang
nationalization, 194
New Armies, 38
New China News Agency, 178
New Democracy, 130, 190
New Life Movement, 60
New Party, 95, 98, 100, 102
New Reforms (Qing), 34, 38–9, 42–3
newspapers, 179, 184
Nie Rongzhen, 122n47
nomenklatura (*bianzhi*), 10–11, 12, 115–16, 167, 173–5, 176, 177
nongovernmental organizations (NGOs), 173, 184–5
nuclear test-ban treaty, 232
Nurhaci, 19

Oboi regency, 29
Office of the President, 55
Oi, Jean, 210n10
one nation, divided country, 9
Organic Law of Judicial Courts, 50
Organizational Clique, 58
Oriental despotism, 27n20
Oxnam, Robert, 29

party committees, 145, 147, 151
patron-client ties, 52, 66, 68, 72, 116, 155, 181, 212
peasants, 143, 158
Peng Dehuai, 121, 122, 123, 138, 139, 155
Peng Ming-min, 87
People's Armed Police (PAP), 165

people's congresses, 126–7
People's Consultative Council, 55
People's Liberation Army, 120–5, 165;
  in Cultural Revolution, 145–8, 154,
  192, 202; declining power of, 221;
  Discipline Inspection Commission,
  171; General Equipment
  Department (GED), 171; and
  Great Leap Forward, 138;
  organizational change in, 171–2;
  in post-Leap period, 141–2;
  relations with CCP, 109, 151–2,
  166–8, 175–6, 231; in regional
  administration, 130
Perdue, Peter, 35–6
police, 50–1, 125
political commissar system, 100–101
Political Council, 47
political economy, 83–5
political parties, 46, 87, 100, 127–8
Political Study Clique, 58
postal stations, 22
price system, 208–9
Prince Chun, 43
production responsibility system,
  207–8
*Proposals for the Second Five-Year
  Plan*, 197
Provisional Amendments for the
  Period of Mobilization for the
  Suppression of Communist
  Rebellion, 76
Provisional New Criminal Code, 50
public security apparatus, 125–6
Pye, Lucian, 218–19

Qianlong Emperor, 25, 30
Qing dynasty. *See* China, imperial

radio, 179, 183
Rao Shushi, 132
Rawski, Evelyn, 24–5
Rawski, Thomas, 210n10
real estate, 214
Red Army (Chinese), 68, 110. *See
  also* People's Liberation Army

Red Army (Soviet), 69
Red Guards, 145, 158
reform, political, 163, 164–5, 186
reforms of 1898, 6
regime change, 4
regional administration, 20–1, 37–9,
  51–2, 112, 130–1, 192
Reorganization Loan, 51
residence permits, 183
residents' committees, 133, 183
reunification, 78, 84
Revolutionary Committees, 145–7
Rowe, William T., 33
rural reconstruction, 61
Rural Work Department, 141n95
Rustow, Dankwart A., 103n48,
  225–6

Salt Administration, 51
Self-Strengthening Movement, 6
Shanxi province, 51–2
Shepherd, John Robert, 35
Shunzhi Emperor, 18, 29
single-party systems, 221–2
social revolution, 134–5
Socialist Education Campaign, 143,
  202
Soong, James, 98
Soong, T. V., 70
sorcery scare (1768), 30
Southern Library, 29
Soviet Union, 68, 112, 133–6, 191,
  193–7
State Council, 117, 133, 139, 147,
  151, 166–70; and CCP, 176;
  Ministry of Personnel, 174;
  reorganization of, 177; Standing
  Committee, 117
State Planning Commission, 115n27
State Press and Public Publications
  Administration, 178–9
State Statistical Bureau, 199
statecraft, 7, 45
state-owned enterprises (SOEs), 210,
  229
strikes, 150

students, 232–3
succession, 4, 18–19
Sun Yat-sen, 43–4, 55, 57. *See also*
  Three People's Principles
Sun Yat-sen, Mme., 192
Sun Zhongshan. *See* Sun Yat-sen

Taiping rebellion, 27n20, 37
Taiwan Garrison Command, 77, 100
Taiwan Independence Party, 96,
  102
Taiwan, 8–9, 233; economy of, 98; and
  imperial China, 35; independence
  movement, 87, 102; mainlanders
  and Taiwanese on, 81, 83; party
  system, 96–7; political economy of,
  83–5. *See also* China, Republic of;
  Guomindang
taxation, 21, 23, 36, 61, 64, 208
television, 179, 183
Third Five-Year Plan (TFYP), 140
Third Line, 202–3
Thought of Mao Zedong, 144, 202
Three People's Principles, 7, 59
Three-Antis campaign, 131, 190
Tian Jiaying, 139n91
Tiananmen demonstrations: (1976),
  152; (1989), 218, 232
Tibet, 233
Tongzhi Restoration, 37
trade, 82, 191, 202, 213
trade unions, 128–9, 151n118
two-line struggle, 195

unemployment, 229
united front, 108, 127–8, 129
United League, 45
United States, 80–1

Village Socialist Education campaign,
  202

Wakeman, Frederic, 27n20
Walder, Andrew, 116
Wang Heshou, 142
Wang Hongwen, 122n47, 150n114

Wang Hsi-ling, 91
Wang Jingwei, 44, 58
Wang Sheng, 91, 92
Wang Zhaoming, 44
warlords, 37, 38
Wei Jingsheng, 220–1, 232–3
Western Hills Group, 58
Whampoa Clique, 58
White Lotus rebellion, 23
Wilbur, C. Martin, 53
Wittfogel, Karl August, 27
women's associations, 151n118
work units, 183, 210–11
workers, 158
Wright, Mary, 39
Wu Jiaxiang, 220–1
Wu Peifu, 52

xiangyue, 21
Xinjiang, 233
xitong, 118, 127–8
Xu Shichang, 47
Xuanye, 18–19

Yan Xishan, 51–2
Yang Xiguang, 159
Ye Jianying, 122, 151
Ye Qun, 148
Yinreng, 19
Yinzhen, 19
Yongzheng Emperor, 19, 22, 25, 29,
  30
Young Communist League,
  128n68
Yuan Shikai, 7, 45–8, 50–3, 71

Zeng Guofan, 37
Zhang Chunqiao, 122n47, 150n114
Zhang Wannian, 181
Zhang Xun, 48
Zhang Zhen, 181
Zhang Zhongli, 31, 32
Zhang Zuolin, 47
Zhao Ziyang, 164, 177, 180, 181, 207
Zhejiang, 150n114
Zhili region, 52

Zhou Enlai, 101n143; and Cultural
Revolution, 146, 147, 148, 149;
death of, 152; and Gao Gang, 132;
and Great Leap Forward, 138; and
Hundred Flowers, 137; and Lin
Biao, 156; and PLA, 121, 123;
rebuilds party-state, 11
Zhu De, 121
Zhu Rongji, 177, 180, 217, 220, 228–30
Zuo Zongtang, 37